11592   MCFed

Timber
in Construction

Edited by
John Sunley and Barbara Bedding

BT Batsford Ltd, London/TRADA

© TRADA 1985
First published 1985

All rights reserved. No part of this publication
may be reproduced, in any form or by any means,
without permission from the Publisher

ISBN 0 7134 5053 3

Typeset and printed in Great Britain by
Butler & Tanner Ltd
Frome and London

for the publishers
B. T. Batsford Ltd
4 Fitzhardinge Street
London W1H 0AH

Contents

Preface

If visitors from another planet came to the earth they would almost certainly regard timber as a miracle material. It grows like a weed across the fertile world and in forms often suited to the needs of man. Many of its fruits are edible, and its bark, leaves, and juices provide by-products like rubber, cork, and scent. Its versatility as a construction and decorative material involves it in some degree in every artefact of man. It can be enormously strong in compression and in tension. Its elasticity enabled the development of hunting-derived sports like archery and fishing, and it can be jointed and worked with simple tools. It is light in weight, sheds water, and can be one of the most enduring of all materials. It floats (except for the heaviest hardwoods), is a fuel, is clean and non-toxic, is a non-conductor, and a high insulant, is self-finished, does not corrode, and under normal conditions will not rot. Finally, it smells good, feels good, and is a pleasure to work with. In all it is an amazing gift from nature, unsurpassed in the benefits it has bestowed upon us.

In architecture it was one of the very first building materials, and is still used as the basic material in about 80 per cent of all homes, providing a high proportion of the contents of buildings made from other materials. One might have thought that the age of high technology would have produced a better alternative material. High technology, however, is also usually high energy consumptive and in this area timber has much to offer. It uses no irreplaceable energy sources to produce and little energy to work. In addition to which, modern techniques of stress grading, jointing, preservation and fire protection have extended its natural qualities and given it far greater structural possibilities.

The Timber Research and Development Association has been largely responsible for the continuous development of timber application and has been resourceful in promoting its virtues.

As a practising architect I have always been drawn to timber construction and have had a lot of pleasure designing with it and watching subsequent construction. It has always seemed to me that those who work timber have an almost intuitive skill and often somewhat reflective temperaments.

Because of the support TRADA has always provided to architects working in timber I was very glad to write this preface, and although there are no specific chapters dealing with architectural design in timber, the selected examples illustrated show the versatility of the material, the inspiration it gives to designers, and the strong character the material imparts to buildings.

This book will be a useful up-to-date reference for all who are tempted to use timber in modern buildings or refurbishment work. It is an attractive and renewable material of great variety and just as modern in application today as it must have seemed when men first left the caves.

MICHAEL MANSER
President, Royal Institute of British Architects
23 October 1984

List of figures

List of plates

List of tables

Introduction

J.B. Lewis
TRADA Chairman 1984–86

This book has been prepared by the Timber Research and Development Association (TRADA) as part of its 50th anniversary celebrations. There has long been a need for an authoritative reference book on the use of timber in construction for architects and specifiers and for students in these fields. This book, with each chapter written by a specialist in the subject, is intended to fill that gap. After 50 years of work in the interests of ensuring the economic use of timber, TRADA is in a unique position to commission such a work.

Generous contributions from members of TRADA facilitated the preparation of the book and allowed copies to be donated to students in the architectural and allied professions. Grateful thanks are extended to all those who contributed. Thanks are also due to the authors and the many companies and individuals who provided information and illustrations used in its compilation.

The association began life as the Timber Development Association, founded to counteract claims and attacks by competing man-made materials. The early years of the association were concerned with publicity and promotion, but a gradual change saw more and more involvement in technical aspects of the use of wood. In 1954 TDA accepted a grant from the Department of Scientific and Industrial Research and moved from London to premises in Buckinghamshire with space for test and research facilities. In 1962 the change was acknowledged and TDA became TRADA. Having outgrown the original laboratories, TRADA moved to its present location at Hughenden Valley in 1967 where it now has purpose-built offices, laboratories and large-scale test facilities.

TRADA has always been at the forefront of timber design, with prototype timber frame houses built in 1963 and four-storey timber frame flats completed in 1965. TRADA has been involved in large-scale timber structures over the years with designs for many large buildings being undertaken. Many of these buildings are illustrated in this book; one of its more notable recent involvements has been with the design of the roofs for the Thames Flood Barrier (Plate 1) where TRADA acted as specialist consultants to the consulting engineers.

TRADA employs architects, engineers, technicians and other specialists working in the interests of timber users, specifiers and suppliers. Its consultancy and advisory services are available to all those concerned with timber and membership is open to companies or individuals who supply, specify, manufacture or use timber.

Building Regulations

The use of timber in construction is, like other materials, to a large extent governed by the requirements of the Building Regulations.

The Building Bill, which is due to come before Parliament in Spring 1985, contains proposals which will have a major effect on the Building Regulations and building control procedures. The Bill and its associated documents were undergoing consultative procedures at the time of this book going to press.

The Building Regulations are being changed in an effort to simplify the system. The main difficulty has been that the whole document is approved by Parliament so that it can only be changed with parliamentary approval and must be produced in a set format. The new Regulations for England and Wales will consist of a group of documents:

- **The Building Regulations** themselves will be approved by Parliament and will be a brief statement of the *functional requirements* of the Regulations. They will also include specific requirements relating to the passage of heat.
- A series of **Approved Documents** giving recommended solutions to the functional requirements. Initially these are being produced by the Department of the Environment Building Regulations division but it is anticipated that in the longer term other organizations, currently the British Standards Institution and the British Board of Agrement, will be approved to produce them. In general, the Approved Documents will not be mandatory, unless compliance with them is made compulsory under the Regulations themselves. At the present time only the document dealing with means of escape from fire is in this category.

In addition to the change in format of the Regulations, major changes to the system of approval and building control functions are included. **Approved Inspectors** will be introduced as an alternative to the local authority building control departments. This is intended to give applicants the choice of either following the present system or using a private inspector to certify compliance with the Regulations and notifying the local authority of the intention to follow this course of action. Inspectors will be approved by 'Designated Bodies': these will be professional institutions where entry is by examination. There is also provision for self-certification by 'approved applicants' in respect of structural and thermal insulation matters only.

The revised Regulations are intended initially to replace the England and Wales Regulations and later the London Building Byelaws. The Scottish Building Standards are also being revised but these will largely follow the previous format and will not be in the same form as the England and Wales Regulations. It appears likely that the Northern Ireland Regulations will follow the England and Wales format when they are revised.

The Approved Documents are largely based on the requirements contained in the 1976 England and Wales Regulations, with only detailed amendment. However more major changes are under discussion relating to some aspects; these may involve surface spread of flame requirements for linings and sound insulation.

Since this book was prepared in 1984, when the 1976 England and Wales Regulations, 1977 Northern Ireland Regulations and the 1981 Building Standards (Scotland) were in force, it is essential that designers and specifiers should check on the detailed requirements of the current Regulations before undertaking specific designs.

Timber Research and Development Association
January 1985

1 Timber

Dr John D. Brazier

John D. Brazier BSc DSc FIWSc is head of the properties of materials section at the Princes Risborough Laboratory, Building Research Establishment.

THE MATERIAL

Timber was man's first structural material and today it is as important as ever for this purpose; it is likely, too, though difficult to prove conclusively, that timber is used for a greater number of products than any other material. What then is this material that has been used longer than most and finds such variety in use? What are the characteristics which make it so valuable and why is it so versatile?

Timber is sawn wood, a material obtained from trees. Wood occurs in all parts of the tree, its roots, main stem and branches, but commercial timber almost invariably comes from the main stem. Branch and root wood are usable and indeed are likely to be used increasingly for fibre products as well as for the traditional use of fuel, but the character of branch and root wood and the economics of production generally preclude their use as industrial sawn wood, especially where there are adequate supplies of stem wood.

Two types of commercial timber are recognized, softwood and hardwood. Softwood is obtained from conifers or cone-bearing trees, usually with needle-shaped or scale-like leaves which persist for many years so that most trees are evergreen; hardwood comes from so-called broad-leaved trees which may be deciduous or evergreen. Softwood and hardwood are botanical terms and do not refer to the density or hardness of the wood. As it happens, most softwoods are fairly soft, though pitch pine and yew might be considered exceptions; in contrast, hardwoods can vary greatly in density and hardness, balsa is a hardwood, as is obeche, but so too are greenheart and lignum vitae.

Wood is composed of cells, made up of a cell wall, which varies in thickness in different timbers, and a central lumen or cavity. Most cells are long in relation to their width and are aligned axially along the trunk, giving rise to the grain of wood. All the cells in wood are derived from a layer of actively dividing tissue called a cambium which lies between the outermost wood and the innermost bark; thus new wood is laid down on that already there, the first formed wood is that nearest the pith or centre of the stem and the latest, that nearest the outside. Wood production often occurs cyclically, ceasing when conditions are unfavourable for growth, due to drought, cold, etc, and these cyclic periods of growth are marked in the wood by distinctive patterns of cells giving rise to growth rings. In temperate timbers such rings are produced annually and this provides a means for determining the age of the tree. Figures 1.1 and 1.2 show the structure of wood.

It is in terms of its function in the growth of the tree that some of the more important characteristics of wood can be understood. The stem has three main purposes in the growth of the tree: first, a structural role, to support the crown of leaves, the food-producing organs of a plant; second, a conducting function, because water – the so-called sap of the tree which is essential for the synthesis of food by the leaves – has to be moved from the roots to the leaves; third, a storage role so that food is always available to the plant, even though the tree may be leafless. The great majority of the cells contribute to the strength of the stem and it is in order to best withstand the bending stresses induced in it by movement of the crown that most cells are aligned along the length of the stem. The whole cross-section of the stem contributes to the structural performance but the other functions are confined to the outer, most recently formed wood. Active conduction is confined to a very narrow outer layer of wood although all the wood in the stem contains water – it is 'green' when felled – and this water may act as a reservoir in times of need. Food storage occurs in a somewhat deeper layer of wood in a zone which is termed the sapwood. Inside this is the heartwood. Heartwood formation occurs when food materials in the innermost sapwood are converted to complex organic substances which may infiltrate and colour the wood giving rise to a colour contrast between heartwood and sapwood. Other changes can occur which effectively block the conducting cells, and wood which has a high degree of permeability in the sapwood becomes impermeable in heartwood. Such changes in colour and permeability do not occur in all woods though in most stems of sufficient size there is a central core of wood with no living cells - the biological definition of heartwood - surrounded by a layer of physiologically active wood - the sapwood.

Heartwood formation is of great importance in the

utilization of wood. Many timbers are used for their appearance and especially their colour. Almost invariably it is heartwood that is sought and the pale sapwood is removed; only exceptionally is white sapwood preferred to coloured heartwood, as in the case of hickory for handles or the clean white of blades from cricket bat willow. For the most part it is hardwoods that are used for their appearance and in which heartwood colour is important; most softwoods are used for purposes where appearance is of little importance and sapwood is normally included. In any event, most softwood timber is cut from trees of comparatively small size with a high proportion of sapwood, and its exclusion would be quite uneconomic.

Besides enhancing appearance, the deposition of heartwood substances and blocking of the tissues to prevent ingress of water can give wood a degree of durability – a resistance to fungal and insect attack which it does not have as sapwood. It is difficult to judge the durability of a timber but, in general, the darker its colour, the more resistant it is to water uptake and the greater its density, the better its durability is likely to be, especially its resistance to decay. However, the only truly effective assessment of durability is by exposure of heartwood in ground contact trials, though exposure to various types of fungi and insects under laboratory conditions can often indicate its likely performance in months compared with the many years that may be needed for a field trial (Figure 1.3). Many such studies have been made and are reported in the technical literature where conventionally timbers are classified into five natural durability classes, according to the life of untreated heartwood in ground contact. Such life expectations are a guide only; pieces of the same timber can differ markedly in their decay resistance and life expectancy is greatly influenced by exposure conditions. The Appendix gives durability ratings for some commonly used timbers.

An important though somewhat different aspect of

performance in adverse conditions is the resistance of wood to fire. Wood is combustible, that is it ignites and there can be a rapid surface spread of flame, but rates of burning are often low with the build-up of carbon on the surface limiting oxygen availability to underlying wood. Thus, in a fire, sections of timber of even modest size will retain their integrity for a long time, outlasting other materials that fracture or deform (Figure 1.4). Ignition and rates of surface spread of flame can be greatly reduced by a variety of treatments, such as the application of surface coatings, or, better, impregnation with appropriate chemicals (see Chapter 3).

The changes which occur in wood on heartwood formation affect not only its durability but also its permeability, or the ease with which liquid can flow through wood. Because of the axial alignment of most cells, movement of liquid is usually much easier along the grain compared with movement across the grain, so that end-grain penetration of preservatives is often much better than that into the sides of a piece of wood. The ability to penetrate wood with a preservative liquid is of great technical importance; timbers which otherwise have a low resistance to insect or fungal degrade can be made highly resistant.

In order to treat wood with preservative, it must be partially dried so that the lumina or cavities of the cells are free of water; even so, the ease with which different timbers can be treated varies greatly. Some are readily penetrated but others, typically those with cells that have been blocked on heartwood formation, are highly resistant with the surface barely penetrated, even though a pressure treatment is used. Timbers are classified as permeable, moderately resistant, resistant and extremely resistant depending on ease of penetration of their heartwood (see Appendix). All sapwood is rated either permeable or moderately resistant and, if effectively treated, wood which is otherwise perishable is rendered highly durable and can have a long life in exacting conditions, as in the case of telephone and transmission poles (Figure 1.5).

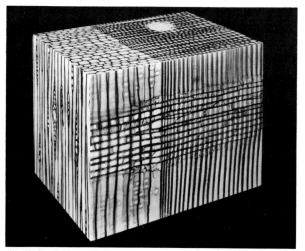

Figure 1.1 _Wood is composed of cells, for the most part aligned axially along the stem, but some, aggregated to form rays, run radially. The illustration, of a piece of pine, shows the boundary between the last formed wood of one year, with thick cell walls, and the first formed wood of the following year, with thin cell walls. The cavity in the cross-section is a resin canal, a common feature of some softwoods._ Photograph: Princes Risborough Laboratory, Building Research Establishment. Crown Copyright.

Figure 1.2 _A segment of a softwood stem showing the wood protected on its outer surface by bark. New growth is produced by a cambium between bark and wood. A wide band of sapwood contrasts in colour with the heartwood. Growth rings are a conspicuous feature and give rise to a characteristic figure on both radially and tangentially cut surfaces._ Photograph: Princes Risborough Laboratory, Building Research Establishment. Crown Copyright.

An exception to the general need to dry wood for preservative treatment is the use of a diffusion method for the penetration of preservative salts. For a successful diffusion treatment, wood must be wet and must be kept wet. Any wood can be treated, though rates of diffusion differ markedly and it has to be remembered that if a water soluble preservative salt is used and the timber later exposed to wet conditions the preservative salt may leach out.

When first converted, wood contains water and drying of wood is an essential process in its preparation for use. Removal of water substantially reduces the risk of fungal attack, provided that the wood is kept at a moisture content below 20 per cent. The weight of wood is reduced by drying and most strength properties are substantially increased; although, exceptionally, sawing wood is more difficult, finishes obtained in machine processing are greatly improved with dry wood. Any impregnation process requires the wood to be at least partially dry and finally, and perhaps most importantly, for wood to maintain its dimensional stability in use and give satisfactory performance in components, it must be at a moisture content in equilibrium with the environment of its use.

Drying of wood requires, initially, the removal of water from the cell cavities and thereafter removal of some of the water from the cell walls. It is when water is lost from the cell walls, below the so-called fibre saturation point, that shrinkage occurs. Expressed simply, the cell wall is made of cellulosic strands in a matrix of hemicellulose, surrounded by lignin and containing water. Removal of water causes the matrix to shrink but this shrinkage is constrained along the length of the cell because the cellulosic strands, mostly aligned in this direction, shrink little in length. Thus the matrix can only shrink between the strands and this gives rise to the familiar cross-grain dimensional change when wood is dried. For complex anatomical reasons, tangential shrinkage (T) around the growth rings is always greater than radial shrinkage (R) across the growth rings – six per cent and three per cent of the green dimensions are average figures when dried to 12 per cent moisture content – but the ratio T/R differs between timbers,

Figure 1.3 *Naturally durable timbers can be used in the most demanding situations without the need for preservative treatment.* Photograph: G. R. Wiltshire & Co Ltd.

Figure 1.4 *The performance of timber in fire is illustrated in this photograph of the aftermath of a fire in a casein glue plant in the USA.* Photograph: Borden Chemical Co.

though a figure of the order of 2:1 is common. Distortion of boards on drying, such as spring and bow, results from the difference between longitudinal and transverse shrinkage, and changes in shape of the section of a piece of timber, such as cup and the diamonding of a square, from the difference between tangential and radial shrinkage. Ease and rate of drying differ greatly between timbers, and kiln-drying schedules have been developed to balance speed of drying, which generally minimizes cost, against likelihood of degrade.

Once dry, timber responds to changes in atmospheric conditions by absorbing or losing moisture leading to small changes in its thickness and shape. The speed of response and extent of this movement differs between timbers; some are particularly stable with a change in volume of less than three per cent when transferred from an environment at 90 per cent relative humidity, to one at 60 per cent relative humidity at 25°C, while others, far less stable, may move by twice this figure over the same humidity range. Particularly stable timbers are needed where movement can lead to problems

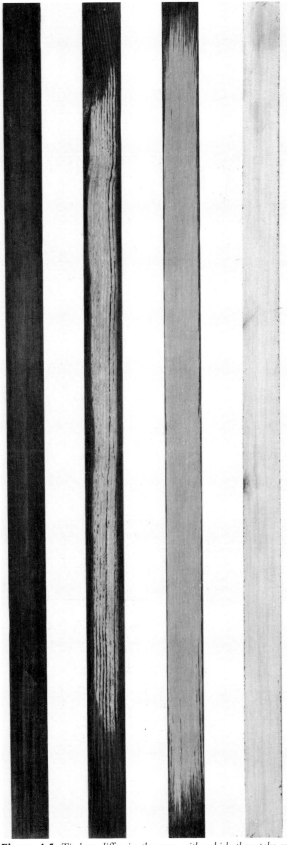

Figure 1.5 *Timbers differ in the ease with which they take up liquids. The illustration shows sticks of timbers rated permeable, moderately resistant, resistant and extremely resistant, cut longitudinally after treatment with creosote. Note the greater end grain compared with side grain penetration in the moderately resistant and resistant samples.* Photograph: Princes Risborough Laboratory, Building Research Establishment. Crown Copyright.

in use, as with some types of flooring, joinery and furniture parts where a snug but not tight fit is needed, or where accurate detail must be maintained, as with engineers' patterns.

When felled, logs may end-split due to the release of stresses in the growing tree. These stresses can be very great, particularly in hardwoods, with the outer part of the log in tension and the inner in compression. In some tropical hardwoods the compression stress is sufficient to rupture the woody tissue and produce a condition known as brittleheart, often characterized by hairline failures across the grain and breaking of the wood with a short, biscuit-like fracture when it is subjected to even modest loads. Misshapen stems and, in particular, those with an off-centre pith, have an abnormal type of wood, known as reaction wood, on the vigorous growth side of the stem. Reaction wood, unlike normal wood, can shrink along the grain, often leading to distortion on drying; it is also characterized by high growth stresses and may split or, when sawn, bind onto or spring away from the saw.

The strength of timber is very variable due, in part, to differences in its properties along and across the grain but also to differences between timbers. Because of the mainly unidirectional alignment of the wood cells and the parallel arrangement of the main structural components of the cell walls, properties such as bending strength, resistance to cleavage and stiffness are many (10–40) times greater when resistance to stress is across rather than along the grain. Thus maximum strength is obtained with straight-grained wood; any deviation of the grain, as with spiral or other cross-grain and localized distorted grain around knots, results in a loss in strength. When used to its best advantage, wood is a remarkably strong material and, when performance is related to weight, wood compares very favourably with many structural materials and particularly so when cost is considered (Table 1.1). However, wood is not only strong but it has the capacity to absorb energy even after failure is initiated. A cellular structure with many cell wall/air interfaces resists crack propagation so that if timber is loaded to failure in bending this is a slow yielding process and there is no sudden fracture as can happen with other materials.

Differences in strength between timbers derive mainly from differences in their densities. Because cell wall thickness and the ratio of cell wall thickness to lumen size vary greatly between timbers, dry wood density can range from as little as $100 \, \text{kg/m}^3$ in balsa to a figure more than ten times this in greenheart, at $1050 \, \text{kg/m}^3$, and $1230 \, \text{kg/m}^3$ in lignum vitae (Figure 1.6). As most strength properties show a linear or near linear relationship to density there is a corresponding range in strength. The presence of water in wood reduces most strength properties, and prolonged exposure at temperatures as low as $60°\text{C}$ or shorter periods at higher temperatures reduce strength and toughness and result in a tendency to brashness; at sub-zero temperatures most strength properties are increased making wood particularly useful as a building material in such conditions.

Wood is only rarely used in the round, as a log or pole, and is normally sawn to size for use. Such conversion may be to boards or planks in which form the timber is often dried and thereafter re-sawn to sizes

Table 1.1 *Comparison of structural performance of European redwood and other building materials*

material	specific gravity (sg)	tensile strength (T) N/mm²	T/sg	modulus of elasticity (E) N/mm² × 10³	E/sg × 10³	cost £/tonne
redwood	0.5	92	184	7.7	15	200
mild steel	7.85	470	60	207	26	400
aluminium alloy	2.7	310	115	70	26	1100
concrete	2.3	4	2	28.6	12.5	82

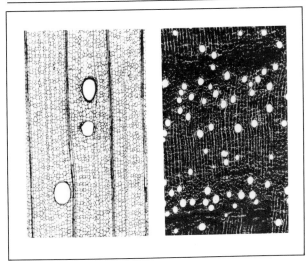

Figure 1.6 *Cross-section of balsa (left) and lignum vitae (right). The very thin-walled cells in balsa give a wood of very low density, about 160 kg/m³ when dry; the thick-walled cells in lignum, which cannot be individually seen, result in a wood of about 1200 kg/m³. In both woods, the large cells are for water conduction.* Photograph: Princes Risborough Laboratory, Building Research Establishment. Crown Copyright.

appropriate to its use; it is a practice adopted where use is in a variety of often fairly small sizes, as with much hardwood. Softwood logs are usually converted directly to section sizes required in construction and joinery, for pallet boards etc, and efficiency of out-turn is obtained by maximizing yields in these sizes. Conversion is more rarely directed to optimizing performance, for the production of quarter-sawn boards for maximum stability or to obtain the most decorative figure from a timber; again, this is more usual with hardwoods because of their higher value, but such conversion is at the expense of yield, it produces narrower boards, and costs are increased because of the repeated turning of logs during sawing (Figure 1.7).

Further processing is by a number of machine operations and it is a feature of timber that it lends itself to

Figure 1.7 *Conversion patterns and the changes in shape which may occur in drying. Logs sawn through and through (top left) give wide boards but these tend to cup on drying (bottom left). Conversion to produce quarter-sawn boards (top right) gives narrower boards but these are more stable on drying and in use (bottom right). Figure of some hardwoods, for example oak and sapele, is enhanced by quarter-sawing.*

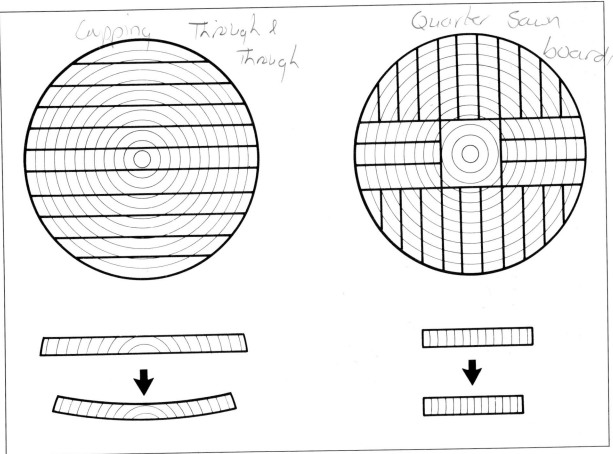

a variety of processes, with the production of elaborate and often detailed profiles, from mouldings to the complex and precise shapes of items such as shuttles, engineers' patterns, musical instruments, etc. Ease of machining is affected by several factors but, in particular, wood density. Heavy timbers are more difficult to machine than those of medium or light weight though lightweight timbers often require cutters to be kept very sharp if a smooth finish is to be obtained. A few hardwoods contain silica in very small amounts but sufficient to cause severe blunting of tools; this effect can be reduced by the use of cutters tipped with tungsten carbide and when long machine runs are required of even moderately hard timbers, tipped cutters are used to reduce wear and the down time of machines. Surface finish is affected by a number of factors; apart from those controlled by the operator, such as cutter sharpness and rate of feed to the machine, characteristics of the wood such as moisture content and grain direction are important. Dry wood finishes better than wet wood, and wood with an irregular grain or with grain deviating around knots is prone to tear. Many tropical hardwoods have an alternating spiral grain which gives an attractive stripe or interlocked figure to quarter cut surfaces but causes tearing of the surface unless special care is taken in planing.

A very few timbers have an irritant effect when they are machined, either from inhalation of dust causing irritation to the eyes, nose and throat, or from an interaction with the skin and a dermatitic response; other timbers, though not generally irritant, can affect individuals probably as a result of sensitization after long exposure. Such effects can be minimized by the use of efficient dust extraction procedures and attention to hygiene, for example with the use of barrier creams.

TIMBERS – SOURCES AND USES

In 1983 the cost of wood and wood products, including paper and board, imported into Britain was $£3.8 \times 10^9$; add to this the value of UK production and the figure exceeds $£4 \times 10^9$. About half this expenditure is on paper and board and about $£10^9$ on solid wood, that is

Figure 1.8 _The majority of softwoods are imported into the UK. Here large sections of Douglas fir are being unloaded._ Photograph: Seaboard International (Timber and Plywood) Ltd.

sawn wood and logs. The volume of solid wood used in 1983 was about $9 \times 10^6 \, m^3$, noticeably up on previous years but below the peak figures of the early 1970s; it is a volume which is difficult to comprehend but if stacked on the playing area of a full-sized football pitch it would reach a height of 1250 metres or over three-quarters of a mile!

About 80 per cent by cost and rather more by volume of this use is softwood. Softwoods are the principal timbers for construction and joinery, as well as for purposes such as packaging, estate work, etc. They come, very largely, from the coniferous forests of the northern hemisphere and there are two main regions of supply, Northern and Central Europe, principally Sweden, Finland and Russia, and North America, mainly British Columbia. Shipments from Europe are dominated by two woods, pine or European redwood and spruce or European whitewood. The character of both timbers varies appreciably depending on its origin – wood from more northerly latitudes is typically slowly grown with a fine texture, while that from further south is often of more vigorous growth, heavier and stronger. However, whatever their origin, pine and spruce in Europe grow to only a modest size, 20–25 metres in height and 30–60 centimetres in diameter, so that sawn timber only exceptionally exceeds a section size of 275×75 mm and most is much smaller. This is in contrast to the growth in the forests of western America where trees 60–80 metres in height and over a metre in diameter are found, though today less frequently than formerly. Thus, for a long time, large sections of up to 300 mm square, and clear, knot-free timber cut from the outside of large old trees could be obtained; such timber is still available, though in limited quantity, and increasing volumes of North American timber are being cut from smaller trees. There is more variety in the Canadian forests with, besides different types of pine and spruce, Douglas fir, hemlock, western red cedar, the true firs, yellow cedar and Port Orford cedar. For many years the supply was dominated by Douglas fir (Figure 1.8), but today western hemlock, usually mixed with amabilis fir (hemfir), and a mixture of spruce, pine and fir are the timbers most commonly shipped. Western red cedar, a lightweight durable wood, is available in modest quantities for exterior cladding, greenhouses, summer houses and similar purposes, but once-important woods, such as Sitka spruce, used for glider framing and racing cars, and yellow pine used for patterns and high-class joinery, are now special-purpose woods which, when available in better grades, command very high prices.

Other woods obtained from elsewhere in America warrant brief mention. In California, American redwood, or sequoia, is a stable, durable, dark red wood used for high-class joinery, and incense cedar from the same state has replaced the original pencil cedar, a juniper, for pencil slats. Pitch pine, once an important timber of the south-eastern and Gulf states of the United States, is now obtained mainly from Central America, principally Nicaragua and Honduras, but loblolly pine (one of the woods of the pitch pine group) has been widely grown in the south-eastern states of the US and plantation trees are being used for sawn wood and plywood.

From southern Brazil shipments of Parana pine – not

a true pine but related botanically to the monkey puzzle – provide a fine, even-textured, almost knot-free wood used for high-class interior joinery. Today, Parana pine is the only important commercial softwood from the southern hemisphere, but within a few years, radiata pine, native to California but extensively planted in Chile, New Zealand, Australia and South Africa, is expected to be available in increasing quantities on world markets, particularly from Chile and New Zealand. Finally, for the UK market, special mention must be made of sawn softwood from the UK forests. Current annual production is about 800,000 m³ but will rise to about twice this figure by the year 2000 and could provide 20 per cent of the national need. Current supply is mainly pine and spruce, but spruce, particularly Sitka spruce, will increasingly contribute to the production, providing a wood for construction as well as for more general purposes.

Hardwoods occur in most parts of the world but are obtained commercially mainly from the northern temperate forests and the tropical rain forests. These two forest types differ in many ways but of special significance for timber supply is that whereas a temperate forest usually has one or only a small number of species which reach commercial timber size, the tropical forest is a mixture of many, often hundreds of species. Thus the temperate forests can be intensively exploited whereas commercial cutting in the tropical forests is normally restricted to a small number of the available species so that the forest is very selectively cut. Yet another difference is the much greater size, both in height and girth, of the trees of the tropical forests compared with those in the temperate forests. However, because the log length extracted from the forest is often determined by factors such as weight, the wheelbase of lorries, road curvatures etc, tropical timbers are not necessarily available in very long lengths though boards are often wider than those obtained from temperate forest trees.

More than 100 different hardwoods are used in the United Kingdom but many are special-purpose woods and about a dozen meet more than 80 per cent of the need (see Table 1.2). More than 50 per cent of the use is temperate forest timber, including that from the British forests; the remainder comes very largely from the tropical forest resource. Hardwood is imported in both log and sawnwood form, but over the years there

has been a steady decline in the log volume so that today it accounts for less than ten per cent of the total value of the hardwood imported.

Temperate hardwoods are obtained from three main regions of the northern hemisphere. Foremost as a source of supply to Britain is Europe, including the British forests, a smaller though still substantial quantity comes from the eastern states of America and the adjoining parts of Canada, and a substantially smaller volume from Japan. Many timbers, for example white oak, beech and ash, occur in all three regions; each is produced by different species in the three areas of supply but differences between, say, the various sources of white oak, result more from conditions of growth, size and age of tree cut, than from inherent differences between the timber of the different species.

Tropical hardwoods, too, are obtained from three main regions of the world. The most important for supply to Britain, as well as to world markets generally, is South East Asia, principally Malaysia, Indonesia and the Philippine Islands. In these and many other South East Asian countries, the forests are dominated by trees of the dipterocarp family and timber such as the various types of meranti, lauan, seraya, keruing, kapur, balau, etc, are all dipterocarp woods. They have a somewhat plain appearance and are used for functional rather than for decorative purposes. Other important South East Asian timbers are teak from Burma and Java and ramin from parts of Malaysia and Indonesia. West Africa, for long the most important source of tropical hardwood for Britain is less so today, though substantial volumes are shipped to mainland Europe. The West African forests were first exploited for African mahogany (*Khaya*) and they have provided many fine mahogany-like woods, such as sapele and utile, red woods such as guarea, makoré, niangon, and a variety of other decorative as well as general purpose woods. Shipments from Latin America are dominated by mahogany (*Swietenia*) from Brazil (Figure 1.9), but the potential of the region for the supply of a variety of decorative and general purpose woods is, as yet, only locally developed.

An analysis of the types of hardwood used in Britain (Table 1.3) shows the major demand is for those in a medium-weight range, between 500 and 750 kg/m³ when dry. This group can be further divided into woods with an attractive colour, often used where appearance is a factor in selection, and woods which are plain and often pale in colour.

The coloured group of woods include the so-called 'red woods' provided by the mahoganies and many mahogany-like woods, and brown woods of the teak, afrormosia and iroko type. Many of these woods are durable and are used for exterior joinery, as well as for furniture and decorative purposes indoors. The volume of red wood used is high, mainly due to good supplies of Brazilian mahogany and red meranti/red lauan but there is a wide choice of red woods available and many contribute to the supply. In comparison, few brown woods are available in quantity and there is a constant search for high quality wood of the teak and afrormosia type; decorative woods, with a walnut-like appearance, command particularly high prices.

Two main types of functional, generally somewhat plain woods can be recognized, those that are durable

Table 1.2 *United Kingdom hardwood use by timbers, 1982*

Timber	Volume (m³ × 10³)
beech	196★
oak	187★
meranti/lauan	123
elm	77†
American mahogany	67
ramin	66
keruing	49
ash	40†
sycamore	35†
iroko	24
African mahogany	19
birch	13
total use in 1982	1144★

★ import and UK production
† UK production only; there is a small import of ash and elm

Figure 1.9 *Brazilian mahogany, seen here, is an attractive hardwood for joinery, furniture and other uses. It is available in good section sizes and excellent quality.* Photograph: Princes Risborough Laboratory, Building Research Establishment. Crown Copyright.

and suitable for outdoor use, and those that are perishable in conditions favouring decay and can be used only in a protected environment. The first group is typified by oak, for long the traditional structural hardwood in exposed situations. Today oak is supplemented for many structural uses, as well as for sills and thresholds, framing of trucks and lorry bodies, estate work etc, by keruing and kapur, Malaysian woods of comparable or better durability, available in large sizes and at modest prices.

The most commonly used general-purpose pale wood for indoor use is beech but other important woods of this type are ramin, birch and ash. These woods, which have a plain appearance, good strength and machine well, are favoured where ease of processing and uniformity of appearance are sought, as in much furniture, as well as for mouldings, handles and turned items. Beech and ash with excellent steam bending properties are used for bent work for chairs, and ash selected for straight grain and good weight has outstanding toughness making it particularly useful for handles of striking tools, garden tools and for sports goods.

In comparison with the volume of medium weight wood used, requirements for both heavy and light weight hardwoods are small. Heavy woods are used where exceptional strength, resistance to wear and long life are required as with harbour, dock and shore defence works, industrial flooring and engine bearers. In the marine environment, greenheart has long been the preferred timber, as it combines outstanding technical properties, particularly resistance to attack by marine organisms, high strength and stiffness, with availability in large sections, up to 400 mm square, and in long lengths up to 18 metres. Other very heavy hardwoods, such as ekki, jarrah, balau, etc are suitable for these purposes but are not available in comparable lengths.

Lightweight hardwoods, such as obeche, jelutong, virola, have a limited market in Britain as mouldings, unstressed parts of furniture, drawer sides, drawing boards, etc, but for many purposes where appearance is of little importance, softwoods, especially spruce, are a cheaper alternative. In some countries of continental Europe, poplar, one of the lightest temperate hardwoods, and some lightweight tropical hardwoods, such as gaboon or okoumé and obeche, are used for plywood; however shipments of tropical hardwood logs for this purpose are decreasing as more plywood is made in their countries of origin. The lightest of all commercial woods, balsa, is used in sandwich construction, for insulation and for modelling.

Table 1.3 *Pattern of United Kingdom hardwood use*

End-use categories	Annual volume* (m³ × 10³)
Heavy woods (>750 kg/m³) for structural use, often in large sizes, e.g. greenheart, ekki, jarrah, balau	<50
Medium weight woods (500–750 kg/m³) a coloured woods with an attractive appearance, mainly for furniture, exterior joinery	
a (i) red woods, e.g. American (Brazilian) mahogany, red meranti/red lauan, utile, sapele, gedu nohor, guarea, makoré, niangon, African mahogany	250
a (ii) brown woods, e.g. teak, afrormosia, cordia, iroko, walnut, paldao, ovangkol, African walnut	50
b plain, often pale woods	
b (i) durable woods, for outdoor, often structural use, e.g. oak, keruing, kapur	250
b (ii) pale, non-durable woods, for use in protected environments, popular for furniture e.g. beech, ash, ramin, birch	350
Lightweight woods (<500 kg/m³), for mouldings, unstressed parts of furniture, etc, e.g. obeche, jelutong, virola	50

* The figures include imports and UK production; they are approximations only, as import or production figures are not available for some of the timbers listed.

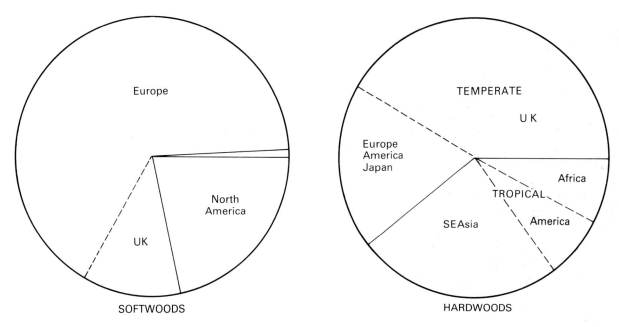

Figure 1.10 *Origins of UK timber supplies, 1982.*

2 Panel products

Anthony B. Hall

Anthony B. Hall BSc AIWSc is a timber consultant specializing in panel products and is the UK technical consultant to Finnish Plywood International.

A feature of solid timber is that it is the product of long, slender logs with both adequate dimension and strength in the direction of the grain and little of either in the direction of the other two major axes. This fact of nature made timber excellent constructional material for struts and ties but did little to advance the use of timber as a diaphragm material to fill the spaces between framing members. This deficiency was partly met by planking – using boards in succession to act as an area infill – but in many instances this solution fell short of the functional requirements.

Following the Industrial Revolution and the consequent changes to industry which it brought during the nineteenth century, the requirement for wood-based panel products to meet many developing uses was identified. Also identified was the need to find uses, in areas of established wood industries, for trees which otherwise had no commercial value. This was coupled to a growing awareness of the relatively large quantity of wood fibre material left after the conversion of timber or as a residue of other factory processes. It was against this background that plywoods and fibre building boards began to be produced in volume from the turn of the century.

Figure 2.1 *Rotary peeling of plywood veneer.* Photograph: American Plywood Association.

The concept of veneer plywood must have been rather easy to visualize. The derivation of veneer from logs had been practised for generations and by this time a range of adhesives of varying type and quality, mainly based on natural products, was available. It was not remarkable to think of combining the two materials to form a panel of bonded multiple veneer layers. The remarkable part of this evolution was the development of the manufacturing process to produce large and consistent quantities of such panels and this owed much to the development of the rotary veneer peeler in the late nineteenth century (Figure 2.1). The manufacturing process, although much refined, remains basically unaltered today. The other major landmark was the introduction in the 1930s of synthetic resin adhesives - by-products of the rapidly expanding oil industry - which included adhesives with a marked degree of moisture resistance.

By its nature plywood takes the best part of a tree, with large diameter straight logs containing a minimum of defects being preferred. Plywood manufacture is therefore centred on those areas where either there is a plentiful supply of logs suitable for peeling or, alternatively, logs which are not wanted for other uses.

Fibre building boards are based on quite a different manufacturing technology and have a different significance to the balance of wood utilization. They are made by reducing timber raw material to fibres and then reconstituting them by a felting operation into sheet form. Because of the degree of reconstitution, fibre building boards can utilize forest thinnings, parts of the tree left after the extraction of sawn lumber or plywood veneer, or other residue from wood processing factories.

In concept, particleboards come closer to fibre building boards than to plywoods and again the idea of reducing wood material to chips and reconstituting these chips to form a panel, after the addition of an adhesive binder, was under consideration at the turn of the century. For a variety of reasons it was not until some fifty years later that chipboard production, mainly for the furniture industry, began in quantity. As with fibre board production, the chipboard process was popular in using raw material which, at best, would otherwise only find a use in relatively low value industries.

The first half of the twentieth century saw the development of core plywoods such as blockboards, battenboards and laminboards with the intended purpose of giving much of the performance of plywood but at a lower cost (Figure 2.2). Latterly the creative energies of the plywood industry have been concentrated on refinement rather than major innovations. Fibre building boards (hardboards, medium boards and softboards) continue to be manufactured generally by the same method, but a major development in the 1970s has been medium density fibreboard, or MDF, the first volume production fibre building board to be produced by a dry process method.

It is the newcomer, the particleboard family, which is the most innovatory product area at present. The range of wood chipboards has been extended from furniture grades to include structural and moisture-resistant varieties in addition to some peripheral developments such as cement-bonded chipboards. There has also been the development, in parallel with wood chipboards, of flakeboards based on larger, geometrically engineered particles.

All types of panel products; plywood, chipboard and fibre building boards, are now produced with low surface spread of flame properties. The treatments are applied to the veneers, particles or fibres before, during or after manufacture and boards are available with Class 1 certification to BS 476: Part 7 'Surface spread of flame test for materials'. Some, in addition, have obtained Class 0 certification to the Building Regulations requirements. The treatments are described in Chapter 3 and products which have obtained Class 1 or Class 0 certification are listed in the TRADA Wood Information Sheet 'Low flame spread wood based board products'.

A recent trend has been the development of board products for specialized applications. These include composite panels incorporating insulation, currently available with plywood or chipboard facings. Other special boards are described within each category.

Sadly, much of the basic development in wood-based panel products took place before the need to classify and document materials logically and systematically had been identified. Too often a new product has been given a name at the development stage based on the company title, a geographical location, a timber species, the intended major use or some similar source to separate it from its fellows and, apt or otherwise, the name has stuck with the product through its market life. In addition, in the case of plywoods, quality and grade classifications have evolved on a local basis or, at best, a national basis with little or no attempt at correlation

Table 2.1 *Popular usage of the major wood-based sheet materials in building, construction and allied applications*

	Plywoods			Chipboards			Fibre Building Boards			
Application	WBP bonded ply	Non-WBP bonded ply	Block-board & Laminboard	Type I	Type II	Type III & Type II/III	Hardboard	Medium board	Insulating board (softboard)	MDF
BUILDING ELEMENTS:										
Sheathing	X					X	X	X	X+	
Flat roofing	X					X			X+	
Roof sarking	X					X			X+	
Cladding	X						X	X	X	
Floor underlay										X
Floor surface (dry)					X					
Floor surface (moisture hazard)	X					X				
Linings – interior partitions and wall panels	X	X	X				X	X	X	
Linings – ceilings & roofs	X	X	X				X	X	X	
STRUCTURAL COMPONENTS:										
Composite beams	X						X			
Truss gussets	X									
Stressed skin floor and roof panels	X				X	X	X			
JOINERY ETC:										
Facias and soffits	X						X			
Staircase construction	X		X		X	X				X
Window joinery				X	X					X
Mouldings and architraves				X			X			X
Furniture and built-in fitments		X	X	X			X	X		X
Door construction	X	X		X			X			X
TEMPORARY WORKS:										
Concrete formwork	X						X	X		
Signs and hoardings	X						X	X	X	
OTHER:										
Shopfitting, display and exhibition work	X	X	X	X			X	X		X

+ Bitumen-impregnated insulating board.

The above table is by no means exhaustive and absence of X does not necessarily imply unsuitability of a material.
Specific designs will be required to meet appropriate regulations and some applications may call for preservative treatment of the indicated material if the timber used in its construction is of limited durability. In many of the applications it will be normal to apply an appropriate surface finish to the material which will require maintenance from time to time.
For further information on the selection and use of sheet materials, please consult TRADA's specialist publications and those of individual manufacturers and their trade associations.

between different producing areas. More recently attempts have been made to rationalize the grading and nomenclature relating to wood-based panel products and these attempts have met with some degree of success. An example of this is the ISO grading of plywood face veneers which identifies broad classifications regardless of species.

PLYWOODS

Sources

Plywoods differ from other wood-based panel products in that they are often identified with the species of timber employed in their construction. For economic reasons they usually originate from the area in which the timber is grown. Some countries with large forest areas and less dense populations produce a large surplus to their domestic requirements whilst others produce almost exclusively for their home market. Britain has

always been a ready market for a wide range of imported plywoods as well as being a producer of a small quantity of high quality plywood from imported logs.

The main sources of plywood imports have traditionally been Canada, Finland and Russia whilst during the 1970s the Far East (Malaysia, Singapore, Korea and Indonesia) emerged as a fourth major market force. Although these areas supply the bulk of the British requirement, imports of plywood are obtained from some forty or fifty countries.

Although superficially competitors, the major plywoods differ significantly from each other. North American plywoods are typically of softwood veneers with pronounced variation in spring and summer growth. Finnish and Russian plywoods are mainly based on birch face veneers of even texture and colour with only small natural defects, whilst Far Eastern production is based on red and white hardwoods. Unlike fibre boards or particleboards it takes little experience to differentiate between plywood types.

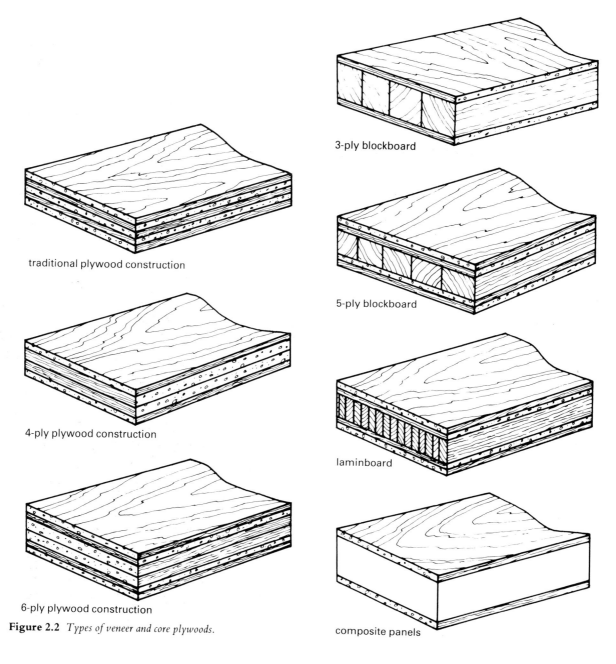

3-ply blockboard

traditional plywood construction

5-ply blockboard

4-ply plywood construction

laminboard

6-ply plywood construction

Figure 2.2 *Types of veneer and core plywoods.*

composite panels

Production

Plywoods of all types, regardless of the species employed as raw material, are manufactured to the same basic process. The logs are conditioned, usually by water or steam treatment, to soften the fibres. After cutting the logs to length, they are peeled to give a continuous ribbon of veneer. The veneer is dried, trimmed, repaired and jointed, after which it is cut into press-size pieces and graded. The plywood lay-up is then prepared by assembling an appropriate stack of dry and glue-spread veneers (Figure 2.3). The assembly is cured in a hot press after which the panels are trimmed to size and, in some cases, sanded. Finally the panels are checked to ensure they comply with the designated grade before being packaged and despatched.

Characteristics of plywood

Although only a very small part by weight of the final product, the adhesive is extremely influential in determining the use to which any plywood may be put. Not so much from structural considerations; it is the wood content which determines strength properties. The role of the adhesive in this respect is to provide a joint which is always stronger than the adjacent timber.

The adhesive's strongest influence relates to the ability of the plywood to withstand degrees of weathering without loss of glue-line adhesion (i.e. delamination). Those adhesives of WBP (weather and boil proof) type as defined in BS 1203 'Synthetic resin adhesives (phenolic and aminoplastic) for plywood' are accepted as capable of providing a bond in plywood which is highly resistant to weather, micro-organisms, water, steam and heat. Other adhesive types, BR (boil-resistant), MR (moisture-resistant) and INT (interior), are progressively less resistant. At present only some phenolic resin adhesives meet the requirements of type WBP and many major manufacturers have standardized their plywood production around these adhesives.

It cannot be overstressed that plywood durability is not determined solely by consideration of the glue type. Also important, if the plywood is not protected or treated, is the natural durability of the plywood's timber content. Some manufacturers using non-durable species can apply protective treatments to plywood veneers during manufacture if requested to do so. Alternatively treatments can be applied after manufacture by impregnation treatments. Specialist advice should be sought from the plywood supplier and preservation company.

Plywood is unique among wood-based sheet materials in having an appearance similar to solid timber. Indeed many plywoods are named by the species employed in their face veneers and marketed on the basis of face quality classification. Different appearance grades of a specific plywood do not usually give rise to different allowable design strengths.

As has already been stated, plywoods are made from both hardwood and softwood species on a basis of their suitability for plywood processing, availability and price. Hardwoods tend to have relatively few and small natural defects such as knots, little difference in annual growth characteristics and even grain, giving a clear, if at times somewhat bland, surface. Conversely, softwood plywoods generally have more numerous and larger defects and a more pronounced difference between spring and summer growth. Indeed, good quality softwood veneers may well be selected for their figure despite the fact that rotary peeling does not usually give the most attractive veneer.

There are really only three distinct categories of face veneer:

> Veneer which is near perfect as peeled.
> Veneer which is imperfect as peeled, but is repaired.
> Veneer which is imperfect as peeled, and is not repaired.

Most plywood manufacturers produce to more than these three basic grades by subdividing them to suit specific market requirements. Good quality face veneers are a very small proportion of total veneer peelings. Matching grades may be used on either face of a plywood. Alternatively a lower grade may be used on the back face. As higher grades are more expensive and their supply often more difficult it is advisable to be aware of veneer gradings and not overspecify.

Most commercial plywoods are laid up with the grain of alternate veneers opposed by 90°, being sequentially parallel to the panel length and width. This method of construction gives rise to a product with well-balanced performance characteristics in addition to added dimensional stability in variable moisture conditions.

Plywood commonly finds use as a flat slab, loaded at right angles to its surface (as, say, is the case in industrial flooring or concrete formwork lining). Most efficient structural utilization is obtained if panels are supported to give two-way spanning, but this is not often achieved in practice. It is a well tested rule of thumb that single-spanning plywoods called to span in excess of 600 mm are seldom structurally economic although on occasions they may be financially expedient. Plywoods also perform well in panel shear (as, say, in the sheathing of timber

Figure 2.3 *Assembly of glued and unglued plywood veneers.* Photograph: American Plywood Association.

framed housing (Figure 2.4) or box-van side panels) and, for example, will often show advantage over other competitive products in not requiring elaborate framing members. Impact strength of plywoods is generally good because of the resistance to penetration of the cross-bonded veneers. Plywood can also be bent along or across its face grain (the latter usually being the easier to achieve) to relatively small radii. High force is required to bend thick boards to their minimum radii and water or steam treatments are used on occasions to facilitate the operation.

Comparative performance data on commercial plywoods commonly available in the United Kingdom is given in BS 5268: 'Code of Practice for the structural use of timber', Part 2 'Permissible stress design, materials and workmanship'. Plywood, more than any other wood-based panel product, is limited by its raw material. Until peeled, the manufacturer will not know the veneer yield he can expect, nor the relative proportions of face and core veneers. He needs this information to determine both his mix of face qualities and also his average production thickness. The effort must then be made to match this yield to his customers' requirements.

The maximum thickness of board that a manufacturer can produce is physically limited by the amount that the press will open. This is usually sufficiently wide to produce a 75 mm panel, but the popular thicknesses fall in the range 4 mm to 25 mm. Plywoods are made to thicknesses below 3 mm but they are not then considered to fall within the classification of standard commercial plywoods.

The two major factors affecting the size of panel produced are firstly the length of the peeler log and secondly the requirements of the purchasing public. The length of the peeler log is set by woodworking requirements and it will be slightly longer than either the length or breadth of the panel to be pressed. The other major dimension is then chosen to give a useful overall panel size. Most presses are set to produce 2440 mm × 1220 mm, but there is a wide range of sizes in use throughout the plywood industry not usually in excess of 3660 mm × 1525 mm. Above this press size, engineering problems mount up rather quickly so it is normal to produce over-press sizes by alternative methods such as scarf jointing panels together. It is not economic to run presses other than full, so if sizes less than full press are required they are usually produced by cutting from full size panels.

Plywood identification

Many plywoods available in the UK are manufactured to national standards of the country of origin, e.g.:

Figure 2.4 *Plywood sheathing in timber frame construction.*

In addition they may be referenced in some performance standards.

Associations representing leading manufacturers operate quality certification schemes to ensure that member companies' production meets published levels of manufacture and performance criteria based on these standards. These schemes, made effective by continuous inspection and testing programmes, are operated notably by the following bodies:

The Council of Forest Industries of British Columbia (COFI)
The Association of Finnish Plywood Industry (AFPI)
The American Plywood Association (APA)

There is at present no common approach to marking of plywoods but major supply sources such as COFI, AFPI and APA member companies employ their own marking systems which incorporate some or all of the following information:

UK	British Standards Institution	BS 1088 & 4079
	British Standards Institution	BS 1455
Canada	Canadian Standards Association	CSA 0121
	Canadian Standards Association	CSA 0151
Finland	Finnish Standards Association	SFS 2415
	Finnish Standards Association	SFS 4091
	Finnish Standards Association	SFS 4092
Sweden	Swedish Standards Commission	SIS 23–42–05
US	National Bureau of Standards	US Product Standard PS 1–83
Malaysia	Malaysian Standards	MS 3.22
Singapore	Singapore Standards	Singapore Standard 1

The Standard governing manufacture and quality control

The place of origin and source

The plywood type

The bond classification

The species and grade of face veneers

In some instances the marking of plywood panels manufactured specifically for structural purposes may give an indication of the performance levels achieved by these panels in a specific end use (e.g. APA Engineered Grades).

The existing situation on the marking of plywoods causes confusion with some specifiers in the UK. There should be an improvement when a British Standard for veneer plywood (BS 6566, due for publication in 1985) is issued. This calls for all boards claiming compliance with the Standard to be marked on back or edge with the manufacturer's name or identification mark together with:

The number of this British Standard.

The panel thickness.

The appearance grades and species category of the face veneers.

The bond classification.

The durability class of the plywood and, if treated, details of the treatment.

Alternative marking will be acceptable under the Standard only on production of an approved manufacturer's certificate. It is anticipated that virtually all plywoods available in the UK will fall within the scope of this Standard.

End uses of plywood

The early days of plywood manufacture were typified by the use of non-durable adhesives and small press sizes (900 mm × 900 mm to 1500 mm × 1500 mm) with major markets in tea chests, furniture and the like. The change to synthetic, durable resins by the North American plywood industry in the 1930s immeasurably broadened the markets for plywoods and the wide adoption of this bonding has led to the domination of today's market by WBP bonded panels. The end-use market is diverse but the building and construction industries are the largest consumers in building components and concrete formwork applications (Figures 2.4–2.7). Other major uses are crates and packages, vehicle body parts, marine fittings, farm buildings and equipment, industrial flooring (Figures 2.8–2.10) and shop and exhibition fittings.

Plywood economics

The production costs of plywood are broadly divided into three major categories: labour, energy and raw material, and in each of these areas plywood is more expensive than other wood-based panel products. It is the generally higher performance of plywood, thickness for thickness, which in many cases makes it cost-effective to the user, and causes it to be selected in preference to less expensive products.

The lower priced end of the plywood market is subjected to continued erosion by the development of other

Figure 2.5 *Plywood box beam arches for a sports stadium in Finland.*
Photograph: Finnish Plywood International.

Figure 2.6 *Plywood sheathing for roof panels to form the dome of a mosque in Luton.* Photograph: Council of Forest Industries of British Columbia.

Figure 2.7 *Plywood used as formwork for concrete.*

Figure 2.9 *Plywood is widely used for packaging.*

Figure 2.8 *Plywood flooring in industrial situations can provide easy access to services below.*

Figure 2.10 *The surface of Hammersmith Bridge in London is plywood panels finished with a patented anti-skid surface.* Photograph: GLC.

less expensive wood-based panel products and some manufacturers have looked to strengthen their market position by providing further services to add value to their standard products, such as:

Cut sizes (i.e. sizes smaller than standard press sizes).
Over-press sizes (large panels, usually formed by the structural jointing of standard press sizes).
Machining and other woodworking (tongued and grooved joints, drill holes, chamfers, bevels and other profiling).
Treatment during manufacture (usually to improve durability or fire performance).
Functional and decorative surface coatings (such as paint, resin, impregnated paper or glasscloth etc).

The provision of services of this kind by the plywood manufacturer means that he is on these occasions providing a component rather than a raw material.

Despite the developments in wood-based panel products, plywood remains structurally the strongest member of the family. It could also make strong claims to being the most durable and creep-resistant as well as being the only panel which retains a 'real' wood appearance. However, plywood manufacture requires large capital investment and production and raw material costs are high. In recent years the industry has displayed considerable ingenuity in minimizing labour costs but it seems unlikely to be able to achieve similar reductions in cost in the future. For a variety of reasons the prospects for special plywood products are much brighter, although they raise additional complications so far as marketing and stocking are concerned.

Core plywoods

The main derivatives from plywood are blockboard, laminboard and battenboard. These products are made by applying veneers to a core made up from solid timber core blocks. Following assembly of the core, application of the face veneers and other finishing operations are carried out in a manner similar to the plywood manufacturing process. The core of laminboard consists of veneers up to 7 mm thickness, blockboard of strips of solid wood between 7 mm and 30 mm wide, and battenboard of block width in excess of 30 mm. Commonly, one or two veneers are applied to each face, with the veneer grain direction perpendicular to the direction of the core strips.

Blockboards and laminboards reached a peak of popularity in the 1960s and early 1970s with supplies mainly from Finland and also from other European countries. More recently, as in the case of plywood, larger quantities have been imported from the Far East and South America.

With the visual appearance of plywood, but usually bonded with interior quality resins, these core plywoods could be used for cabinet work, especially doors, without framing members, and the ease with which they could be cut and fixed on site made them particularly popular for built-in fitments. Alterations in building practice, away from the use of built-in units and towards the use of factory prefabricated units have caused a decline in core plywood consumption, and the long term prospects of these products are open to question. Their sole purpose is as plywood substitutes and their only justification is if they can carry out the plywood function at a lower price. Whilst plywood labour costs have been kept in check, core plywood costs have not – mainly because of problems in automating core construction. The low return presently obtained on these products gives little encouragement to manufacturers to invest in this direction.

Blockboards are generally produced with plywood face veneers, but they are also available faced with more decorative veneers. In such instances it is normal to apply the exotic veneer as a post-manufacture operation. Also available is a range of resin/paper surfaces and other overlays and finishes.

Laminboard is generally considered to be an upmarket blockboard due to its more refined core construction. As it is more expensive than blockboards, it has not been widely used for house fitments, and its major outlet is in high class cabinet work where it is usually overveneered. It has always been favoured by musical instrument manufacturers, many of whom hold the strong view, based on experience, that laminboard is more dimensionally stable than any other wood-based sheet material. It must be added that there is no scientific evidence to support this view.

Over the past decade there has been a limited production of plywood veneered particleboard. Its introduction has been successful and although it has not yet met with universal acceptance, it may well be a pointer to a future growth market for plywood veneers.

CHIPBOARDS

Production

In the manufacture of chipboard, appropriate raw materials such as forest thinnings and industrial wood waste are converted into wood chips by mechanical chipping machines, after which the chips are screened and dried. The graded chips are then mixed with a controlled quantity of resin; in the proportion of about eight per cent by weight. The coated wood chips are then formed into boards, usually by curing between the plates of a heated platen press. An alternative method of manufacturing thin chipboards is to form them around a heated cylinder before reconverting the panels to a flat shape.

In platen press production there are three basic methods of laying up the chips for pressing (Figure 2.11):

Single layer. The distribution of chips is random, giving consistent density throughout the thickness of the board.

Multiple layers. Graded chips are deposited in layers, normally fine chip surfaces with larger chips in the core to give varied density through the thickness. A three-layer system is most common.

Graded density. The method of distributing the ungraded chips gives a smooth, unlayered transition from fine surface chips to coarse core chips.

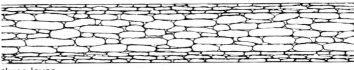

single layer

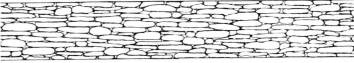

three-layer

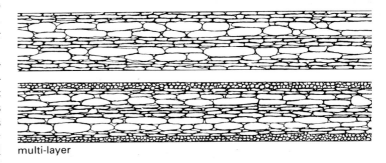

multi-layer

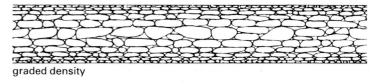

graded density

Figure 2.11 *Basic methods of laying up chipboard.*

After pressing, boards are trimmed and sanded on both faces to the required thickness (Figure 2.12).

Chipboard types and their sources

In addition to a substantial domestic production of chipboards, the UK imports the majority of its requirements from Europe, particularly Spain, Belgium, Sweden, Finland and West Germany. Unlike plywoods, chipboards are not named by either the species used in their production or by their country of origin, but are usually given a mill or company name. A problem for chipboard in its early days was that, among the general specifying public, there was little awareness of brand or type. Large users, such as furniture manufacturers, were more knowledgeable and indeed were often influential in the manufacturer's decisions as to what should be produced.

This matter has become more regularized with the broadening of chipboard use into areas other than furniture and DIY, and further benefit was derived from the publication, in 1979, of BS 5669 'Specification for wood chipboard and methods of test for particleboard' which identified four types of chipboard:

  Type I   Standard (furniture and general purpose chipboards).
  Type II Flooring (mainly for domestic house floor coverings).
  Type III Improved moisture resistance.
  Type II/III Combining the strength properties of Type II with the improved moisture resistance of Type III.

Work is already in hand to revise BS 5669:1979 to include chipboards in excess of 25 mm thickness and also flakeboards and waferboards. Consideration is being given to the introduction of a structural chipboard category.

Characteristics of chipboards

Types I and II chipboards are considered suitable for interior use in dry conditions and are usually bonded with urea-formaldehyde resins. Type II is usually of greater density than Type I. Panels of Type III and II/III have improved moisture resistance and can be used in more exposed conditions or where occasional wetting may occur. The improvement in performance is obtained by the use of more moisture-resistant resins such as phenol-formaldehyde or melamine-formaldehyde either as replacement to, or fortifiers of, urea resins. It is not yet possible to make a direct comparison between the resistance to weathering of a Type III chipboard and a WBP bonded plywood.

Chipboard surfaces are not generally considered to be attractive in themselves. Unlike solid timber or plywood they do not present a 'woody' appearance. Faces vary from fine particles to larger chips but chipboards always look like a reconstituted product. The view on edge is also not attractive and not surprisingly, therefore, chipboard is seldom left in its manufactured state when used in a decorative application. It does however make an excellent substrate for a variety of finishes. It naturally follows that chipboards are not sold by appearance grades and, for example, BS 5669:1979 makes no distinctions on the basis of appearance.

In general, chipboards are less strong and less stiff than plywoods because of their shorter fibre length. The chipboard manufacturer can produce a higher strength

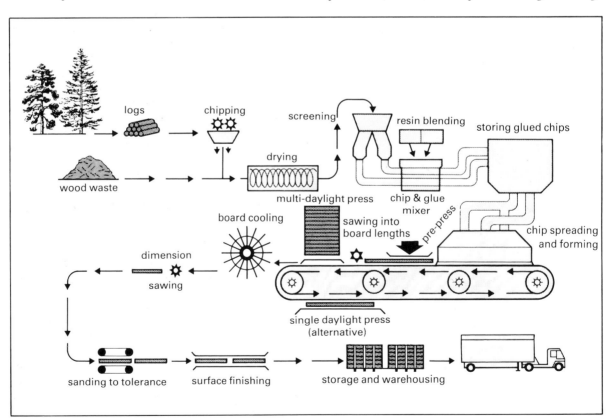

Figure 2.12 _Chipboard production._

panel by varying the chip finish and lay-up and also by increasing the resin content, and high strength chipboards well overlap the performance levels of less strong plywoods. Higher strength chipboards are not necessary for existing chipboard market areas, but are being investigated with a view to market development.

Chipboards, like plywoods, have good strength in flat plate bending and in panel shear. They are less capable of resisting impact damage and suffer a little in being less effective in holding standard fasteners such as screws, nails and staples. They are also more creep-prone under prolonged loading than long-fibre boards and solid timber, but this can be catered for in design. It is not normally practical to flex other than thin chipboards into a curve.

The choice of press size for platen press chipboard production is, for a variety of technical reasons, broader than the choice open to plywood manufacturers. Multi-daylight press installations are usually based on a module of 2400 mm × 1200 mm panel production, for example, 1200 mm line width × 4800 mm length (rather than 2400 mm × 2400 mm which would double the width of the whole production line) (Figure 2.13). In addition, large single daylight presses have been commissioned with a line width of 2500 mm and a length of 14,400 mm. This large press area gives considerable size flexibility. 2400 mm × 1200 mm panels can be produced by single saw cuts, or alternatively a wide range of non-standard boards can be cut with minimum wastage. It also permits production ex-press of large, unjointed chipboard panels – something not yet possible in plywood production. A limitation to this benefit is that equipment used in subsequent surfacing of chipboards is often limited by cost and other factors to a 1200 mm or 1850 mm width. Alternatively, presses are based on an 1830/1850 mm width with varying lengths, so that 1830/1850 mm × 2440/2750/3050/3660 mm can be obtained depending on the overall size of the press. While these sizes are mainly aimed at the furniture industry, they are also finding a market in the construction field. Another recent development has been the introduction of single daylight continuous presses with a fixed width but permitting any length to be cut without waste.

Similarly to plywood, the range of thicknesses of platen pressed chipboards commonly on offer is 6 mm to 25 mm, the popular thicknesses being in the range 12 mm to 25 mm, but thicker panels up to 70 mm can be manufactured in some presses. Thicker chipboards do raise problems in manufacture and cause additional expenses. For example it can take two hours to set up a single daylight press when changing from standard to extra-thick panel production. Similar costs are incurred when changing back. The manufacturer may therefore be reluctant to produce thick chipboards unless a large production run is possible, but there are other manufacturers who specialize in the production of these thick panels.

Uses of chipboard

All of the early development of chipboards was directed at the furniture industry. The late 1960s saw the development of the domestic flooring market for chip-

Figure 2.13 *Multi-daylight press for chipboard.* Photograph: Chipboard Promotion Association.

board and these two uses dominate the market today, taking some 80 per cent of the UK's chipboard. The popularity of the product for flat cabinet work is easy to understand and will continue whilst this style remains fashionable. In addition to boards designed to meet individual furniture manufacturers' specific requirements, a wide range of surfaced chipboards is available to manufacturer and DIY enthusiast alike. These include pre-primed or pre-painted boards, wood veneers, decorative melamine foils, decorative vinyls – both smooth and textured, paper faced, hardboard faced and plywood veneer faced, with a preponderance of melamine faced boards (Figure 2.14).

Chipboard manufacturers would like the security of a broader-based market and, further, would like to see any market extension concentrated upon value-added boards.

Developments on the building and industrial side of the market have included the extension of domestic flooring from first floor joisted floors to include solid ground floor systems (Figures 2.15 and 2.16). Also higher strength flooring grades have found application in some industrial flooring situations (Figure 2.17). The introduction of the moisture-resistant Type III chipboards has led to their use in applications as diverse and demanding as concrete formwork (Figure 2.18) and farm buildings. A drawback at the moment is the absence of BSI or similar authoritative design data for the various types of chipboard classified in BS 5669:1979.

Figure 2.14 *Selection of particleboards*. Photograph: Crown Copyright.

Figure 2.15 *Chipboard domestic flooring*. Photograph: CPA.

Figure 2.16 *Chipboard overlay on solid floor*. Photograph: CPA.

Figure 2.17 *Chipboard industrial flooring*. Photograph: CPA.

Chipboard economics

Compared with plywood, financial aspects of chipboard production are very favourable. Capital costs, energy, labour and material costs are all substantially less and there is an ever-increasing prospect of raw material availability as forest husbandry becomes more scientific. There is of course increasing competition for this raw material from other markets – pulp and paper, fibreboards, flakeboards etc – but the main barrier to the full exploitation of chipboard, which potentially is highly flexible with regard to both input and production, lies in the fact that chipboards have a poor profit record. For the past ten years prices have ranged from average to poor. This is due to over-production rather than competition from other materials. The major period of mill starts was in the late 1960s and early 1970s and the subsequent lack of profit has given little confidence to make capital investment in the form of new mills. However, wherever possible mills have updated their existing plant and machinery to improve the quality of their production.

Other particleboard products

Recalling that today's wood chipboards were developed with furniture uses in view, and are characterized by small surface particles and larger chips in the core, it comes as no surprise that a major separate production has developed based upon wood particles which have

Figure 2.18 *Chipboard used for concrete formwork.* Photograph: CPA.

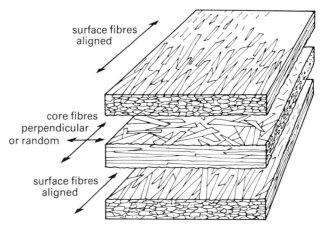

Figure 2.19 *Typical oriented strand board (OSB) composition with parallel fibre alignment in surface layers and perpendicular (or random) core fibre alignment.*

HARDBOARDS

Production

The raw material of hardboard, which is mainly forest thinnings, is chipped down mechanically to around 25 mm square and 3 or 4 mm thick and is screened prior to reducing the chips to fibres. There are two principal methods of fibre production; the defibrator method, in which steamed chips are fed between mechanical grinding discs, and the explosion method, which is based on the ejection of chips from a steam-heated pressure vessel. The resultant fibres are then mixed with water and other additives and the pulp generated is deposited on the wire mesh carrier of a forming machine. After removal of much of the water, the wet pulp layer is fed into a high temperature press. Following this stage, tempered hardboards are oil-impregnated to give a retention of some 7 to 9 per cent by weight. Heat treatment and conditioning are then applied to bring the panels to a satisfactory moisture content (Figure 2.20).

Sources of supply

In addition to some domestic production, hardboard is supplied to the UK by more than thirty countries. Major exporters to Britain include Sweden, Finland, Spain and Portugal. As with chipboards, hardboards are mainly marketed under mill or company names which often give little idea of the origins of the product. Although some brands are known because of their long presence on the UK market there would appear to be little brand identification by the general purchaser and specifier.

Characteristics of hardboards

Since hardboards are not dependent on added resins to achieve a bond between fibres, there is no classification of them by adhesive type comparable to chipboards or plywoods. Hardboards are generally durable and classification to BS 1142: 'Fibre building boards', Part 2: 'Medium board and hardboard' is based on bending strength and limits the weight variation and dimensional response to water immersion or humidity change.

substantially greater fibre length and which are intended to meet the growing 'structural' market for particleboards. These boards, generically classed in the UK as flakeboards, are bonded with moisture-resistant adhesives and are seldom graded by face appearance. Waferboard from Canada is a typical example with flakes of at least 30 mm in length. A recent further development has been the production of boards with aligned particles so that the grain of the wood strands is preponderantly in one direction in any one layer of the panel thickness – thus to an extent emulating a three-ply plywood. This group of products is known as oriented strand board or OSB (Figure 2.19). It is perhaps a little early to know whether the expense of aligning strands is cost-effective, but it is quite clear that flakeboards are a significant and permanent addition to the particleboard range of products.

Another allied development is cement-bonded chipboard, which is not always classified as a particleboard because of its high proportion (60 to 70 per cent by weight) of cement. It is substantially more dense than standard wood chipboards and somewhat difficult to work but has the advantage of being highly fire-resistant. The main uses to date of this product are for linings and partitions in buildings.

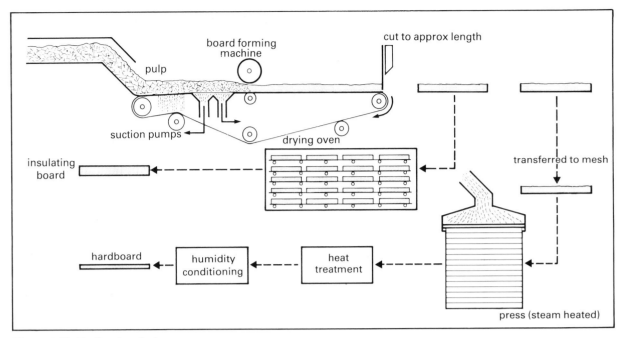

Figure 2.20 *Hardboard production.*

The front face of hardboard is extremely smooth, with a fine mesh pattern on the reverse. Duo-faced hardboards are also available. The face is homogeneous and does not show any distinct signs of its timber origins. The colour ranges from light gold to dark brown for standard hardboards and dark brown to near black for the tempered varieties.

Because of their relatively slender thicknesses hardboards are seldom used unsupported to span horizontally in load situations. Their high panel shear strength however makes them particularly useful as vertical skins in beams, framed panel constructions such as partitioning and sheathing (Figures 2.21, 2.22). Design data for type TE tempered hardboard is included in BS 5268: Part 2: 1984.

Thicknesses of hardboard range from 1.3 mm to 12.7 mm, but the most popular thicknesses are in the range 2.0 mm to 6.4 mm. Press sizes vary widely but are usually either modular on the standard building panel size of 2440 mm × 1220 mm e.g. 1220 mm × 3660 mm and 1700 mm × 4880 mm or on standard door sizes – a major market for standard hardboard.

The labour input in hardboards is moderate, as also are energy and material costs. However, hardboards as a product range have an undeservedly low market image and profitability has for many years been variable, with poor financial results being achieved during prolonged periods of overproduction. Hardboard has few obvious competitors, with the possible exception in more recent years of thin chipboards.

In addition to standard and tempered hardboards, a wide range of value-added products is available ex-mill. They include duo-faced (i.e. smooth on both faces), sealed, primed, pre-painted, surface laminated (including melamines, PVC, paper/metal foils and fabrics), moulded, embossed and perforated boards.

Figure 2.21 *Hardboard web structural box beams.* Photograph: Hirn Construction Ltd.

Figure 2.22 *Tempered hardboard I beams partitioning in an attic conversion.* Photograph: FIDOR.

Uses of hardboard

Tempered hardboards are mainly used where both high strength and resistance to moisture are required. They are suitable for internal and external wall linings, claddings, soffits and fascias and also find applications in agriculture for farm buildings and as dividers for animal stalls, storage bins and silos. Standard hardboards are used in a variety of interior applications such as wall and ceiling linings, panelling, partitioning, joinery, furniture, caravan interiors, underlays for floor coverings, flush doors, shopfitting and exhibition work (Figures 2.23 and 2.24).

Hardboard economics

Hardboards are versatile, effective and inexpensive and few inroads have been made into their traditional markets by other competitive materials. The broad market front gives protection to the sales situation, but the long-term prospects of the products are probably more limited by manufacturing aspects than by market forces.

The wet processes used to produce hardboards and most other fibreboards utilize equipment of high capital cost. Because of the relatively low profitability of hardboards in recent years, there has been a reluctance to invest in new plant. It remains to be seen whether by 'natural wastage' an undersupply situation develops with a consequent firming up of prices, giving confidence to the investor to make the necessary repairs and modernization to keep his plant in economic operation.

Other fibre building boards

Medium board and softboard (or insulating board) are fibreboards which are allied to hardboards and are manufactured by a similar wet process – although in the case of softboard, the press stage is omitted. Medium boards are subdivided into two categories:

LM medium boards. Of lower density with colour grey to light brown and having a smooth velvety surface.
HM medium boards (or panel boards) which are of higher density than the LM variety and resemble standard hardboard in surface appearance.

Softboard is a low density sheet material usually used for insulation purposes. Its colour ranges from cream to mid-brown. Softboard insulating boards are also available in either pre-decorated or bitumen-impregnated forms. Figure 2.25 illustrates fibreboard densities.

The major newcomer to the ranks of fibre building boards is medium density fibreboard, or MDF which is manufactured by a dry process and incorporates glue. Although only available in quantity in the UK for some five years it already represents over ten per cent of the fibre building board market and there is considerable additional capacity available to support a larger market penetration.

The fibres for MDF are prepared as in hardboard production. They are then dried and impregnated with adhesive and press-cured using either heat or radio-frequency treatment to produce a board of homogeneous

Figure 2.23 *Manufacture of hardboard faced flush doors.* Photograph: FIDOR.

Figure 2.24 *Hardboard underlay used in office refurbishment.* Photograph: FIDOR.

cross-section with both faces smooth (Figures 2.26 and 2.27). Thicknesses range between 4 mm and 35 mm and common sheet sizes are 1220 mm or 1525 mm wide × 2440 mm or 3050 mm long. A particular feature of MDF is the quality of cut achieved when machining, particularly on the edge (Figure 2.28).

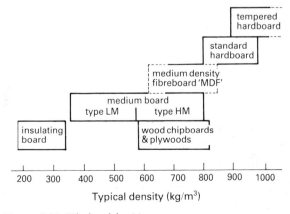

Figure 2.25 *Fibreboard densities.*

Figure 2.28 *Machined MDF panels.* Photograph: FIDOR.

Figure 2.26 *Formation of MDF mat.* Photograph: Seaboard International (Timber and Plywood) Ltd.

128

Figure 2.29 *MDF stair treads.* Photograph: FIDOR.

Figure 2.27 *MDF mat pre-pressed before final pressing. At this stage the mat is electronically scanned to ensure correct composition.* Photograph: Seaboard International (Timber and Plywood) Ltd.

It is perhaps too early to see the precise position MDF will occupy in the market. To date, informed opinion suggests that the largest volumes are being used in the UK as alternatives to solid timbers in applications such as skirtings, mouldings, architraves, door frames and joinery rather than, for example, as a substitute for chipboards in furniture. The present relative costs of MDF and furniture chipboard would support this opinion. If there is a change in fashion in popular furniture, MDF may well be better placed to cover the change than are chipboards. This would lead to a considerable expansion of MDF's role. Otherwise a steady substitution at the top end of the furniture market is envisaged, together with a development and extension of the timber substitute market (Figures 2.29 and 2.30).

Figure 2.30 *The sides, arms and legs of this chair are MDF finished with high gloss polyester.* Photograph: FIDOR.

DECORATIVE VENEERS

Although geometrically similar to plywood veneer, the production of wood veneer for decorative purposes bears little relation to commercial plywood veneer production, despite the fact that the decorative veneer may well ultimately provide the surface for a wood-based panel.

The art of cutting exotic woods into veneers is an old one. Early furniture makers discovered that judiciously placed cuts through some timbers could expose very attractive and decorative surfaces. Several factors, depending on species, may contribute to this, including growth irregularities and defects, colour variation and the arrangement and jointing of veneers.

Veneers may be produced from the log by rotary peeling as for plywood veneer, but few timbers display their best figuring on their tangential face. Consequently most decorative veneers are produced, after the log has been halved or quartered, by advancing it against a fixed knife blade to produce a slice. Veneers produced in this way are usually between 0.5 mm and 1 mm thick. The Appendix shows timber species which are available as veneer. The more common veneers such as sapele and teak types are bonded to chipboard cores in large quantities for DIY and general renovation applications.

When veneering plywood, the decorative veneer is normally laid at right angles to the adjacent veneer. To avoid instability a balancing veneer should be applied to the back of the board. If the panel is to be decorative on one side only, a cheaper veneer of similar thickness and physical properties is used as a balancer (Figure 2.31).

SPECIFICATION AND PURCHASE

When purchasing wood-based panel products, it is necessary to give an accurate and concise specification to the supplier. Normally the specification will require the following:

> Size of board. Length × breadth (giving due regard to grain direction in the case of plywoods).
> Nominal thickness.
> Grade or quality (using ISO or BSI classifications or National Product Standards).
> Brand or trade name of product.
> Bond classification (when appropriate).
> Any special instructions.

When specifying a component to be fabricated from a wood-based panel product it would be normal to accompany the specification with an appropriate detailed working drawing, showing dimensional tolerances and any special requirements.

Figure 2.31 *Selecting and matching burr veneers for furniture.*

Obtaining supplies of a chosen material, to the required grade and in the required quantity at the required time can raise problems in some instances. The manufacturer will usually be the fabricator of a mass-production panel product; most board factories having an output of between 10,000 and 150,000 cubic metres annually. In addition to his major production, he may also produce more specialist board products in smaller quantities for more limited end uses. His production, if he is an overseas manufacturer, will be sold to an importer who, in turn, will sell on to, say, a large user or a small timber merchant. A similar procedure is likely to be followed for a product manufactured in the UK.

The importer and the merchant would like ideally to carry a complete selection of all the goods on offer, but the high outlay required prevents this. The special products of most board manufacturers can be obtained on six to eight weeks delivery but will not normally be held in stock and, for example, the ability to inspect, sample and test is inhibited. However, some importers are developing specialist departments to cover these types of product.

The main business of manufacturers and importers is related to high volume lines and they prefer to deal in these products in bulk (35-tonne lots, say, for the manufacturer and multiple pallet loads for the importer). Their approach on quantities tends to be more flexible over special products. The merchant deals in smaller quantities and may well be prepared to trade in as little as single boards if necessary. Some importers have a merchanting side to their operation, which often leads to a more flexible attitude on quantities.

3 Treatments

Dr Gavin S. Hall

Gavin Hall BSc(Hons) MF DFor FIWSc is head of the technology department at TRADA.

This chapter deals with materials (usually liquids) that are put into, or onto, timber and wood-based sheet materials in order to modify their properties in some way. There are three categories of such treatment which are commercially important; important to such an extent that timber with a long desired service life is rarely used without at least one of them. These will be considered in more detail in the following pages as:

treatments to prevent fungal and insect attack
treatments to improve behaviour in fire
application of finishes to give resistance to weather and to provide decoration.

There are other forms of treatment available for timber but typically these are for speciality end uses and are applied on a limited scale. A few examples are:

- impregnation with plastics materials to improve properties such as resistance to wetting, dimensional stability under changing humidity and wear resistance. The impregnation techniques are similar to those for vacuum-pressure impregnation with preservatives but on a small scale. The plastics vary but include phenolic, epoxy and methacrylate resins, polymerized in the wood by heat, chemical reaction or radiation. The wood may be in the form of veneers or solid and species which absorb liquids readily are usually chosen. Golf club heads, cutlery handles, forms, and flooring boards are examples of this treatment finding commercial use.
- treatment with ammonia in gas or liquid form in order to plasticize the wood and facilitate bending to sharp radius curves. The timber, which is usually of a permeable type and of small cross-section, regains most of its original strength and rigidity once the ammonia has evaporated.
- treatment with gaseous or liquid chemicals which induce chemical changes in the wood making it more dimensionally stable when exposed to varying relative humidity conditions. Such processes are known as acetylation and cross linking; they have had little commercial application for reasons of cost and occasional adverse effects on other properties of the wood.
- steeping in, or impregnation with, polyethylene glycols in order to prevent shrinkage and consequent distortion and splitting. Unlike acetylation treatments, PEG, as it is popularly known, keeps the wood in the green or swollen condition, but the swelling liquid is PEG, not water, and PEG, particularly of the higher, more waxy grades, does not evaporate significantly so that the wood does not dry out. This technique is sometimes used for turnery and carved items but its most common application is in the preserving of wooden artefacts, particularly those recovered from under water.

WOOD PRESERVATION

'Preservation', when used in the timber context, has a more restricted meaning than the dictionary definition. The British Standard Glossary BS 6100 Part 4 defines wood preservation as 'technology of preserving wood from deterioration and destruction by living organisms by the application of wood preservatives'. The organisms concerned in this biodeterioration are primarily insects and fungi but others such as marine borers and bacteria can be important in special situations of storage or use.

The spores by which fungi colonize new food sources are ubiquitous and insects capable of destroying wood and its derivative products if conditions are favourable are also widespread. Therefore protecting wood by antiseptic measures alone is not usually practical, although there are three measures which can prevent the biodeterioration that they cause. The first is to create and maintain conditions which are unfavourable for the insect or fungus; the second is the use of naturally durable (i.e. resistant to biodeterioration) timbers; thirdly, susceptible timbers can be rendered resistant or almost immune by being treated with chemicals which repel or kill the destructive organisms.

All fungi and most insects which infest and destroy wood are using the chemical constituents of wood as food; many such insects also use it to protect themselves from predators. Besides food, they require reasonable temperatures (which usually prevail and which it is impracticable to control), oxygen (which is rarely inhibit-

Figure 3.1 _Gun deck of HMS Victory. (By permission of the Commanding Officer, HMS Victory.)_ Photograph: BRE Princes Risborough Laboratory. Crown Copyright.

ing except when timber is deeply buried or immersed) and sufficient moisture to allow them to develop. Insects are much more tolerant of low moisture content than are fungi which typically will not thrive below a wood moisture content of 20 per cent. It follows that deterioration by fungal attack, resulting in mould discoloration, sap-stain or decay, can be prevented by keeping the wood dry. Where feasible this should be a primary aim whatever other measures are taken.

Although wood preservatives may come out of a tin, wood preservation does not. That is to say, there is much more to the technology of wood preservation than the mixture of chemicals described on the label. It starts at the design stage and continues through choice of materials to the ensuring of good workmanship on site.

Design can prevent timber in service getting wet from rain, condensation or the ground. Where timber components such as exterior joinery are inevitably going to get rained upon, their design should be such as to shed as much of it as possible and prevent the water penetrating the component from where it may take months to evaporate. Design can also be important where the insect hazard is from subterranean termites for instance, but in temperate countries the opportunities are limited.

It is sometimes feasible to prevent decay and insect attack by employing timbers which by the nature of their chemical constituents, are naturally durable (see Chapter 1). This is particularly true of hardwoods, some of which are extremely resistant to attack and can have almost indefinite life even under hazardous conditions (Figures 3.1, 3.2). However, many of the commercially

important timbers are not sufficiently resistant without preservative treatment for use in situations where there is a risk of decay (e.g. fence posts, railway sleepers) or may be at risk (sole plates, exterior joinery) (Plates 1–5). Insect attack of timber in service is fortunately less significant than decay in the UK and certainly far less important than in tropical and sub-tropical regions.

Wood preservatives are poisons designed to inhibit attack or, in the case of remedial treatments applied to already infested wood, to kill the insect or fungus. To be effective over decades and to be safe and practical in

Figure 3.2 _Timber bridges are becoming increasingly popular. They can be constructed using naturally durable timbers as in this bridge at Kendal where hewn greenheart sections form the structural elements._

use, a good wood preservative formulation must aim for a number of desirable properties such as permanence, low mammalian toxicity, absence of side effects such as corrosivity towards metals, paintability, gluability and, of course, good effectiveness against a wide range of organisms, good availability and acceptable cost. There is no ideal wood preservative. Those which have survived in the wood preservative industry from the many historic and later candidates are those which give the best compromise between the various features outlined above.

As well as describing briefly which these wood preservatives are, it is appropriate to consider how they are applied to timber and panel products since in practice, the two are related and best considered together.

It may be stating the obvious but all commercial preservatives designed for long term preventive (as opposed to curative) effect are applied as liquids. Some, known as tar oil types, are liquid in their natural state although some of these require heating to lower their viscosity. Others are water soluble chemicals (usually inorganic), applied in water solution and known collectively as 'water borne' or WB for short. The third main category is known as organic solvent or OS because the active chemicals are made up into a solution in organic solvents of the white spirit type before being applied to the timber. A still small but apparently growing class of preservatives which upsets this neat categorization are those applied as oil in water emulsions. Essentially these are OS types where emulsions are used to substitute water for some of the expensive OS carrier.

Figure 3.3 *Brushing or spraying is the least effective method of applying wood preservatives. However it is often the only course available for remedial treatment.* Photograph: Rentokil Ltd.

The least effective methods of applying wood preservatives are brushing or spraying. In many cases, the treatment is merely cosmetic in wood preservative terms and for protection to be maintained, periodic reapplication is necessary. The reason for this is that timber is a relatively impermeable material and the limited amount of fluid that can be applied by brush or spray remains near the surface from which evaporation and/or leaching is most rapid. This is not to say that such superficial applications of wood preservatives have no role to play; indeed for remedial treatment *in situ* there is really no practicable alternative (Figure 3.3). One way in which the loading can be increased without the need for repeated 'coats' is to apply the preservative thickly in the form of a stiff emulsion. As this breaks down, the active ingredients are able to migrate into the timber giving greater penetration than is possible with low viscosity materials.

Considerably better but still a relatively superficial method is dipping of timber in a preservative fluid. Dipping in this context means immersion in the fluid for less than about ten minutes. Longer than this it is termed 'immersion' or 'steeping'. Dipping is widely practised in tropical countries to protect freshly cut wood from stain, mould and insects during storage and transportation, but the desired protection is short-lived and the process not really one of true preservation. The chemicals used in this case are carried in a water 'solvent' and usually comprise sodium pentachlorophenate (possibly with some sodium borate) and an insecticide such as dieldrin or gamma-hexachlorocyclohexane. A similar formulation, but using pentachlorophenol instead of the sodium salt, is still used by some UK joinery manufacturers to treat windows and other exterior joinery components. Such preservatives are of the OS type. The treatment involves immersing a weighted package of components or assembled units in a tank of the preservative for a minimum period – usually three minutes (Figure 3.4).

Preferably this immersion process is regulated automatically to avoid the temptation of giving the load a quick dip in the solution. Even this would be better than brushing or spraying because the end grain of the timber, which is particularly vulnerable in service to absorbing water and therefore at risk from decay, also absorbs more preservative. However, dipping for three minutes has been found to be the minimum acceptable time for joinery components, after which the treated wood is stored in a ventilated, covered area in order to allow the carrier solvent to evaporate. This leaves the active chemicals deposited in water-insoluble form in the wood. Gluing and painting would be affected if the majority of the solvent were not allowed to evaporate before further processing was carried out.

Next in order of effectiveness, and using the same type of organic solvent formulations, are the variations on the treatments known as double vacuum. In its simplest form, this involves loading the timber, plywood, etc into a treatment 'cylinder' (which may be square or rectangular in cross section!), drawing a vacuum on the 'cylinder' which is then filled with preservative fluid before the vacuum is released (Figure 3.5). Atmospheric pressure is allowed to act on the fluid for a period of about 20 minutes, forcing in the preservative solution.

After this, the residual fluid is pumped back into a storage tank and a final vacuum is drawn to remove excess fluid from the surface and outer layers of the timber. After return to atmospheric pressure, the cylinder is opened, the timber removed and allowed to dry in the same way as for immersion treatments. The variations involve different levels and durations of vacuum and, for those species which resist penetration by fluids, e.g. European whitewood, the augmentation of the 'pressure' phase to two or three atmospheres. Treatment durations vary from about a half to two hours depending on species and the use for which the timber is destined. This form of treatment with organic solvent borne preservative is considered appropriate for all but the most demanding service conditions. This is brought about in part by the use of low viscosity organic solvents with high penetrating ability. For long-term protection of components exposed to the weather, the protection of a paint or similar coating is required and this form of treatment is not considered suitable for ground contact or immersed end uses.

The wood preserving industry and the technology on which it is based are concerned with impregnating the appropriate amount of preservative chemical into the outer zones of the timber treated to a depth and at a concentration that will prevent deterioration for at least the desired service life of the components. If timber were absorbent like brick, simple dipping would suffice. Different species of timber vary considerably in their resistance to absorbing liquids. Some, such as the sapwood of European redwood, are sufficiently permeable to be completely penetrated by the simpler forms of double vacuum treatments. Others resist all but the most superficial impregnation even when high pressures and prolonged treatment periods are employed. Fortunately, most such timbers are resistant to decay and insect attack by virtue of their chemical composition, but where such timbers do require to be treated, specialized methods have been developed. These include oscillating pressure treatments, the use of liquefied petroleum gas as a carrier for the preservative chemicals, or the use of very high pressure treatment which would crush most timbers.

Where service conditions put most demands on the decay resistance of timber or plywood (e.g. ground contact, cooling tower fill, marine use), vacuum pressure impregnation treatments with water-borne preservatives or creosote are specified. These processes are similar to those of the double vacuum treatments which employ above-atmospheric pressures, but the treatment conditions imposed are more severe (up to 14 atmospheres imposed pressure) and the durations several times longer. When creosote is chosen, so-called 'empty-cell' processes are often used to minimize subsequent bleeding of the considerable volumes of the preservative that are injected. These empty-cell processes are characterized by the omission of the initial vacuum stage (or even a partial pressurization of the wood) before the preservative fluid is introduced. This facilitates the recovery of excess liquid during the final vacuum stage.

It may seem unusual that mixtures of inorganic salts such as copper sulphate, sodium dichromate and arsenic pentoxide, all water soluble, should be used for demanding wood preservation under conditions where water soluble materials can be dissolved out. The secret

Figure 3.4 *Immersion treatments are widely used for treating joinery components with organic solvent preservatives. This is often carried out in the equipment used for low pressure application of organic solvent preservatives.* Photograph: Fosroc Ltd.

Figure 3.5 *Pressure treatments are the most effective method for protecting timber against severe decay hazards. Timber is loaded into the pressure cylinder for treatment.* Photograph: Hickson's Timber Products Ltd.

lies in the ratio in which the chemicals are mixed. Once in the timber they react to form a water-insoluble complex which is nevertheless toxic to wood-destroying organisms, both insect and fungal. These preservatives are known as copper-chrome-arsenic or CCA preservatives and have a long history of effective use. The salts are applied as a two to three per cent solution in water using vacuum pressure processing that involves an initial vacuum stage that may be as low as 80 per cent. This combination achieves deep penetration without exces-

Table 3.1 *Characteristics of preservatives*

Type of preservative	Typical characteristics				
	Suitable for ground contact	Coloured	Paintable/ gluable	Strong odour	Cause swelling
Tar oil	Yes	Yes	No	Yes	No
Organic solvent-borne	No	No	Yes	Yes/No	No
Water-borne	Yes	Yes	Yes	No	Yes
Emulsions	No	No	Yes	No	Yes

sive concentrations of chemical. Four to ten kilograms of salt per cubic metre of wood are typical retentions, the amount being specified in accordance with the end use.

It is obvious from the brief consideration above, that the preservative treatment of wood is not an all or nothing affair. In some cases, such as timber used in contact with the ground, a known decay hazard exists, the extent of preservative penetration and its concentration necessary to give it protection can be judged, and the processing appropriate to this and the size and species of timber employed to achieve it applied. At the other end of the scale, uses of timber can be identified or naturally durable species specified where no preservative treatment is necessary. Between, there exist many circumstances of timber use where, due to inadequacies of design, workmanship or maintenance, or change of use, a decay hazard may arise intermittently. In such circumstances, such factors as the consequences and financial implications of deterioration, the cost of treatment and the ease of reinstatement must be weighed up by the specifier. The Building Regulations, NHBC and some British Standard commodity specifications require preservative treatment in some situations. For less defined circumstances there is, fortunately, an increasing amount of guidance available from BSI, TRADA, the British Wood Preserving Association and others to help the specifier make a judgement. Both the guidance and the more detailed coverage of the subject is commended to anyone with a responsibility for specifying timber or wood-based boards. Tables 3.1, 3.2 and 3.3 summarize the characteristics, methods of application and categories of end use respectively.

Table 3.2 *Methods of application of wood preservatives*

Application methods	Use situations
Brush/spray	Superficial/cosmetic treatment, treatment of cut surfaces
Dipping	Thin components, e.g. woven fencing panels; minimum treatment for exterior joinery components/assemblies (NHBC)
Immersion	In OS types – cladding of permeable species
Double vacuum	OS types – carcassing, external joinery, panel products
Vacuum pressure	Tar oil and water-borne – heavy duty treatments for high stress situations, e.g. sole plates, fence posts, transmission poles, marine timbers
Diffusion	Similar to double vacuum (using special water-borne preservatives) for difficult timbers
Sap displacement	Development process for round timber, e.g. transmission poles

Table 3.3 *Categories of need for preservation treatment for building components*

Categories of need for preservation (based on BS 5268: Part 5)	Building component examples* (assuming timber with low natural resistance)
Preservation unnecessary	Interior joinery; floorboarding; interior wall studs
Preservation optional	Roof timbers (pitched); ground floor joists; tile battens
Preservation desirable	External wall studs; timbers in flat roofs; cladding
Preservation essential	Sole plates; loadbearing joinery; timber in contact with ground or concrete below dpc.

* See BS 5268: Part 5 and BS 5589 for full specification guidance

FLAME RETARDANT TREATMENTS

Timber is rarely the material first ignited in an accidental building fire. Such fires usually start in the contents of buildings, often the furnishings, but under the influence of flames and heat radiated from such a fire, timber and wood-based boards will, in their natural or conventionally decorated state, start to burn and contribute to the developing fire. In situations where large areas of timber room linings are used, this contribution could become significant in influencing the course of the fire and the speed with which it got out of control. The tendency of such lining materials to spread flame across their surface when subjected to imposed radiant heat and a pilot flame is known as the 'surface spread of flame' property of that material or product. The BS 476 Part 7 test (Figure 3.6) used in the UK to evaluate this property is unlike that used in other countries, most of which have their own tests.

What flame retardant treatments do for timber is to modify, either physically, chemically or both, the process of combustion of that wood surface exposed in the test (or real fire) in such a way as to suppress flaming. The way that the various treatments available do this varies with their type. In some cases, the mechanisms are very complex and imperfectly understood. It is almost certain that most of the early flame retardant treatments and even some of the recent ones have been arrived at by trial and error rather than from first principles.

Flame retardant treatments for timber and board products are available either as post-manufacture treatments or as part of board manufacture which will up-

Figure 3.6 *Testing the surface spread of flame properties to the requirements of BS 476 Part 7.* Photograph: Warrington Research Centre.

grade from the inherent Class 3 surface spread of flame to Class 1 of BS 476: or even Class 0 as defined in the Building Regulations. Thus timber can be brought up to that performance level one below non-combustibility by the appropriate choice of treatment.

They are of three distinct types. For solid timber, impregnation processes very similar to those described for CCA preservatives can be used with water-borne chemicals; for reconstituted boards like chipboard or fibre building boards, chemicals of a similar nature can be incorporated during manufacture; and for all products, including those already installed, specially formulated paints and varnishes are available which combine a decorative role with that of upgrading the flame spread behaviour of the product.

As with wood preservatives, no ideal treatment exists. The specifier must decide which to require on the basis of cost, appearance, resistance to moisture and several other factors unrelated to actual flame retarding capabilities. These latter will have been validated by independent test for a representative range of timber substrates, and certificates attesting to this are available from the manufacturer on request.

All the types of flame retardant available in the UK and which meet the Class 1 performance requirement are suitable for interior use provided that the prevailing relative humidity is not above about 80 per cent. For exterior use, the choice is extremely limited but then it might well be argued that the flame spread test is hardly relevant to that type of situation. There is, however, one impregnation treatment and one type of surface coating which claim to have weather resistance, in which case they certainly should have sufficient resistance to moisture for high humidity indoor uses such as swimming pool halls (Figure 3.7).

With new building work, the choice lies between all

Figure 3.7 *The timber in this swimming pool was treated with a moisture-resisting flame retardant impregnation treatment.* Photograph: Koppers Company Inc (UK) Ltd.

three types of flame retardant treatment whereas for *in situ* upgrading, only surface coatings can normally be contemplated. It has been known for panelling to be removed, treated with an impregnation type flame retardant and reinstalled, but this is unusual and obviously the risk of damage is high. If board materials are to be used, then assuming that the supply situation is good, the most straightforward way of achieving the Class 1 (or Class 0) requirement, is to specify boards with the desired appearance and with built-in Class 1 performance. However, the range is more restricted than with 'natural' boards and stocks of what tend to be regarded as special items are not necessarily kept. TRADA issues leaflets in its Wood Information series which give information on the types produced for both board products and treatments available for upgrading timber and boards. Table 3.4 summarizes some of the characteristics of flame retardants. Where it is decided for reasons of

Table 3.4 *Summary of characteristics of flame retardant treatments*

Types	BS 476 Pt 7 Class 1	BS 476 Pt 6 Class '0'	Moisture resistant	*In situ* application	Need decoration/ protection
Impregnation treatments					
1 Salt-type	Yes	Some	No	No	Yes
2 Moisture resistant type	Yes	Yes	Yes	No	No
Incorporated into boards	Yes	Some	No	No	Yes
Surface coatings					
1 Clear intumescent	Yes	Some	No	Yes	No
2 Opaque intumescent	Yes	Some	No	Yes	No
3 Opaque	Yes	No	Some	Yes	No

cost, availability, flexibility, or convenience to specify a treatment to be carried out on standard materials, the first choice is between impregnation treatments and surface coatings. There is no doubt that, when applied correctly and well maintained, a surface coating flame retardant can perform very satisfactorily both as a decorative finish and, in the unlikely event of a fire, as a means of isolating the timber lining from the fire and so delaying its involvement. They are not foolproof materials, however, and require more care in application and use than a conventional paint or varnish. Also, they need to be maintained carefully if the flame spread protection effect is not to be reduced. There is considerable prejudice against surface coatings for new work, notably amongst building control officers. This stems from the difficulty of identifying the treatment as to type and quantity applied. Once applied, they resemble conventional varnishes, gloss or emulsion paints depending on the type and, unlike these, require to be applied at a

minimum rate, not just enough to cover, if they are to give the required degree of protection. There is also the worry about what happens when redecoration time comes around – will they be stripped off and replaced by a non-flame retardant finish? They have been shown to be capable of being overpainted to a limited extent without having their protective properties impaired, but the worry still remains.

Before leaving the surface-coating flame retardants, a word on how they react in a fire is in order. Most examples of this type are what are known as intumescent finishes. This means that on exposure to heat at temperatures typical of the early stages of a fire but well below that which would cause ignition of timber, chemicals in these coatings release gases which cause the heat-softened coating to froth or intumesce. What develops is a carbonaceous crust of foam, several millimetres thick, which insulates the timber surface from the fire (see Figure 3.8). This is a very simplified ex-

Figure 3.8 *Samples before and after surface spread of flame test – from left to right: untreated – exterior grade varnish – flame retardant clear finish – flame retardant impregnation treatment – flame retardant emulsion paint – flame retardant semi-matt paint.*

planation and, in reality, the products are much more complex. A theoretical benefit of this type of coating is that it delays the onset of charring of the timber and may contribute a few minutes to the burnthrough or fire resistance. However, such an effect is rarely significant and such protection should usually be viewed as a bonus rather than something to be relied upon to achieve a required period of fire resistance. Having said that, there are very similar systems of thicker and more active intumescent coatings and materials which have a very important role in fire resistance, notably in fire door design and protection for structural steelwork.

A variety of simple inorganic chemicals, such as ammonium sulphate, ammonium phosphate, sodium borate and various chlorides and bromides modifies the combustion of wood in such a way that flaming and flame spread is reduced. In CCA preservative terms, high concentrations of these chemicals are required to suppress the natural flaming inclination of the wood – some ten times the 4 kg/m^3 loading of CCA. At these concentrations, Class 1 and even Class 0 performance is possible from a wide variety of timber species and board products.

Proprietary formulations are used for such treatments and these consist essentially of mixtures of salts similar to the above, perhaps with additional components to give fungal resistance, reduce corrosive effects and so on. Unlike CCA preservatives, these mixtures do not 'fix' in the timber to become insoluble, but remain water soluble and vulnerable to wetting and high humidity. Some form of protection in the form of paint, varnish or stain finish is desirable even in an interior environment if the treated product is to remain decorative. Being impregnated into the timber in water solution, it follows that the timber must be redried before use. There are no organic solvent-borne flame retardants that will achieve Class 1 surface spread of flame to BS 476 Part 7. There is one process, however, which uses organic chemicals in water solution for vacuum pressure impregnation. After impregnation, the active ingredient is still water soluble but the timber or board is then kiln dried and, when at a low moisture content, the temperature in the kiln is increased. This causes the chemical to polymerize inside the wood to give a leach-resistant treatment that will even retain its flame retardant properties outdoors for a considerable time. The treatment chemicals are clear so that a good decorative effect can be maintained. Inevitably, this process is slightly more expensive than the salt-type impregnation flame retardant treatments but in some service conditions it is the only process currently commercially available that can be performed. Under more mild conditions, the salt-type treatments will perform as perfectly adequate flame retardants as long as manufacturers' recommendations are followed.

FINISHES

The need to decorate wood surfaces has already been touched upon in connection with flame retardant surface coatings. Sometimes the timber, plywood or chipboard is used merely as a neutral background to a paint finish which obscures it. In many cases, it is desired to exploit the attractive appearance of the wood or panel by using a clear varnish or translucent stain type of finish. A secondary function of the finish is that it will protect the wood surface. This is particularly true outdoors, but even indoors, protection against abrasion, water staining, knocks and dirt getting ingrained is an important function of the finish.

Seals for industrial timber floors represent perhaps one of the few situations where the protective function is dominant and decorative value minimal. In most cases they are equally important.

There are few, if any, finishes that do not change the appearance of the wood to which they are applied to some degree in colour, sheen or texture. Varnishes and polishes are often said to 'bring out the colour or grain', an effect which is due to the displacement of air in the surface fibres with the synthetic resins contained in the finish. This is usually thought to be a desirable characteristic, but the clearer the varnish initially and the greater its ability to resist yellowing as it ages, the better.

The selection and use of wood finishes indoors present few problems. The conditions of use are not usually too demanding and finishes can often be applied under controlled or at least, favourable conditions. Matt, eggshell, silk, gloss, white, red, green, clear, highly film-forming, penetrating and finishes with a whole variety of other attributes are available to choose from (Figure 3.9). Care with preparation, including checking that the moisture content is appropriate to the service conditions, is necessary if the full decorative value of the wood is to be exploited. A varnish brings out the defects as much as it does the grain!

Finishes for outdoor timbers face a much harder (and shorter) life. The overall problem is weathering. This is a combination of factors including the chemically degrading effect of ultra-violet light, fluctuating moisture content leading to cracking, the leaching action of water which removes soluble chemicals, the development of micro-organisms resulting in mould, stain and increased porosity, and the stresses imposed by changing temperatures.

Untreated wood exposed outside, however 'durable' its classification may be, will soon lose its colour and develop surface checking. If continued for months and years, such exposure will result in soiling of the wood surface and gradual loss of fibre. It usually follows that some form of protection is required to prevent this weathering although this 'erosion' is said to occur at only 6 mm per century and untreated wood components have performed satisfactorily without finishes for decades.

Most finishes for outdoor timbers are still applied on site – with all the problems that this entails. Factory finishing is increasingly being looked to in order to provide exterior finishes with increased initial life before maintenance becomes necessary. Greater control of the preparation and finishing operation is possible with factory application of even conventional paints, varnishes and exterior wood stains. The practice of applying one or two coats of such finishes to joinery, cladding, etc before it is sent to site, to be followed by any localized repair and a final finishing coat after installation is fortunately growing. Nevertheless, it is still discouraging to do so when faced with the unthinking or uncaring storage and treatment such components receive on some building sites. In this respect, the UK lags far behind its continental neighbours who regard the installation of fully finished joinery components into fully prepared openings as the norm.

From the brief outline of the weathering process to which exterior building components are subjected, it is obvious that a wood finish for use outside should protect the wood from wetting and rapid changes of moisture content and from at least ultra-violet light. Additionally, it might contain chemicals to discourage micro-organisms, and light colours will control surface temperature to some extent.

The choice of finish is broadening as the requirements of a good exterior finish are being recognized more widely by specifiers and finish manufacturers. It used to be a choice between gloss paint, varnish and exterior wood stain. Now there are many textured finishes, paints specially formulated for exterior service, and a wider range of exterior stain formulations to choose from. White alkyd gloss paint is still available of course, and widely used, but its deficiencies as a finish on timber used outdoors are being more openly talked about.

The first choice facing the specifier is whether to dis-

guise the timber or board substrate in terms of texture and/or colour, whether to modify the colour whilst still allowing the texture and grain pattern to show through, or whether to try to preserve the appearance of the wood as naturally as possible. Such decisions will dictate the type of product as paint/textured finish, exterior wood stain, or clear 'stain' or varnish. Within each of these categories there is a seemingly bewildering range of commercial products, many making enthusiastic claims, and varying widely in price and the aggression with which they are promoted. Also, the scene changes quite rapidly. A UK consumers' organization and TRADA attempt, periodically, to give guidance on specific types of finish (currently paint and exterior wood stains respectively) (Figure 3.10). Such evaluations are to be commended because it is obviously not practical to attempt to provide this guidance here.

To add to the confusion which arises from the recent development of new products, the terminology has not been adequately standardized. For this reason, a brief description may be in order – starting with paint because everyone knows what paint is!

Pigment bound in a resin, dissolved or dispersed in a solvent which may be organic or water constitutes a typical paint. The object is to get a continuous, level and more or less uniform thickness of pigment bound with resin adhering to the surface of the wood on the one face and presenting a decorative and protective surface on the other. Conventional paint systems dry by solvent evaporation and the coating is built up from primer, undercoat and top or finishing coat. Weathering and oxidation cause the paint film to embrittle over the years, and because the film is relatively impermeable to water vapour, moisture arising from condensation or leakage through joints tends to get trapped behind it. This may lead to blistering, loss of adhesion, cracking and flaking with the result that maintenance can often require stripping back to bare wood and recoating from scratch.

Varnishes are similar to the paint described above, except that the film contains more resin and no pigment. It may contain ultra-violet light absorbers, plasticizers and other ingredients to make and keep the dried film flexible and able to accommodate movement of the wood. However, varnishes tend to suffer from the same limitations as paint plus the added disadvantage that discoloration due to fungal stains or water penetration cannot be masked on retreatment as they can with paint. It follows that maintenance of varnish has to be anticipatory if costly restoration of appearance is to be avoided. Also, because they contain no pigment, their limited ability to reflect or screen out damaging light leads to earlier deterioration of the film and possibly also of the wood beneath it. Varnishes are usually best reserved for timber protected from direct exposure to the weather and where frequent maintenance with a high standard of workmanship can be relied upon.

Exterior wood stains were originally promoted as alternatives to exterior varnishes, but have developed into perhaps the most important class of exterior finishes for wood. They are available in a wide range of colours and vary between those which penetrate the surface of the wood to leave very little surface film, and those more resinous formulations that resemble translucent paints.

Figure 3.9 *Finishes for interior timber are available in a wide range of types. Specialist floor finishes provide a hard wearing surface.* Photograph: Jewell Harrison.

Figure 3.10 *Proprietary exterior wood stains are subjected to weathering trials at TRADA.*

Figure 3.11 *Sample boards illustrate the water repellent properties of exterior wood stains.*

They are not without their limitations, however, and it would be wrong to view them as the ultimate answer to exterior finishing of timber. They would benefit from greater durability particularly of their protective value which relies on water repellency (see Figure 3.11). They have the advantage of allowing the wood to 'breathe', i.e. lose moisture vapour which would otherwise accumulate, but this allows moisture contents to fluctuate more than with paint or varnish. Also they offer less protection to glazing sealants than do paints

and interact to a greater extent with the design of the component. One of their primary virtues is their ease of retreatment since they erode rather than fail by cracking or flaking.

Increasingly, products are coming on to the UK market with properties intermediate between conventional paints and exterior wood stains. These are the so-called opaque versions of stains, some of which are labelled microporous paints by their manufacturers. They are probably better considered as exterior paints, that is

47

paints formulated with exterior performance and durability specifically in mind. They are typically less glossy than conventional paints and their hiding power may be less. Single formulation, as opposed to primer, undercoat and top coat, is usual. They claim ease of maintenance and a resistance to the normal form of 'paint-type failure' on prolonged weathering.

There is considerable promise that these finishes and exterior wood stains, between them, will provide most of the answers to the finishing of exterior woodwork. However, development work is continuing and a steady evolution of improved products can be anticipated to complement this very demanding end use of timber and wood-based board products (Figures 3.12, 3.13). Table 3.5 is an attempt to generalize the characteristics of the main types of finishes for wood.

Figure 3.12 *Exterior wood stains are particularly effective on sawn boarding, used here to surround the balcony of a timber frame house in Surrey.* Photograph: Michael J. Barrett.

Figure 3.13 *Exterior wood stains provide protection for timber in severe environments. The National Trust for Scotland's Visitors' Centre at Ben Lawers is situated at 1400 ft in the Grampian mountains; the European redwood boarding was treated with a dark water repellent stain which has weathered to a natural looking silver grey colour.* Photograph: Jewell Harrison.

Table 3.5 *Characteristics and uses of the main types of finishes for timber*

Types of finish	Interior	Exterior	Protective	Decorative	Clear	Stain	Opaque	Approx. exterior service life (years)	Exterior joinery	Cladding Boarding	Cladding Plywood	Application Factory	Application Site
Paint (primer, undercoat, topcoat)	Yes	Some	Yes	Yes	No	No	Yes	5	Some	Some	No	Yes	Yes
Varnish	Yes	Some	Yes	Yes	Yes	Some	No	2	No	No	No	(Yes)	Yes
Exterior wood stain	Some	Yes	Yes	Yes	Some	Yes	No	4	Some	Yes	Yes	Yes	Yes
Exterior paints	—	Yes	Yes	Yes	No	No	Yes	5	Yes	Yes	Yes	Yes	Yes
Textured finishes	—	Yes	Yes	Yes	No	No	Yes	15	No	—	Yes	Yes	(Yes)
Floor seals	Yes	No	Yes	Most	Most	Some	Some	–	–	–	–	(Yes)	Yes

48

4 Specifying timber

Brian Keyworth

Brian Keyworth DipArch RIBA was manager of TRADA's building development department and is now in private practice. Prior to joining TRADA he was principal architect at the Midlands Housing Consortium having previously worked in various private practices.

In a technological age it is very easy to take for granted those elements which have always existed and in the building industry this tends to apply to traditional materials such as brick and timber. It is not until it is necessary to write a precise specification that the information shortfall becomes apparent and sources of guidance are sought. Timber in particular is not usually imported with a precise 'end use' classification but is made available via merchants to the specifier or user with the onus upon them to determine its final form. A floor joist, for example, is formed only when the appropriate section of timber is cut and fitted into place. Most timber importers and merchants have considerable knowledge which is available to their customers, but there is a gap between their expertise in timber buying and the user's need for correct and economic specification for all types of timber.

Timber is used in the building industry for structural members, for joinery and trim and for claddings and linings. For each of these end uses there is an appropriate grade and quality, in terms of appearance, durability and efficient use of the material. There is no advantage to the user in specifying a better quality than is necessary for satisfactory performance. The specification requirements for most end uses are set out in the relevant British Standards and guidance information is provided in publications by TRADA, BRE and organizations representing overseas suppliers. Specification is, however, complicated by the fact that timber is generally imported using commercial grade descriptions which differ from those specified in British Standards and that the grades also vary depending upon the type of timber and its country of origin.

Timber can be divided botanically into 'softwoods' and 'hardwoods'. These terms are in themselves confusing since some softwoods are harder than some hardwoods and vice versa. Softwoods are produced from coniferous trees and hardwoods from deciduous trees and both classes contain timbers which vary in colour, weight, strength and resistance to decay (see Chapter 1). The names given to a species may also vary depending upon its country of origin which will have given its own common name. The standard names for most timbers in common use are given in British Standards 881

and 589 'Nomenclature of commercial timbers'. Additional information on the properties, characteristics and uses is given in the TRADA series of Red Booklets on 'Timbers of the World' and the BRE publications, 'Handbook of hardwoods' and 'Handbook of softwoods'.

It is important that when specific names are quoted they should be from the Standard in order to avoid confusion. To illustrate this: one of the commonly used softwoods in Britain is termed European redwood in the British Standard. It comes from the species *Pinus sylvestris*, which is called (amongst other names) deal, Swedish pine or Scots pine.

Softwood is used for almost all structural purposes and a considerable proportion of the joinery and trim in this country. Due to its climate, size and geography, Britain can never be self-sufficient in timber production – approximately 90 per cent of requirement needing to be imported. Softwood imports come primarily from Scandinavia, Russia and Canada and timber is an important factor in the economies of these countries. In the days when virgin forests were available, there was a plentiful supply of large sections of timber which were used by the building industry of the time. This supply situation has gradually changed since the turn of this century and large sections are less readily available in commercial quantities making it necessary to consider timber from smaller trees. However, more detailed technical information on the properties of timbers and the introduction of stress grading has resulted in efficient designs without the previous over-specification.

Softwood is normally sawn in its country of origin into square-edged sections in a range of standard sizes and marked on its end grain with the shipper's mark (Figures 4.1 and 4.2).

Timber from Northern Europe is graded at source using commercial quality grades and these are the grades used by buyers and importers. It is common practice not to separate the better grades but to sell them as a grouped grade described as 'unsorted quality'. In this quality redwood and whitewood are kept separate. The lower quality grades are sold separately and can include mixed redwood and whitewood species. In addition to these commercial grades a limited amount of timber for

Figures 4.1 and 4.2 *Imported softwoods showing shipping marks.*

structural purposes is stress graded to BS 4978 'Timber grades for structural use' in its country of origin and exported in that form.

Canadian and North American softwood is generally separated at source into structural or joinery grades. Most is imported as sawn material either stress graded or separated into commercial grades.

The terminology of commercial grading varies according to the country of origin. It will be appreciated that these terms, whilst of general interest to the specifier, are not suitable to describe requirements fully and it is therefore essential to refer to the relevant grades appropriate to the end use in the British Standards.

Hardwood is imported from many parts of the world, including Europe, but mainly from the tropical or semi-tropical areas. There are numerous species available and by comparison with the well-developed sawmilling industries of the softwood exporting countries, many hardwood producers are still relatively less sophisticated. Most hardwoods are imported in specific thicknesses but random widths, which are within an agreed and accepted range. They may also be imported as cut-to-size dimension stock or as logs sawn through and through. Other hardwoods include temperate species such as beech, walnut, elm, oak, which are used mainly for veneers and quality joinery. British grown hardwoods typically will be sawn through and through and cut to size on order (Figure 4.3). These are often available from specialist companies who deal with a particular market as well as from the companies who import hardwoods.

The majority of hardwoods used by the building in-

Figure 4.3 *Through and through cut British logs.* Photograph: Mallinson Denny (UK) Ltd.

dustry are for joinery, except for some species such as keruing and balau from South East Asia; iroko and celtis from West Africa; and jarrah and karri from Western Australia, which are used structurally. These timbers are available in long lengths, free from growth defects, making them ideal for long span or heavily loaded beams, joists or posts. Structural hardwoods should be specified in accordance with BS 5756 'Specification for tropical hardwoods graded for structural use' which gives grading rules for a single visual stress grade designated 'Hardwood Structural' (HS) grade and the species should be named in the specification. The Code of Practice for the structural use of timber, BS 5268 Part 2 currently includes grade stresses for 12 hardwood species graded to BS 5756 rules. These are indicated in the Appendix which gives details of the properties of some commonly used timbers.

STRESS GRADING

All load bearing timber is stress graded, i.e. graded for strength in order to allow its more efficient use. Higher stresses and moduli of elasticity may be used in calculations because the size and position of defects in the timber, which affect its strength, have been assessed.

Grading may be carried out visually by trained and registered stress graders or by the use of an approved stress grading machine. All structural timber has characteristics which affect its strength. The effect of growth characteristics such as knots, wane and slope of grain are taken into account when producing stress values and the grading rules define the allowable size, type and number of defects for each species grade.

Machine grading is based upon the relationship which exists between the strength and stiffness of timber. Each piece is fed through a series of rollers and the machine automatically loads and measures the deflection. The machine is programmed to the appropriate grades and automatically assesses each piece of timber over its full length. A visual inspection is also carried out by the operator to ensure that no timber with unacceptable defects is accepted by the machine.

Softwood for structural purposes must be stress graded in accordance with BS 4978, the Canadian NLGA rules, the American NGRDL rules, or the Economic Commission for Europe grades. BS 4978 defines two principal grades, General Structural (GS) and Special Structural (SS). When these are met by machine grading the initials become MGS and MSS. Two other machine grades are included in the Standard, M50 and M75.

All stress graded timber is clearly marked to show the grade and the company's or the grader's identifying mark. When timber is visually stress graded at source it also carries a mark to identify the country of origin (Figure 4.4).

In the UK the training of visual graders and their certification is controlled by TRADA, which operates a quality assurance scheme permitting the use of the TRADAMARK (Figure 4.5). BSI controls and approves stress grading machines through its Kitemarking system. Machine graded timber is marked with the number of the machine and the Kitemark instead of the grader's mark (Figure 4.6).

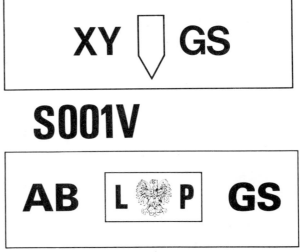

Figure 4.4 *Stress grading marks for timber visually graded overseas to BS 4978.*

Figure 4.5 *The TRADAMARK for visually stress graded timber.*

Figure 4.6 *The Kitemark for machine stress graded timber.*

Every piece of structural timber should be marked somewhere along its length, when inspecting on site, however, it should be remembered that it is possible for the marks on the piece to be removed when it is cut to fit.

Machine stress graded timber may, in addition to the stamp mark, be marked along its length or towards one end with a splash of coloured dye to indicate its grade. The relevant colours are green for MGS, blue for M50, purple for MSS and red for M75. Timber which has been machine graded in its country of origin is similarly marked to UK graded timber but will also have a mark identifying both the country and the approving authority.

Timber graded in Canada and the USA to the National Lumber Grading Authority (NLGA) rules or the

Figure 4.7 *North American stress grading marks.*

National Grading Rules for Softwood Dimension Lumber (NGRDL) is also clearly marked. Each piece of timber will bear a stamp showing the registered symbol of the grading agency, the identity number of the sawmill or the grader, the grade, the species or species group and on surfaced timber reference to whether surfacing was done on dry or green timber (Figure 4.7). Currently stress graded softwood imported from North America is visually graded; it is likely that in the future machine graded timber will also be available. The grades are different from BS 4978, the grades being defined as categories, primarily related to end uses. The categories currently imported into Britain are:

Light framing	(for timber 38 mm to 89 mm in both thickness and width) Light framing is subdivided into Construction grade for load bearing members, and Standard grade which is a general purpose timber for wall plates, noggings etc.
Structural light framing	(for timber of similar size to light framing) used for special structural applications (such as trusses, stressed skin panels etc) generally subdivided into Select Structural, No 1 and No 2 grades.
Structural joist and plank	(for timber 38 mm and thicker, and 114 mm and wider). Generally used, as its name indicates, for joists and beams, it is subdivided into Select Structural, No 1 and No 2 grades in respect of structural values.

The grading rules are applied to all softwood species. A number of species have similar strength properties and are grouped together and marketed in species groups. The three main groups are hem-fir, spruce-pine-fir (S-P-F) and Douglas fir-larch (D-fir-L).

SATISFYING STRUCTURAL DESIGN REQUIREMENTS

Designs for structural timber elements of a building are either produced in accordance with the 'deemed to satisfy' permissible span tables quoted or 'approved

documents' referred to in Building Regulations or by designing in accordance with the relevant British Standard BS 5268. This Standard, to be published in seven parts, is a compendium of Codes, Part 2 covering the general structural use of timber for elements such as studs, joists and beams, as well as fabricated components such as wall panels, box beams and glued laminated structures. Other published parts include related information in respect of the design of trussed rafters, timber preservation and fire resistance.

BS 5268 both replaces and extends the information previously contained in Code of Practice 112. In the time since that earlier Code was produced many changes have taken place in the grading and supply of timber, both in respect of the materials and their use. A greater variety of timber species is now used and this led to a need to simplify the method of specification by grouping the available options. A series of nine strength classes groups the individual species and grades quoted. The strength classes include timber graded to overseas standards in addition to the UK BS 4978 grades and cover the whole range of structural timbers from the lowest grade softwood to the densest highest grade hardwood.

Each timber is given a strength classification according to its grade stress and a particular strength class can contain both different grades and species. Equally, a species may occur in more than one strength class depending upon its grade. Table 4.1 shows typical strength classes and grades of some commonly used timbers. The use of strength classes does not affect the stress grading of timber. BS 5268 refers to BS 4978 for softwoods, BS 5756 for hardwoods and to the overseas grading rules.

When specifying structural timber for a situation where appearance is unimportant, the designer need only define the required strength class (based on tables or calculations) leaving the supplier to satisfy this requirement in the most economical manner from the timber available. Where the appearance of the timber is critical the specifier should state the species required as well as the grade to satisfy the strength class used in the engineer's calculations.

FIRE RESISTANCE OF TIMBER

It is common practice to specify timber components for situations in buildings where a predetermined period of fire resistance is required (Figure 4.8).

Fire resistance is defined as the ability of an element to carry on performing a building function in spite of being exposed to a fully developed fire. It is thus a property of the elements of building construction, not materials. In consequence, to state that a specific size section of timber has x minutes fire resistance is misleading. It may contribute x minutes to the fire resistance of a load-bearing stud wall but several things, particularly its support and fixings, can alter this contribution.

The appropriate tests for fire resistance are contained in BS 476 Part 8★ 'Test methods and criteria for the fire resistance of elements of building construction' and ISO Standard 834, the two being essentially harmonized. Test methods have been defined for most common elements e.g. walls, floors, doors, glazing, beams and columns.

★ To be replaced by BS 476: Parts 20, 21, 22 and 23.

Table 4.1 *Typical strength classes and grades of some commonly used timbers. Softwoods graded to BS 4978 and NLGA or NGRDL rules, hardwoods graded to BS 5756*

Standard name	Strength class								
	SC1	SC2	SC3	SC4	SC5	SC6	SC7	SC8	SC9
Douglas fir (Canada/USA) joist & plank grades	No 3		No 1 No 2	SEL					
Hem-Fir (Canada/USA) joist & plank grades	No 3		No 1 No 2	SEL					
Redwood (Europe)			GS/M50	SS	M75				
Whitewood (Europe)			GS/M50	SS	M75				
Scots pine (British Isles)		GS	M50/SS		M75				
Spruce (British Isles)	GS	M50/SS	M75						
Teak					HS				
Opepe (West Africa)						HS			
Iroko (West Africa)					HS				
Jarrah (Australia)					HS				
Karri (Australia)							HS		
Keruing (South East Asia)							HS		
Balau (South East Asia)								HS	
Greenheart (South America)									HS

(softwoods: Douglas fir to Spruce; hardwoods: Teak to Greenheart)

Structural elements are required to maintain their load bearing capability for the appropriate period and separating elements must resist the passage of fire or excessive heat. The principle is one of maintenance of structural stability and containment of the fire for the specified period of fire resistance, giving occupants the opportunity to escape and allowing fire fighting to take place.

The key word for timber's performance in fire resistance is 'predictability'. Although it burns, this occurs at a predictable speed known as the charring rate. The thermal insulation properties of timber are such that the timber just a few millimetres inside the burning zone is only warm. This is in contrast to high thermal conductivity materials which heat up more uniformly giving rise to problems of expansion and loss of strength over the whole section.

Different timbers char at varying rates, largely as a function of their density, with the higher density timbers charring more slowly. For common softwoods above a density of 420 kg/m^3 this rate of depletion is taken as 20 mm in 30 minutes from each exposed face. Species below this density have been awarded a rate of 25 mm in 30 minutes and certain hardwoods used for structural purposes merit rates of 15 mm in 30 minutes (oak, utile, keruing, teak, greenheart, jarrah).

This rate of charring is little affected by the severity of the fire. Therefore for an hour's exposure the depletions are 40, 50, and 30 mm respectively. This enables the fire resistance of simple timber elements such as beams and columns to be calculated. The predictive method is published in BS 5268 Part 4 Section 4.1.

The estimation of the fire resistance of composite elements such as floors and walls is not as advanced as for beams and columns because of the complexity of interactions between the different components. Considerable reliance has still to be placed on prototype testing in this area, but as knowledge increases, the accuracy of prediction improves. However, it is unlikely that a prediction of the performance of a novel construction would be sufficiently precise, and prototype testing will be required.

The fire resistance of timber constructions can be calculated in the case of beams and columns or obtained from a growing list of 'type' constructions which have been tested by organizations such as TRADA.

AVAILABLE TIMBER SIZES

The sizes and lengths of timbers available are obviously limited to the dimensions of the trees from which they have been converted. Most European softwood imported to Britain comes from Sweden, Finland and the USSR. Smaller quantities come from Yugoslavia, Czechoslovakia, Poland and France. Generally the trees in Europe are smaller than those in Western Canada and the sawn timber is therefore generally of smaller dimensions. The main species from Europe are redwood and whitewood and these are widely used for building; the

Figure 4.8 *The lecture theatre at TRADA where exposed structural timber has been used.*

Table 4.2 *Basic sizes of sawn softwood (from BS441: Part 1: 1978) (cross-sectional sizes mm)*

mm	75	100	125	150	175	200	225	250	300
16	▭	▭	▭	▭					
19	▭	▭	▭	▭					
22	▭	▭	▭	▭					
25	▭	▭	▭	▭	▭	▭	▭	▭	▭
32	▭	▭	▭	▭	▭	▭	▭	▭	▭
36	▭	▭	▭	▭					
38	▭	▭	▭	▭	▭	▭	▭		
44	▭	▭	▭	▭	▭	▭	▭	▭	▭
47*	▭	▭	▭	▭	▭	▭	▭	▭	▭
50	▭	▭	▭	▭	▭	▭	▭	▭	▭
63		▭	▭	▭	▭	▭	▭		
75		▭	▭	▭	▭	▭	▭	▭	▭
100		▭		▭		▭		▭	▭
150			▭			▭			▭
200						▭			
250								▭	
300									▭

*This range of widths for 47 mm thickness will usually be available in constructional timber quality only

The smaller sizes contained within the dotted lines are normally, but not exclusively, of European origin. The larger sizes outside the dotted lines are normally, but not exclusively, of North and South American origin

lower grades for carcassing, the better quality material for joinery.

Widths in excess of 225 mm (up to 300 mm) can be difficult to obtain and may command a higher price than smaller sections. Lengths of up to five metres are available but, again, there is a cost penalty for the longer lengths and it may be difficult to obtain these in any quantity. Finger jointing does allow long lengths to be specified and well-made joints to BS 5291 'Finger joints in structural softwood' are equally as strong as the timber.

Trees in North America are generally larger than those in Europe and larger sections and lengths may be available from this source. The species commonly imported include western hemlock and amabilis fir (imported as hem-fir); Douglas fir and western larch (imported as D-fir-L); and western white spruce, Engelmann spruce, red spruce, black spruce, lodgepole

Table 4.3 *Sizes of surfaced Canadian timber (CLS sizes) mm*

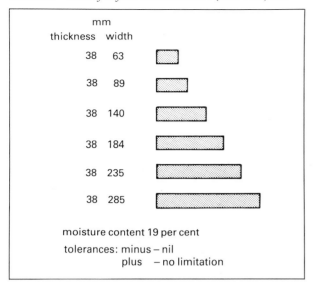

mm
thickness width

38	63
38	89
38	140
38	184
38	235
38	285

moisture content 19 per cent
tolerances: minus – nil
         plus – no limitation

pine, jack pine, alpine fir and balsam fir (imported as spruce-pine-fir). Spruce-pine-fir is available in widths up to 300 mm and lengths up to a maximum of approximately 9 m. Again, there may be a cost premium on the larger sections.

Softwood imported into Britain is normally sawn to the sizes given in BS 4471 'Dimensions for softwood' Part 1 'Sizes of sawn and planed timber' (Table 4.2) although not all of the sizes shown are readily available. The sizes stated in the Standard are basic sawn sizes for timber with a moisture content of 20 per cent.

In addition to the sawn sizes, the Standard also refers to timber machined in Canada to the requirement of the Canadian Lumber Standard (CLS timber). This is construction quality timber, stress graded to the NLGA rules and machined on all four sides with rounded arrises of not more than 3 mm radius. Most of the CLS timber imported into the UK is kiln dried at source to approximately 19 per cent moisture content. The available sizes are shown in Table 4.3. BS 4471 also defines two other timber processes: regularizing and planing.

Regularizing is a process by which the width of a sawn section of constructional timber is made uniform throughout its length. It is used to produce accurately dimensioned timbers for structural purposes and is normally carried out only on the two faces of the timber section where accuracy is important. It removes 3 mm (5 mm is allowed for dimensions over 150 mm) from the relevant dimension of the timber and a working tolerance of plus or minus 1 mm is allowed. Regularized sections should be specified by quoting the expected finished dimensions of the piece, e.g. 50×195 mm regularized, 50×97 mm regularized.

Planing requires the timber section to be surfaced on at least two opposite faces and it is normal to machine all four faces (processed all round). The allowable reductions in size are set out in BS 4471 (Table 4.4). Planed sections may be specified by quoting the sawn size from which the finished section is machined; e.g. Ex 50×100 or by giving the finished dimensions, e.g. 46×96 mm par, or by quoting both sawn and finished sizes if appropriate. A working tolerance of plus or minus 0.5 mm is allowed.

Dimensional availability of hardwoods is more complex to define since it is so much related to the type and species required. Discussion with the specialist hardwood importer is much the best way to establish availability for any given species. Structural hardwoods such as keruing, jarrah, iroko, balau and karri are available in long lengths (6 to 8 metres) and large sections. Joinery hardwoods are usually in smaller sections.

FINGER JOINTS

Finger joints are self-locating end joints formed by machining a number of similar tapered symmetrical fingers in the ends of timber members which are then glued and interlocked under pressure (Figure 4.9). The profile of the fingers may be visible on either the width or depth faces of the timber member. The requirements for the manufacture of finger joints are set out in BS 5291 'Finger joints in structural softwood' and joints to this standard are acceptable in structural softwood members designed in accordance with BS 5268 Parts 2 and 3.

The performance of finger joints is determined by strength tests and an efficiency value for a joint is established by comparing the strength of jointed sections and pieces of defect-free unjointed timber. The relative strength of the joint can then be related to the strength of each of the various grades of softwood.

In order to maintain the necessary standards of pre-

Table 4.4 *Reductions from basic sizes to finished sizes by planing of two opposed faces (from BS 4471: Part 1: 1978). All dimensions in millimetres*

	Reductions from basic sizes			
	15 up to and including 35	Over 35 up to and including 100	Over 100 up to and including 150	Over 150
Constructional timber	3	3	5	6
Matching interlocking boards	4	4	6	6
Wood trim not specified in BS 584	5	7	7	9
Joinery and cabinet work	7	9	11	13

Note: Floorings and wood trim are covered by separate British Standards:
Flooring: BS 1297   Wood trim: BS 584

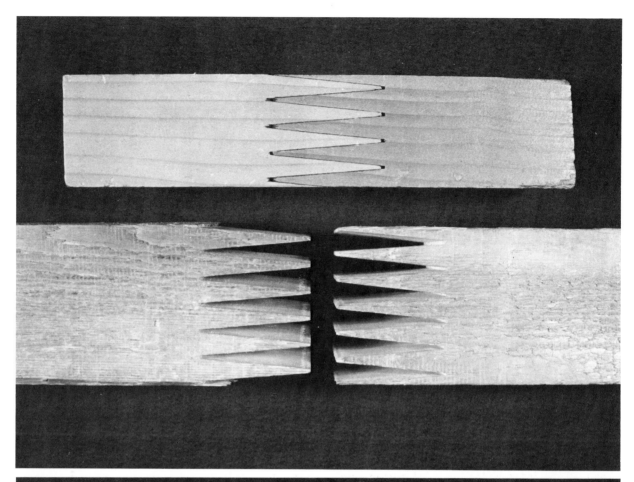

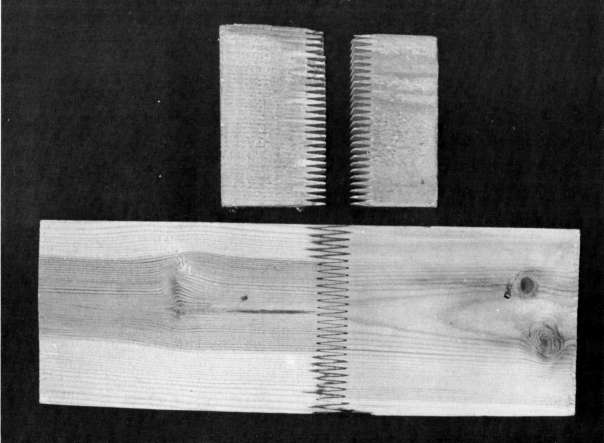

Figure 4.9 *Finger joints in timber.*

cision it is essential for the joints to be made in a suitably equipped workshop under the supervision of trained and qualified staff. Joints can only be tested by a destructive strength test on random selected production samples so it is essential to be able to rely on adequate quality control in production and the British Standard recommends that specifiers should make use of independent quality certification. A quality assurance scheme of this type is run by TRADA and joints produced within the scheme are marked denoting this, as well as identifying the manufacturer of the joint, the type of adhesive used and compliance with BS 5291. The length and pitch of the finger joint can vary, dependent upon the manufacturer and upon requirement and it is not normally necessary for the specifier to make any reference to this.

Finger joints can enable longer lengths of timber to be used than would otherwise be available or used in order to cut out a defective piece of timber from an otherwise acceptable length. In theory it would be possible to have a section of timber made up from a number of finger jointed sections, provided the joints were at least one metre apart to satisfy the British Standard, but in practice the cost of the joints precludes this and it is not common to see more than one joint in any piece.

In addition to the structural joints referred to above, it is becoming common to see finger jointed sections used in the manufacture of joinery items and trim, when a smaller version is used. Reference is made to these in BS 1186 Part 1. These joints are fully acceptable when the joinery item is decorated with an opaque finish such as paint but can, if required, be excluded from the specification for clear finished joinery.

GLUED LAMINATED MEMBERS

One method of obtaining large sections of timber for structural purposes is to glue laminate a series of precision cut smaller sections to form a member of large cross-section and, when required, long length (Figure 4.10).

A glued laminated member can have a straight or curved profile or can be made with a variable section to suit the fabrication of tapering beams or portal frames. Because any size of member can be produced, transport and manufacturing facilities are the practical limiting factors. Since members are factory produced, high standards of quality, accuracy and finish can be achieved. Chapter 6 discusses and illustrates the uses of glulam members.

In general terms, section sizes range from 75 mm × 150 mm upwards and large members measuring over 500 mm × 2 metres and spanning approximately 30 metres, have been made. Off-the-shelf glued laminated beams of up to approximately 120 mm × 600 mm are available in Britain. Most laminated members are fabricated from softwoods, generally redwood or whitewood or western hemlock or Douglas fir. Hardwoods are used but are more expensive and would need to be justified by need for special strength or appearance requirements.

The design of glued laminated structures is referred to in BS 5268 Part 2. Three grades of timber for lami-

nating are specified, termed LA, LB and LC, which are obtained by selection from commercial grades or by referring to the rules set out in BS 4978. A laminated member may comprise only one grade or may have a combination with higher grades at the outer layers with lower grades in the middle where stresses are lower.

Adhesives used in the construction of laminated members must be strong enough to provide a joint at least as strong as the timber in shear parallel to the grain. They must also be creep-free under load and have sufficient durability for the member's end use. Dependent upon these conditions the adhesives used are casein, urea formaldehyde resins, phenol, resorcinol or melamine or a combination of these. These adhesives are specified in BS 1204 Part 1 'Specification for gap filling adhesives' which covers the synthetic resins, and BS 1444 'Cold setting casein adhesive powders for wood'.

The manufacturing procedure for laminated members depends upon the volume of the work and the production facilities, but the procedure must comply with BS 4169 'Glued laminated structural members'. Whilst high quality work can be obtained with simple equipment there is a tendency towards large-scale production using complex equipment with a high standard of quality control.

When required by the end use condition, glued laminated members can be preservative treated in a similar manner to solid sections. BS 5268 Part 5 'Preservative treatments for constructional timber' and BS 1282 'Guide to the choice, use and application of wood preservatives' give guidance. The type of preservative needs to be chosen with regard to the adhesive and whether

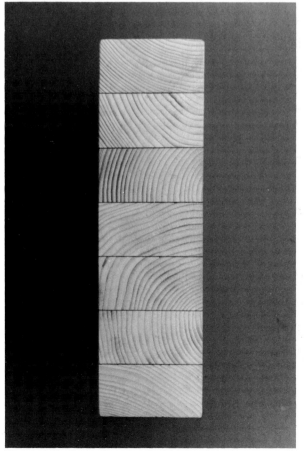

Figure 4.10 *Section through a glued laminated member.*

the treatment is to be applied to the finished members or the individual laminations before assembly. Advice from both the adhesive and preservative manufacturers should be sought where appropriate.

It is normal practice to treat laminated components after manufacture and therefore before specifying pressure treatments for large members it is advisable to check there is a plant which can accommodate the size. The majority of preservatives have no effect on the efficiency of the glue lines after they have cured but compatibility should be checked with the manufacturers. Treatment can be carried out on the individual laminations before they are glued but in this case it is essential that the compatibility of the preservative treatment and the glue is checked beforehand.

SPECIFYING MOISTURE CONTENTS

The wood of all trees when felled contains a considerable amount of moisture, amounting to as much as 150 per cent of the oven dry weight, i.e. the weight of wood after it has been dried in a ventilated oven until no further weight loss occurs. It is therefore necessary to dry timber to a moisture content related to the humidity conditions of its ultimate use. This is achieved by one of two methods, air drying or, more commonly today, kiln drying. In Britain's climate, air drying cannot produce moisture contents sufficiently low to satisfy requirements for internal use in centrally heated buildings. Kiln drying makes it possible to control the humidity, temperature and ventilation and so reduce the moisture content of the timber to meet almost any requirement (Figure 4.11). It is not sufficient to specify 'kiln dried' timber, the moisture content required must always be stated. Table 4.5 gives details of typical requirements.

Although timber may have been dried to the correct moisture content for its use there will still be small changes with variations in atmospheric conditions (e.g. seasonal changes). These will cause small dimensional changes in the cross-section of the timber. The length along the grain is effectively not changed. The detail design of the timber element should ideally take account of this small movement if it is critical. Different species have different movement values. The Appendix gives values for some common timbers.

Measuring moisture content

The moisture content of timber can be measured by oven testing or by the use of an electrical resistance moisture meter. Oven testing involves cutting samples from the wood to be tested, weighing the cut samples, drying them at 101–105° C and re-weighing them. The moisture content is then calculated by the following formula:

$$\frac{\text{Initial weight} - \text{Final weight}}{\text{Final weight}} \times 100 = \text{percentage moisture content}$$

Electrical resistance moisture meters work on the principle that the drier the timber the greater the resistance to the passage of electrical current. The meter normally has needle electrodes which are pressed into the wood and measure the electrical resistance between them (Figure 4.12). The standard needles penetrate approximately 6–8 mm into the wood and indicate the moisture content of the wettest zone through which they pass (including surface moisture if this exists).

Figure 4.11 *Timber being loaded into a drying kiln.* Photograph: Mallinson Denny (UK) Ltd.

Table 4.5 *Typical moisture content specifications (per cent)*

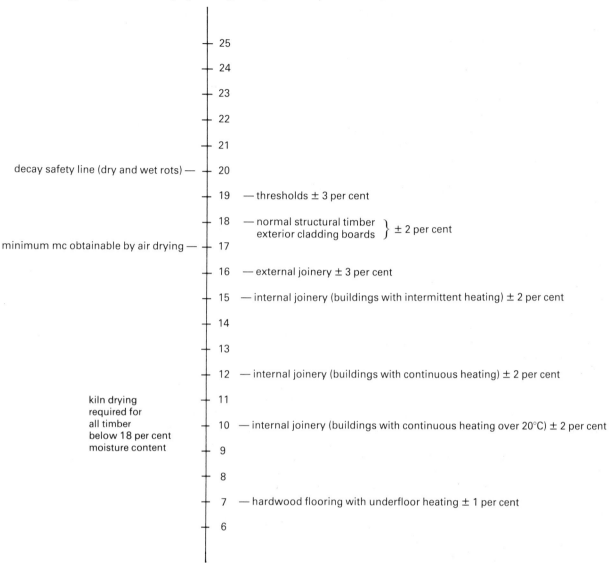

Longer needles with insulated shanks are also available so that the meter reading will indicate the condition of the wood in the region of the tips.

A meter of this type should normally give acceptably accurate readings in the range of 7–25 per cent moisture content which is suitable for most conditions in which timber is used. Meters of this type can be used on all kinds of timber but caution is necessary when checking timber which has been wetted by sea water or water-borne chemicals for preservation or flame retardant purposes since these treatments can cause falsely high readings with resistance type meters.

Panel products must be regarded as separate materials and not merely as the timber species from which they are made. The moisture content readings obtained with a resistance-type meter can be erratic and they should not be regarded with confidence unless the manufacturer has produced calibration charts for the particular product being tested.

The reasons for this are not known conclusively but it is thought that the presence of soluble chemicals in, for example, the gluelines of certain types of plywood may affect the readings obtained. The effect encountered with some varieties of exterior plywood can be particularly severe. Resistance-type meters may, in extreme cases, indicate moisture content values approximately double those obtained by oven drying methods. Examples of meter readings indicating values of 20 per cent moisture content, when actual values of 10 per cent were determined by oven drying tests, have been encountered.

It is not possible to apply a universal correction factor to meter readings since the magnitude of the error varies with the type of adhesive used, the possible presence of additives and the history of the board. When using a moisture meter on plywood, particularly on exterior types, view high moisture content readings with suspicion and use them at best as an indication, never as an accurate measure. Where any doubt arises obtain specialist advice, and, if necessary, carry out oven drying tests.

DURABILITY AND PRESERVATIVE TREATMENT

Timbers of different species vary considerably in their natural durability. Whilst it may be attractive to specify

Figure 4.12 *An electrical resistance moisture meter in use.*

only timbers with high natural durability it is not necessarily economic and may be impracticable. Timbers with low durability may be used provided they have been treated with a suitable preservative if they are to be used in situations conducive to decay. Further details of needs and preservative types are given in Chapter 3.

The durability characteristics of the more common softwoods and hardwoods are included in the Appendix. Further details are given in PRL Technical Note 40 'The natural durability classification of timber'.

JOINERY TIMBER

This section aims to deal with the timber specification of joinery items. Information on other aspects of joinery specification is given in Chapters 8, 9 and 10.

Specification of timber for joinery purposes is greatly simplified by reference to BS 1186 'Specification of quality of timber and workmanship in joinery' which applies to both hardwoods and softwoods. The Standard is in two parts; Part 1 deals with material quality and Part 2 with workmanship. The revised edition of Part 1, on which this section is based is due for publication in 1985.

Defining the quality required by reference to this Standard is more precise and therefore preferable to spe-

cifying by means of commercial shippers' marks. Most European softwood used for joinery is imported as 'unsorted' quality, that is, a mixture of the best four commercial qualities, but the actual quality of 'unsorted' timber varies according to the country of origin and the individual shipper, thus making it an unreliable specification standard. It is one of the skills of the experienced importer's buyer to know which commercial quality from the individual mill or port will meet the required end user standard.

North American softwood for joinery is graded in different ways, the best quality being termed 'clears and door stock' and being broadly equal to European 'firsts'; the second quality is termed 'select merchantable' and is broadly equivalent to European 'unsorted' material. Hardwoods are usually graded FAS (firsts and seconds). Firsts provide a high percentage of clear material to be achieved by cutting and will also provide long lengths of clear timber. Seconds will provide a lower percentage of clear material and shorter lengths of clear timber.

BS 1186 Part 1 describes the quality of timber required for various types of joinery and defines quality in terms of allowable or non-allowable characteristics such as knot size, type, location and frequency, sapwood, shakes and splits and rate of growth. It also defines the acceptable moisture content of the timber components at the time of their acceptance by the first purchaser (usually the building contractor).

Qualities of joinery timber for differing purposes are defined in the form of classes which must be quoted in the specification. Four classes are included in the revised version of the Standard which allow varying amounts and sizes of timber defects or characteristics on the faces of the timber component:

CLASS CSH	CSH stands for clear softwood and hardwood and should be specified only for joinery made from 'CLEAR' grades of timber.
CLASS 1	Specified for high quality or specialized joinery. This quality of timber may require special selection and may therefore have a cost penalty compared to lower grades of the same species. The use of laminated timber is allowed and this may be necessary to achieve the standard consistently and economically. Class 1 is appropriate to both hardwoods and softwoods.
CLASS 2 CLASS 3	These classes would normally be specified for general purpose joinery using species such as European redwood or European whitewood or using hardwood. They apply to both solid and laminated timber. Class 3 allows greater limits of knot size than Class 2, otherwise the classes are similar.

Within each class there are variations in the acceptability of defects and natural characteristics depending whether they occur on exposed, semi-concealed or concealed surfaces of the finished component. An exposed face is a surface which will be visible after the component has been installed in the building. A semi-concealed surface is one which is not normally visible when the component is in a closed position but which becomes visible when the component is opened (for example, at a door or window jamb). A concealed surface is one which is never visible when the component has been installed (for example, the back face of a door or window frame).

It is of course possible to specify the timber quality required for purpose made joinery by adopting the most appropriate BS 1186 class but amending the requirements in respect of any specific item. For example, by precluding finger jointing or laminating on joinery to be clear finished or by applying a more rigorous limitation on knot spacing than is accepted by the Standard. However, care must be used in doing this to ensure that the specific requirement is defined. It would be helpful in such a case to reproduce the relevant clauses from the Standard together with clear identification of the amendment in the written specification for the work.

In old specifications it was commonly inferred that the material to be used should always be the very best quality available. It is rarely possible to afford to do this today and there is, in any case, no real advantage in requiring a higher quality than is necessary to satisfy the end use. When deciding the quality of material required it is important to be aware what is achievable from the timber selected. Although it would in theory be possible by rigorous selection to achieve any species/class combination it would only be economically justifiable in exceptional circumstances to require, for example, CSH (clear) grade in European redwood. It would normally be preferable to select an alternative species (such as hemlock or Douglas fir) if this grade requirement were required.

The other properties which should be considered when specifying joinery timber are strength, durability, workability (especially if the component is of complex detail), dimensional stability and of course appearance. BS 1186: Part 1 includes in its appendix a table giving some guidance information on the characteristics of the more commonly specified timber species together with an indication of their suitability for various uses. Information on species not included is normally available from TRADA or the BRE Princes Risborough Laboratory. When the precise appearance of the timber is important to the finished project, the only totally reliable solution is to inspect and select the timber at the merchant's prior to its use and/or to require a sample for general approval with the manufacturer's acceptance that production will be of similar quality.

Dependent upon the quality and type of work, it may not be necessary to specify the species of softwood to be used but simply to define the BS 1186 Part 1 Class (or classes if they vary on different parts of the finished component). When hardwood is specified it is normally necessary to name the species (using BS 881 and 584 nomenclature) in addition to defining the BS 1186 class of the timber.

The specification should also indicate whether preservative treatment is required on timber components used in external situations, and, if so, specify the type to be used. Irrespective of the durability of the timber species, sapwood is not considered durable and should either be excluded from the specifications for external components or preservative treatment specified. Information on the relevant types and methods of preservative treatment is given in Chapter 3.

5 Historic development of timber structures

Dr David T. Yeomans

David T. Yeomans BSc PhD AMICE is lecturer at the Liverpool School of Architecture, specializing in building conservation. After obtaining his degree in civil engineering he worked for Ove Arup and Partners before embarking on a university career, first at Oxford School of Architecture and now at Liverpool.

The design of long spans in timber must be influenced as much by the availability of timbers large enough to cope with the spans envisaged as by the normal structural considerations of load transmission. In Britain oak was the basic structural timber during the Middle Ages. It was readily available throughout the country and was sufficiently durable. The management of woodland by coppicing ensured that timbers of large enough scantling were available for most building purposes but large structures must have presented a special problem. Structural timbers of great length or girth would have required the felling of complete trees and the size of timber would be limited by the size of tree available. At some times and in some areas such building needs would have also been in competition with the needs of shipbuilding. For medieval builders their problem was to roof the open halls and barns, churches and cathedrals of the period and one can see the development of these roofs as attempts to increase the possible spans with the timbers available.

The rafters of a roof tend to deflect under the weight of the covering, a more severe problem the longer the span and hence the length of the rafters. There are two ways of overcoming this, either some form of strutting is added between each pair of common rafters, or purlins are used with frames provided at intervals to carry the purlins. For both types of roof, either tie beams must be provided to counter the outward thrust of the rafters or the walls must be buttressed. The particular methods adopted for early roofs depended upon the traditions of the region with common rafter roofs being more usual in the south and east of England while purlin roofs were used elsewhere.

The Brandons, in their book on medieval church roofs, illustrated a number with common rafters braced either with simple collars or with collars and scissor braces (Figure 5.1). As the rafters had to span between the outside faces of what might be substantial stone walls, their effective span could be reduced with 'ashlar pieces'; vertical timbers strutting the rafters from the inside face of the wall. The rafters and ashlar pieces were connected together across the wall with short horizontal pieces to form a triangular assembly resting on either one or two wall plates. The scantlings used for all the members of this kind of roof were frequently no more than 125 mm square and although the spans shown by the Brandons were quite modest, between 3.5 and 4.5 m, this method of roofing might be extended to much greater spans with little or no increase in the size of timbers.

The common rafter roofs of Westminster Abbey span almost 11 m with collars and scissor braces to rafters no more than 205 mm square at their bases. Ely Cathedral, with only a slightly smaller span of 10.4 m, has rafters only 125 mm square and braced with two collars, scissor braces and ashlar pieces (Figure 5.2). With 60 degree pitches rafters had to be the same length as the span and obtaining timbers of such prodigious length could not have been easy.

However, with the strutting used for these steep pitches, the bending caused by the weight of the covering would be small and wind forces would be the principal loading. The scissor bracing would have been more effective in resisting this than simple collars and they were each joined to the rafters with notched lap joints allowing some tension to be developed in the bracing members.

A difficulty with common rafter roofs is preventing racking of the trusses. Boarding to carry a lead covering would provide longitudinal stiffness and the problem would be lessened if the roof was contained by the walls of end towers. An apsidal end with its half conical roof must, however, produce some longitudinal thrust and at Westminster braces were added in the eighteenth century to check the racking movement of the fourteenth-century roof.

The other great medieval structures were the monastic barns, the warehouses of their extensive estates. These estate farms were large businesses, and as the lands might be far from the abbeys that owned them, some of the barns contained accommodation for a resident 'manager'. There is a room complete with a fireplace above the waggon porch at Bredon barn and traces of similar accommodation can still be seen at Great Coxwell. The produce from the latter was sent to London where Farringdon Market takes its name from the town of Faringdon on the edge of the former monastic estate. These structures still dominate the small settlements in

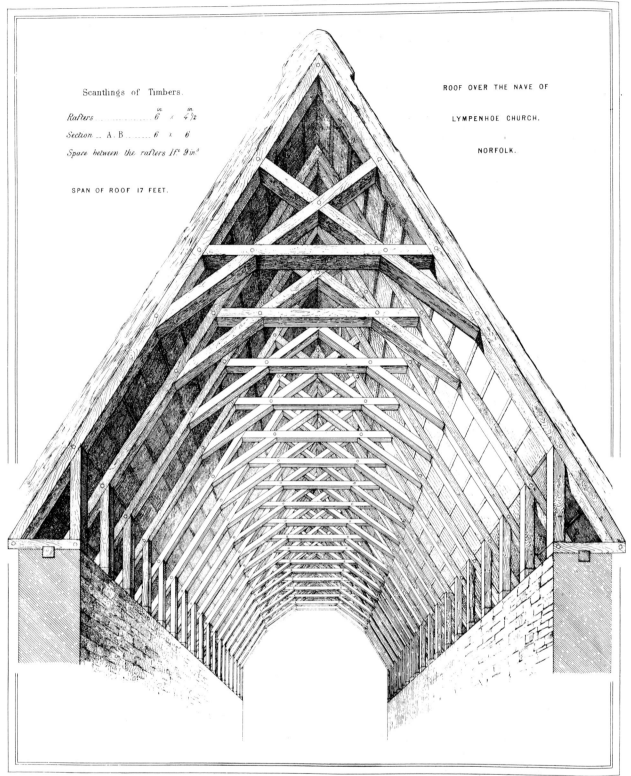

Scantlings of Timbers.

Rafters .... 6^{in} x $4\tfrac{1}{2}^{in}$

Section _ A . B .... 6 x 6

Space between the rafters 1 ft 9 ins

SPAN OF ROOF 17 FEET.

ROOF OVER THE NAVE OF

LYMPENHOE CHURCH,

NORFOLK.

Figure 5.1 *Lympenhoe Church, Norfolk. Drawing by Raphael and J. Arthur Brandon from* Open timber roofs of the Middle Ages.

which they now stand but some of the largest of the great barns, like Beaulieu St Leonards which was 68.3 m long and 20.4 m wide, have unfortunately been lost. The size of this barn can still be seen from the surviving stone walls even though the timbers have gone. The largest barn in England was probably Cholsey barn, demolished in 1815, only 16.5 m wide but over 91.5 m long. Of course the outward form and structure of barns

were similar to those of the halls of the great houses of the time, large rectangular spaces open to the roof; but the barns are the more remarkable simply because of their great size.

Although these barns had structures which were similar in scale to the roofs of the cathedrals, they adopted quite different solutions to the problem of covering a wide span. There were two basic approaches. The most straightforward took advantage of the fact that the roof was lower and could be supported from the ground and simply had two rows of posts dividing the floor of the barn into a 'nave' and 'aisles' (Figure

63

5.3). This type of structure is now called aisle framing and total widths in the region of 18 m were common with this method. But even with the intermediate supports their construction must still have been a major undertaking. Both stone barns and completely timber framed barns used the same basic structure but while the walls of the former could help to give some stiffness to the frames, additional bracing was needed in the timber buildings to ensure overall stability. Like the cathedral roofs, the wind forces on these buildings would have been substantial and bracing was an important part of the frame.

The aisle posts were connected together first with roof plates; effectively two long timbers running the length of the barn, although in practice each was formed of several lengths of timber scarf jointed together. This created two longitudinal frames which were then joined with tie beams set over each pair of posts. This assembly was then stabilized by braces from each of the posts to both the tie beam and roof plate. In barns with stone walls a simple aisle tie joined each post to the wall plate so that clear passages were left along the sides of the building. However, in timber barns the framing stood on a series of sole plates that formed part of the aisle framing. This also included braces so that the aisles were divided into separate bays. Although there were several variations in the carpentry, a curved brace commonly joined each sole plate to the corresponding aisle post, passing the aisle tie and lap jointed to it.

Although the rafters of these barn roofs were the same size as those of church or cathedral roofs, the timbers of the main frame which support the roof were necessarily larger than these roof timbers. The tie beams and roof plates approached 300 mm square while the posts were larger still. The aisle posts, cut from the trunk of a tree, were placed 'upside-down', i.e. with the root end uppermost so that its great girth could be used to form the complex joint at its head. This had to accommodate two tenons set at right angles to each other, a lower one to fix the roof plate and an upper one set inside and above the former to fix the tie beam. Further restraint was provided at this point by a lap dovetail joint where the end of the tie beam sat over the roof plate (Figure 5.4). If a purlin roof was used there would also have to be provision for the principal rafters to be joined to the tie beam.

Many large timber framed barns survive in Kent, often still part of working farms. Unlike the stone barns these have low walls and hipped roofs. In most of the Kentish barns the frames carry crown post roofs (Figure 5.3). Above the wall plates are common rafters with

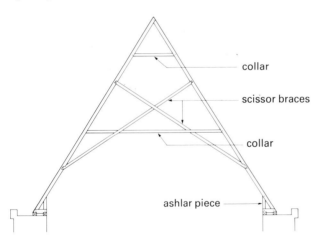

Figure 5.2 Ely Cathedral, Cambridgeshire. The fourteenth-century scissor braced common rafter roof above the nave was originally open but was boarded in during the nineteenth century.

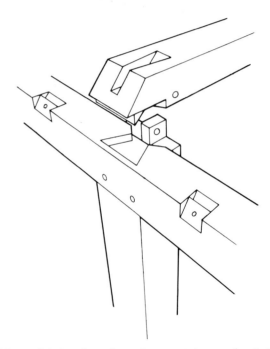

Figure 5.4 *Lap dovetail joint between tie beam and roof plate in aisle frame construction.*

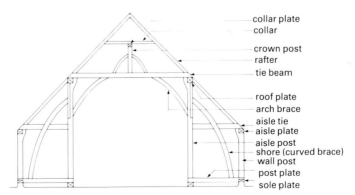

Figure 5.3 *Construction of a timber aisled frame building with a crown post roof.*

64

Plate 1 The roofs of the Thames Flood Barrier are fabricated from twinned rib members of glued laminated iroko — a West African hardwood. The roofs are stiffened by doubly curved edge members.

The roof surfaces are of double curvature with three layers of European redwood, glued together to form a stiff shell, sheathed in stainless steel.

Architects: GLC Architects department
Consulting engineers: Rendal, Palmer and Tritton
Specialist consultants: TRADA.

Plates 2 – 3 Non durable timber used out of doors and in contact
with the ground will need preservative treatment for long life.
These examples of playground equipment were part of the
Liverpool Garden Festival.

Plate 4 The footbridge in the grounds of the Royal Victoria
Infirmary at Wylam, Northumberland is constructed from keruing
with utile used for the handrail.

Photograph: Ove Arup and Partners.

Plate 5 *(Opposite)* Alternatively, less durable timbers treated with preservatives can be used, as in this glulam bridge fabricated from European redwood and built for the Countryside Commission for Scotland at Glencoe.

Photograph: Jewell Harrison.

Plates 6 – 7 Eccentric glulam arches form the sports hall at Stockholm University, spanning 47m.

Photographs: Jeremy Preston.

Plate 8 *(Above)* Typical trussed rafter roof.

Photograph: Gang Nail Ltd.

Plate 9 *(Left)* English oak panelling and doors were used in the renovation of the 'Old Combination Room' at St. Catherine's College, Cambridge. Four carved door heads, preserved from a demolished building, circa 1631, were repaired and combined with the new work to form the heads of the new doors to the room. Seventeenth-century carved panels from two fireplaces and windows were incorporated in the entrance lobby. The panelling was fabricated in the joinery works then dismantled and re-erected on site.

Plate 10 *(Top)* Purpose-made framed and panelled folding doors are used here to divide the sitting room from the stairs and dining area.

Plates 11 – 12 Purpose-made stairs are combined with decorative hardwood flooring (see Chapter 8) to create two very different entrance halls.

Plate 13 *(Above)* Panelling in wych elm, Central Criminal Court, Old Bailey.

Plate 14 *(Left)* The Visitors' Centre at the Bowood Estate in Wiltshire was designed to blend in with the surrounding woodlands and the Capability Brown landscape of the estate.

Plate 15 *(Left)* The building has a central cruciform column of laminated whitewood with laminated beams branching out to support the roof.

Bowood Visitors' Centre

Architects: Graham Moss Associates
Consulting engineers: Harvey McGill and Hayes
Photographs: Peter Cook.

Plate 16 *(Below)* Tollymore Teahouse in the Tollymore Forest Park, County Down, Northern Ireland is designed using round timber poles with 'boy scout' construction joints. The pyramid roof structure is supported on posts, braced externally by diagonal timber poles.

Plate 17 *(Opposite Top)* The diagonal bracing on the building is continued in the structure of the bridge which leads visitors from the car park to the teahouse.

Plate 18 *(Opposite Below)* The pyramid structure of the roof can be seen in the construction of the building.

Tollymore Teahouse

Architects: Ian Campbell and Partners
Structural engineers: Blyth and Blyth Associates in association with Dr J R Gilfillan
Quantity surveyors: McNeil and Ritchie.

Plate 19 *(Above)* An office, showroom and warehouse built for a timber company in Tonbridge, Kent is designed as a 'billboard' for the imaginative and colourful use of timber and timber products. Structural laminated and lattice beams are stained red.

Plate 20 *(Right)* The external panels and doors are demountable so that a variety of products can be displayed. Various configurations of timber boarding are decorated with coloured and natural exterior stain finishes.

Office, showroom and warehouse

Architects: Masini Franklin Partnership
Engineers: Shippen/French Partnership
Quantity surveyors: Monk Dunstone and Associates.

Plate 21 TRADA headquarters building is a timber framed
structure with load bearing timber framed panels faced with
meranti plywood decorated with exterior stain finishes.
TRADA headquarters

Architects: TRADA.

Plate 22 The Burrell Collection in Pollock Country Park, Glasgow houses the art treasures bequeathed to the City by Sir William Burrell. Externally the predominating materials are stainless steel and glass but once inside the extensive use of laminated structural timber becomes apparent. The courtyard features laminated whitewood principal rafters with steel tension rods supported on slender concrete columns.

Plates 23 – 24 The North section, or terrace, features a timber and glass screen with views of the woodlands beyond. Pre-cambered flat roof beams intersect with secondary beams; these are all laminated whitewood with tongued and grooved boarding forming the ceiling.

Plates 25 – 26 *(Opposite and Left)* The cranked beams across the daylight galleries have bolted joints with a concealed central steel plate. This detail is a development of the flat roof construction rather than of the trussed system used in the courtyard.

Plate 27 *(Below)* The pitched roof to the restaurant area incorporates 'Invar' steel stiffening rods to the beams.
Burrell Collection

Architects: Barry Gasson Architects
Consulting engineers: Felix J Samuely and Partners.

Plates 28 – 29 Bulls Wood House, near Haywards Heath, Sussex is an unusual form of timber frame construction. Built on the post and beam principle, the structural frame and external cladding is all Western red cedar. The load bearing beams are laminated timber with tongued and grooved cedar boarding to ceilings.

Architects: Michael Twigg, Brown and Partners
Photographs: Michael J Barrett.

collars with a collar plate that runs the length of the roof under the collars. The collar plate is supported by the crown post which stands on a tie beam. This is braced to both the beam and to the collar plate so that this assembly braces the rafters against racking.

At Cressing in Essex there are two remarkable timber barns which form two sides of the present farmyard. Although they are framed slightly differently, they each have pairs of long bracing timbers in each frame; so-called passing braces, that run from wall post to roof, passing aisle ties, aisle posts and tie beams and crossing each other near the top. Both barns have hipped roofs but with small gablets above the level of the roof collars. Bracing against racking in one of the barns is effected with purlins and long curved 'wind braces' in the plane of the roof while the other barn has a crown post roof with a crown post standing on each of the tie beams. Further west the timber framed barn at Harmondsworth in Middlesex, almost 61 m long and now the largest surviving timber framed barn in England, has a purlin roof and is half hipped i.e. hipped above the purlins (sometimes called a jerkinhead roof).

There is one variation of aisle framing that does not have the arrangement of timbers that has been described so far. The posts of the barn at Great Coxwell (Figure 5.5) are framed directly into the tie beams, so creating a series of transverse frames, rather than being joined by the roof plates into two longitudinal frames. These transverse frames are then joined longitudinally by the roof plates which are above the ties. This kind of framing has been called 'reversed assembly' because it reverses the normal sequence of plate and ties and it suggests a quite different tradition of carpentry. Reversed assembly was not confined to stone barns however. The timber framed barn at Belchamp St Paul in Essex is framed in this way and it is thought that this is an earlier method which was superseded by normal assembly. At Great Coxwell the roof plates are not only carried by the transverse frames, they are further assisted by long curved members between each frame that stand within the wall and curve inward at the eaves to follow the line of the roof. These have a striking resemblance to timbers used in the other, quite different method of roof framing: the cruck frame found in other districts.

It will be apparent that the timber barns referred to so far have been generally in the south and east of the country. In these areas box framing was used for the smaller domestic buildings. In the north and west upland regions of England however, cruck framing predominated for both large and small buildings. With this method the same basic frame could be used for a wide range of sizes of building, from the small cottage to the large hall or barn, only larger timbers being used for the larger spans. Again the same basic construction could be used whether the walls were stone or timber framed. Although the two carpentry traditions are quite different and clearly originated in different areas, it is important to realize that a sharp boundary cannot be drawn between the two. There are areas in which both are used and one can see influences of one upon the other.

Cruck frames (Figure 5.6) resemble the 'A' frames used today except that curved rather than straight members were preferred so that they followed as closely as possible the line of wall and roof. Timbers for the

Figure 5.5 *Interior of the barn at Great Coxwell, Oxfordshire; originally a Cistercian barn, now a National Trust property.* Photograph: Jewell Harrison.

frames were cut from the trunk and main branch, or possibly from a naturally curving tree. This was then split down the centre to produce a matching pair of 'cruck blades'. They were then joined at the top to form an arch-like structure. Although this produced an inherently stable frame, the blades were usually joined together a little below the apex with a short collar. Larger frames might also be joined with a cross beam at about mid-height which might in some cases be extended beyond the blades to support a wall plate or even used to carry upper floor joists. These cross members presumably made the frames more rigid and so easier to erect. Each frame was first assembled while laid flat on the ground with the various members pegged together and the completed frames were then reared into position.

Erection began at one end of the building with the first frame needing temporary bracing to keep it upright. As the second frame was reared into position it was joined to the first with a pair of purlins and this assembly was then made stable by 'wind braces'; short, often curved, timbers fastened between the purlins and the cruck blades. As subsequent frames were reared they would be attached to the already assembled structure by further lengths of purlins (Figure 5.7). This sequence can be seen in the assembled structure because the fixing pegs in the frames were necessarily driven in from the top as they were laid on the ground. Thus as the frames were reared into position the heads of these pegs were on the side towards the end of the building that was

erected first. The frames carried not only the purlins of the roof but also the wall plates that supported the feet of the rafters so that the wall was not load bearing, simply being an infill between the wall plates and the sole plates on which the whole structure stood.

Naturally there were variations in the details of these frames. The blades might be joined directly at the apex or might not meet but be connected by a short yoke. The ridge purlin might be carried by the blades, by this yoke or even by a short post standing on the yoke. Where a cross beam was used there might be braces between it and the blades. Alternatively, where there was no cross beam or where it was not at the same level as the wall plates the latter were carried on cruck spurs; short cantilevers of timber fixed to the cruck blades with notched lap joints. It might not always have been possible to obtain timbers with sufficient curvature to fit the desired cross section of the building. In such cases the roof purlins could not be directly supported by the cruck blades so that raising pieces had to be added between the blades and the cruck spurs to carry the purlins.

The largest cruck barn in England is Leigh Court barn, Worcestershire (Figure 5.8). This has a span of 10.4 m and a height from floor to ridge of 11 m. A yoke connects the blades at the top with a strut to carry the ridge purlin. A cross beam at about mid height is connected to the blades with curved arch-like braces. Although cruck frames were used with stone walls this barn has timber walls about 3 m high set on a stone plinth. The cruck blades have very little curvature so that while the upper of the two pairs of purlins is sup-

ridge purlin

cross tie beam

purlin

wind brace

cruck spur

wall plate

wall post
cruck blade

sole plate

Figure 5.6 *Cruck frame.*

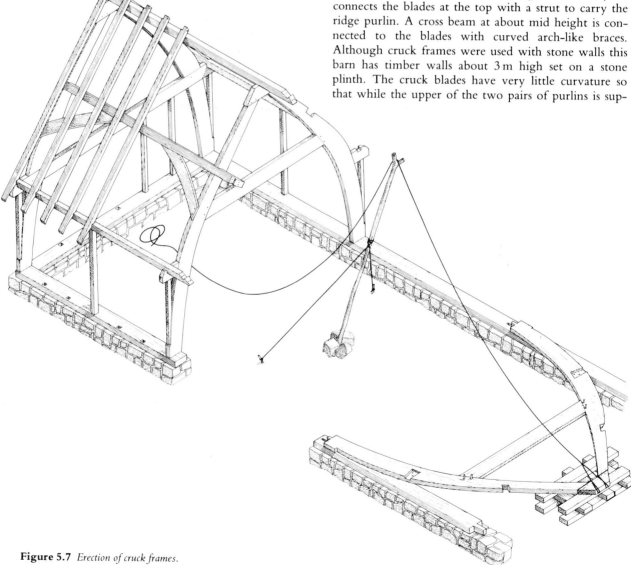

Figure 5.7 *Erection of cruck frames.*

ported directly by the blades, raising pieces are used for the lowest pair.

Remembering that it took one tree to provide each pair of cruck blades, cruck buildings of this scale could not have been common, but similar spans could be achieved with smaller timbers. By separating the blades and connecting across the top with a beam, much larger spans could be built with the timbers available. The basic assembly of three members, a pair of blades and a cross beam, then needed knee braces to be added to form a stiff frame called a 'base cruck' that could be reared into position just like a full cruck (Figure 5.9). Above the cross beam there might be either a purlin or a common rafter roof so that longitudinal timbers joining each of the frames at their knees would serve either as purlins or roof plates. In purlin roofs a further upper pair of purlins would be needed and there were two common ways of supporting these. Either a frame of tie beam and principal rafters was set above the first pair of purlins or a cruck-like frame, called an 'upper cruck' was stood on the cross beam. In the former there would be two members set one above the other, the cross beam of the base cruck and the tie beam of the roof frame above, clasping the lower pair of purlins between them (Figure 5.10). Where an upper cruck was used the cross beam of the base cruck acted as the tie for the upper part of the roof and the curve at the feet of the upper pair of blades enabled them to be supported inside the line of the lower pair of purlins.

This description of the base cruck suggests that it evolved from the full cruck as a means of increasing the possible spans with the timbers available. However, Middle Littleton barn has features which suggest another possible line of development. The barns of Bradford-on-Avon and Middle Littleton (Figure 5.10) are both similar in width to Leigh Court but one can see that they use smaller timbers although their carpentry is much more complex. Both of these barns use another device for increasing the size of the structure. In a completely timber framed base cruck building the wall plate would be supported on cruck spurs in the same way as with a full cruck. These two barns, however, have stone

Figure 5.8 *Leigh Court barn, Worcestershire; England's largest cruck barn.* Photograph: F. W. B. Charles.

walls which carry the wall plate. Moreover the height of the buildings has been increased by raising the feet of the blades on these walls. The barns are different, however, in that Bradford-on-Avon has upper crucks to support the upper part of the roof while Middle Littleton has a tie beam and principal rafters.

A curious feature of Middle Littleton barn is that the bays at each end of the building are framed differently from the rest. Here, instead of having base crucks to support the roof plate, the last frames have aisle posts. There are also truncated aisle posts set against the gable wall supported on corbels (Figure 5.10). This is unusual but not unique because a similar combination of base crucks and aisle posts was used for Siddington barn, Gloucestershire. Bearing in mind the cruck-like members at Great Coxwell that help to support the roof plate mid-way between the aisle posts, one may imagine that

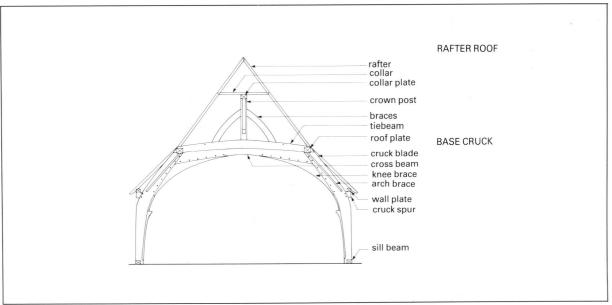

Figure 5.9 *Base cruck construction.*

Figure 5.10 *The base cruck barn at Middle Littleton, Worcestershire; a National Trust property.* Photograph: Martin Charles.

Figure 5.11 *Starston Church, Norfolk; a very simple arched braced roof. Drawing by Raphael and J. Arthur Brandon from* Open timber roofs of the Middle Ages.

the base cruck was seen by some carpenters as a way of improving upon the aisle frame. By using base crucks instead of posts to carry the roof plate, the floor of the barn could be freed from obstructions. Looked at in this way Middle Littleton appears as an intermediate form where base crucks have been used for most, but not all, of the frames.

Both full crucks and base crucks are arch-like structures that must exert some horizontal thrust at their supports. Where they rest on the ground this would have presented no problem, but where they are raised the walls must be capable of resisting this outward thrust. The only structural advantage that cruck frames then have over straight principal rafters is that they bring the horizontal thrust lower down the wall which may then be braced more easily by buttresses. Where straight principal rafters were used without tie beams there was a problem of transmitting their thrust to the wall if they were simply attached to wall plates. A more effective connection between the wall and the principal rafters could be provided with arch braces that then had much the same effect as raised cruck blades. A long mortice was cut in the bottom of the principal rafter and the arch brace tenoned into this and fixed with several pegs. Below the wall plate the brace was similarly fixed to a wall post so that the latter could transmit the outward thrust to the wall (Figure 5.11). In some roofs the arch braces extend to the apex while in others the principals were also braced near the top with a collar and then the arch braces would be framed into this.

This arrangement resulted in an elegant structure suitable for the open roofs of churches or halls where the opportunity might be taken to apply decorative carving to the timbers. Decorative tracery might be used in open spandrels between arch braces and principal rafters or to

fill between the collar and the apex of the roof. Wind braces in roofs of this type might also be decoratively carved. But the most decorative of roof types to be developed was the hammerbeam roof, common in East Anglian churches but widely distributed throughout Britain and capable of the most extraordinary elaboration.

It is not certain how the hammerbeam developed but one possible method that has been suggested is that it came from the arch braced roof. Large timbers would have been needed for the arch braces, as much because of their depth as their length. The size required for these could be reduced by dividing them into two with a short cantilever projecting from the wall and attached to the wall plate (Figure 5.12) i.e. a hammerbeam. This would have had the added advantage that the wall post could be framed into it rather than into the principal rafter and this might have simplified the process of assembly. With the arch brace interrupted by a beam there was no need for it to form a continuous curve. Rather a more pleasing effect could be obtained by extending the hammerbeam and bringing the upper part of the arch brace away from the wall to make a distinct break in the curve. A post, called a hammerpost, might then be added between the outer end of the hammerbeam and the principal rafter for the arch brace to be framed into.

Some credence is given to this suggested line of development by the presence of a number of churches in which simple arch braced principals alternate with hammerbeams, but it should be noted that some authors have suggested quite a different origin which takes account of the similarity between some hammerbeam roofs and the queen post form of roof. In contrast there are also some hammerbeams that have been used with very shallow pitches, rather like tie beam roofs. The wide variety of hammerbeam types seems to suggest that either they were developed separately, each from a different original type of roof or, more likely, that having been developed from one earlier roof form they were then applied within different carpentry traditions for their decorative possibilities.

Like other types of roof, decorative tracery was used to infill the spaces between the structural timbers although it is questionable how structural some of these were. Indeed, the behaviour of hammerbeam roofs has caused much debate. There are of course two problems to solve; the actual behaviour of the structure and the behaviour that was assumed by its builders. It is not possible to consider the second question here and different answers have been proposed for the first. At one time it was thought that the bracket-like assembly provided some assistance to the principal rafter. The assumption was that the hammerbeam, balanced across the wall post, carried a downward force from the hammerpost which was then counterbalanced by the load of the principal rafters at its other end. However, it now seems likely that in most cases the hammerbeam assembly does little to assist the principals. The best known hammerbeam roof is at Westminster Hall, completed by Hugh Herland in 1394, and has a span of 20.7 m with additional arch braces (Figure 5.13). In this structure these arch braces may help the roof to resist wind loads.

Westminster Hall has angels at the ends of the ham-

ROOF OVER THE NAVE OF
CAPEL S⟋ MARY'S CHURCH,
SUFFOLK.

Figure 5.12 *Possible development of hammerbeam roofs. Drawings by Raphael and J. Arthur Brandon from* Open timber roofs of the Middle Ages.

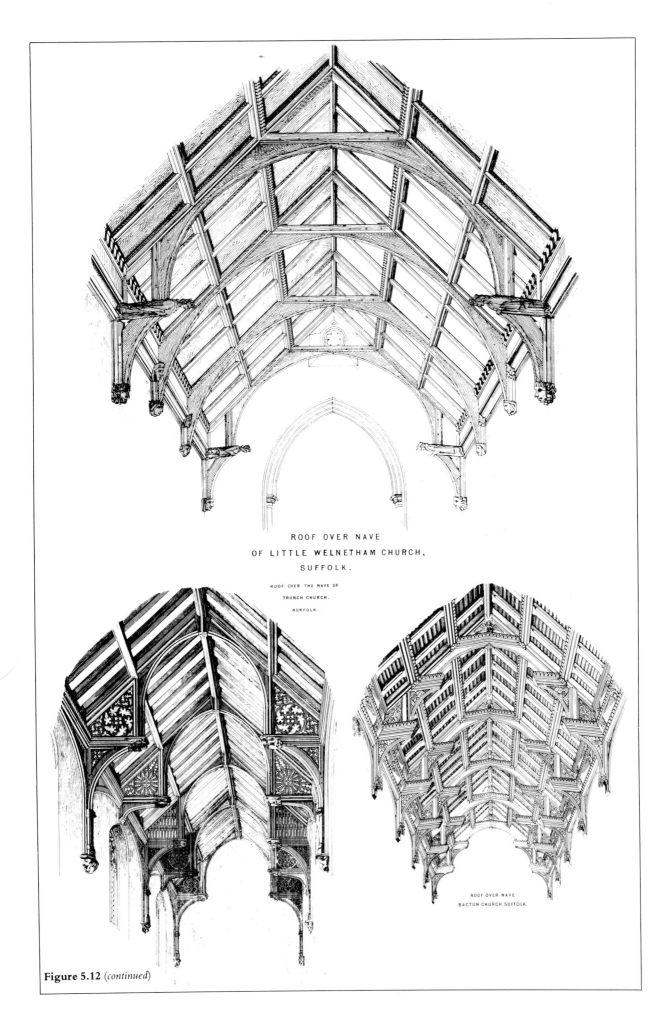

ROOF OVER NAVE
OF LITTLE WELNETHAM CHURCH,
SUFFOLK.

ROOF OVER THE NAVE OF
TRUNCH CHURCH.
NORFOLK.

ROOF OVER NAVE
BACTON CHURCH. SUFFOLK.

Figure 5.12 (continued)

71

Figure 5.13 *Westminster Hall roof. Drawing by Viollet-le-Duc from* Dictionnaire Raisonné de l'Architecture.

merbeams which are a feature of many church roofs; a kind of visual joke suggesting that they were supporting the roof on their backs. Another common decoration device was to extend the hammerpost below the beam to form a decoratively carved pendant. At Wethersden, Suffolk, the church roof has seated and standing figures carved into both the hammerposts and wallposts. In East Anglia many 'double hammerbeams' were built in which a second hammerbeam and hammerpost were jointed into each principal rafter. Of course the additional hammerbeam serves no structural purpose. Even today these are dramatic roofs but when they were built they may also have been richly painted (Figure 5.14).

The end of the seventeenth century saw a radical change in roof structures. Until then roofs for the majority of buildings had relied upon simple king post, or more commonly, queen post frames or 'trusses'. In both of these the principal rafters were strutted from the tie beam so that the latter carried loads in bending. With the tie beam acting in this way the span of the roof was limited by the longest length of timber that could be obtained for this member. In the seventeenth century the modern form of king post roof was introduced, i.e. the type of king post truss with which we are familiar today.

In this type of structure the struts which relieve the principal rafters of the load from the purlins are carried not by the tie beam but by the king post. The king post was widened at the bottom with 'joggles' for these struts to bear upon and they therefore tended to push the king post downward. At the head of the king post similar joggles enable it to be trapped by the principal rafters. These thus acted as a simple arch supporting the king post which therefore acted in tension (Figure 5.16). In this structural arrangement there was no bending on the tie beam which had simply to resist the outward thrust of the principal rafters and it now acted just as a tie rather than also as a beam. Increased spans were therefore possible, partly because the tie beam, not having to carry any bending loads, could be smaller, and also because a scarf joint could be made to transmit tensile forces so that the tie beam might be made in two halves. No longer was the tie beam supporting the king post: the reverse was true.

Ideally the timbers of a king post truss should be arranged so that the principal rafters are strutted where they carry the purlins i.e. close to their mid-point if there is one pair of purlins. Shallower roof pitches and increasing spans both present some difficulties. It is easy to arrange to strut the centre of the principal rafters if the pitch is about 45 degrees, but as the angle is reduced it becomes more difficult to do this for the angle of the struts must also be reduced. Moreover, while the force in the principal rafters will increase with shallower pitches, it becomes more difficult to make an effective joint at their feet to transmit this force to the tie beam. Larger spans may require two pairs of purlins so that the principals may need additional strutting while the tie beam, which carries the weight of a plaster ceiling, may require more support than just the central king post.

Eighteenth-century roof structures show various attempts to overcome these difficulties. Some involve careful detailing of the joints of the trusses, others modifications to the layout of the members, while, more radically, the queen post truss was developed for larger roof structures.

Inigo Jones introduced this new form of king post truss into England from Italy. Few of his buildings still have their original roof structures but the evidence that we have suggests that he was not a very skilful structural designer. Drawings survive of his roof for the Banqueting House, Whitehall, perhaps his most important building, completed in 1622 (Figure 5.15). The span of the roof was over 15.2 m and it had three pairs of purlins. Secondary posts were hung from the principal rafters both to give additional support to the tie beam and to carry a second pair of struts to assist the principals.

Unfortunately, the detailed design was weak because the main struts from the base of the king post did not support the secondary posts directly. Instead the struts and the secondary posts were separately attached to the principals. Weakness in this roof was noticed in the 1720s when repairs were put in hand, but the roof had eventually to be replaced by Soane early in the nineteenth century. Weakness in another large roof by Inigo Jones over the Queen's House, Greenwich, completed in 1617, had been recorded by the end of the seventeenth century and this roof also has not survived. His roof for St Paul's, Covent Garden (Figure 5.16), com-

ROOF OVER NAVE
KNAPTON CHURCH, NORFOLK.

Figure 5.14 *Knapton Church, Norfolk. Drawing by Raphael and J. Arthur Brandon from* Open timber roofs of the Middle Ages.

pleted in 1632, had also to be repaired but it was eventually destroyed by fire.

Christopher Wren's roofs show that he had a far clearer understanding of the behaviour of trusses. His carpentry details are better and, as we shall see later, he was able to develop new truss forms. Because of the large number of buildings that he designed, which included the many churches rebuilt after the Fire of London and the Royal Hospitals, he must also have been influential in disseminating knowledge of these new forms through the carpenters that were employed. Rather than looking at his earliest building, one of his later structures shows how the king post truss might be adapted for long spans. The roof of Trinity College library, Cambridge (Figure 5.17), built between 1676 and 1684, spans 12.2 m. The trusses carry two pairs of purlins and have secondary posts and struts to assist them. One can see how the struts are arranged to prop the principals close to the purlins and that the inner pair bear under joggles at the head of the secondary posts. In this way they support the secondary posts directly while the outer pair of struts are carried on the joggles at the feet of these posts. This detailing means that there is no additional bending on the principal rafters, nor need a joint be made at the top of the posts to carry tension forces.

Metalwork began to be commonly used in these trussed roofs. Metal straps at the feet of king posts were used to 'truss up' the tie beam and so help carry the weight of the ceiling. Because the lower pitches which were now favoured made it difficult to form a satisfactory joint between the feet of the principal rafters and the tie beam, metal straps were used to hold down the principals and prevent their kicking up out of the joint. These can be seen in the Trinity roof (Figure 5.17). This roof also has metal straps to join the two halves of the tie beams but this is an unusual feature because scarf joints could easily be made which would transmit the tensile forces. Metal strapping also began to be used at the head of the king post although it is difficult to understand the reason for this since the Trinity roof has proved perfectly satisfactory without. Hawksmoor often used Y-shaped metal straps here and a good example of this is seen in the roof of St Paul's, Deptford, which, although designed by another architect, Thomas Archer, was probably built by one of Hawksmoor's carpenters between 1712 and 1730 (Figure 5.18).

A good example of how the forces in the truss were understood by some designers is shown in Gibbs' design at St Martin-in-the-Fields (Figure 5.19). A difficulty with long spanning trusses is that there is likely to be some initial deflection because of movement at the joints as they take up load. In the portico of St Martin's, completed in 1726, there is a single truss spanning 18.2 m which has two pairs of secondary posts and inclined

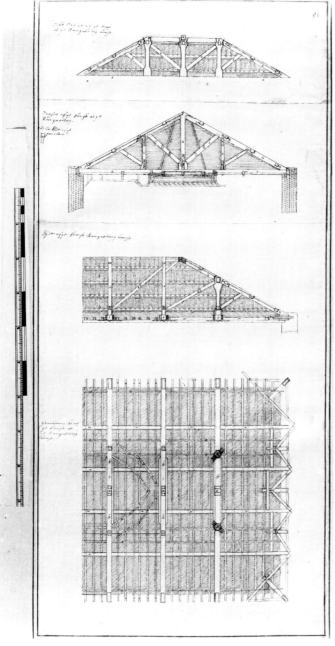

Figure 5.15 *Drawing by Webb of Inigo Jones' roof for the Banqueting House, Whitehall. Drawing: Devonshire Collection, Chatsworth. Reproduced by permission of the Chatsworth Settlement Trustees.* Photograph: Courtald Institute of Art.

struts. The latter must exert some horizontal thrust which must be transmitted to the principal rafters at one end, and apart from the inner pair of struts, to the tie beam at the other. This would normally be done via the tenons at the ends of the posts and such a small area of timber would be liable to crushing. The tenons might be relieved by notching the posts into the tie beam and principals in order to give a larger bearing area. While Gibbs did this at St Martin's he also added straining members just above the tie beam and below the principals to relieve joints of this horizontal thrust. A further refinement in the truss was that a slot was cut in the head of the king post and wedges were driven in to tighten it against the ends of the principal rafters and a similar detail was adopted for the inner pair of posts.

Unfortunately, in spite of these precautions, the truss failed early in its life because of a poorly designed scarf joint in the tie beam.

Because Wren came to architecture from a background in science and mathematics he understood the behaviour of the truss sufficiently to have the confidence to modify its form in only his second building. In the Sheldonian Theatre, Oxford, which was completed in 1669, he both added a pair of secondary posts and divided each principal rafter into two so altering the outward form of the roof (Figure 5.20). One can see in this an apparent arch shape which may well have been the analogy he had in mind in designing this structure. Faced with a span of about 21 m it would have been difficult to obtain single timbers for the tie beams and so he devised an arrangement using seven pieces for each. Four timbers were let into the sides of the posts and so directly supported by them. Below these were three timbers arranged to pass under each of the posts while joined to the upper timbers on either side in such a way as to be able to transmit the tensile forces and so form a continuous tie. This ingenious arrangement attracted considerable attention at the time but unfortunately the structure was replaced in the nineteenth century.

In a later Wren building this form was modified to produce a queen post truss. A flat-topped roof was used for the Painted Hall at Greenwich Hospital in about 1710 and one can see in this structure how the form may have been derived from the design of the trusses of the Sheldonian roof by combining the two middle sections of the principal rafters into a single 'straining beam' (Figure 5.16).

The advantage of this arrangement was that it lowered the profile of the roof. The number of joints was also reduced so simplifying the carpentry. In the Painted Hall roof the queen posts are suspended from the timber arch by metal straps although this was an unusual detail. A very short 'king post' was used, also suspended from the straining beam by a metal strap although in some of the roofs of Wren's London churches where queen post trusses were also used this central post was omitted altogether. By the time this roof was built Hawksmoor was in charge of the day-to-day construction of the buildings at Greenwich so that this development may well be his design.

None of these queen post church roofs has survived, except St Bennet's, Pauls Wharf, completed in 1783 and we know of them only through nineteenth-century measured drawings. St Bennet's is untypical being much higher than the rest and may be more easily compared with the roof of the hall at Chelsea Hospital built between 1682 and 1691 (Figure 5.21). Of all the Wren roofs that have survived, this is the most dramatic. The huge roof space is more like a barn than an attic and when it was first built it was used as dormitories for the nurses. There is far less metal strapping used in this roof than in the roof at Greenwich and the joints between posts, straining beam and principal rafters are formed entirely by the carpentry.

Apart from its ability to form lower pitches and provide usable attic spaces, the queen post truss offered other advantages over the king post form. Because the arch of timber supporting the roof was formed of three

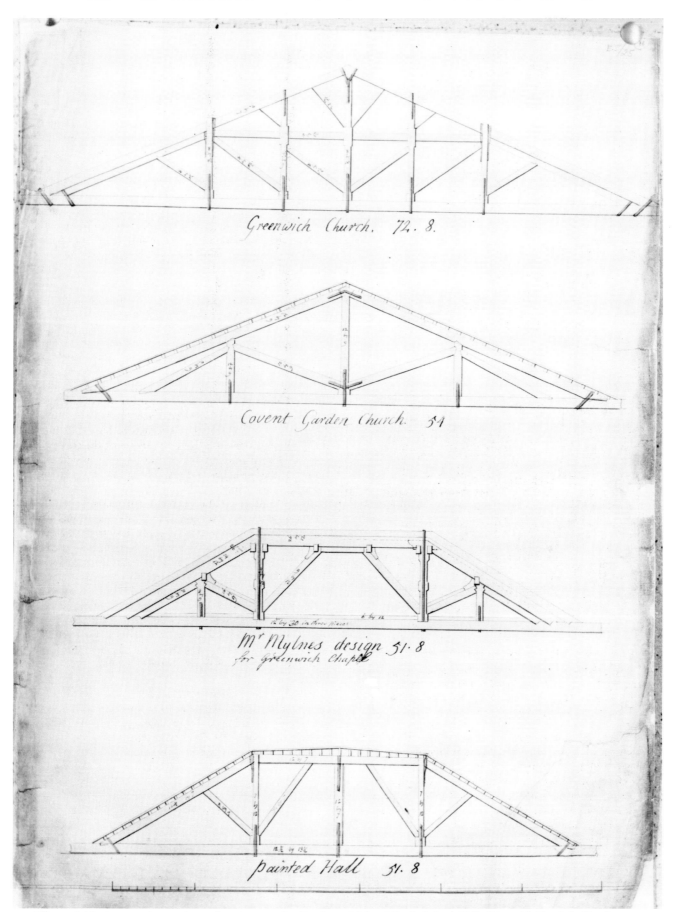

Greenwich Church. 72. 8.

Covent Garden Church. 54

Mr Mylnes design 51. 8
for Greenwich Chapel

Painted Hall 51. 8

Figure 5.16 *A survey drawing by William Newton showing the roof structures of: Hawksmoor's St Alphege, Greenwich; Inigo Jones' Covent Garden Church; an unexecuted design by Robert Mylne; Wren's Painted Hall, Greenwich Hospital. The first two have since been destroyed by fire.* RIBA Drawings Collection.

Figure 5.17 *Roof of Trinity College library, Cambridge.* Photograph: Jewell Harrison.

Figure 5.18 *Roof of St Paul's, Deptford, showing Y-shaped metal straps.* Photograph: Jewell Harrison.

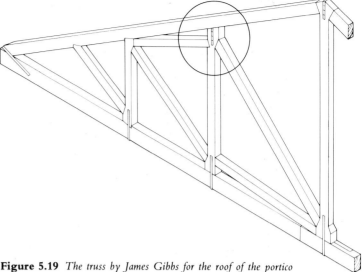

Figure 5.19 *The truss by James Gibbs for the roof of the portico over St Martin-in-the-Fields, London.* Photograph: Jewell Harrison.

pieces rather than two, they could be correspondingly shorter. Two posts were supported by this arrangement so that the tie beam was divided into three spans rather than two. In some long spanning roofs a central post was also added, strutted like a king post from the base of the two queen posts (Figure 5.22). Although used at first with flat lead roofs over the straining beam the queen post truss was eventually combined with long principal rafters to support simple ridged roofs, sometimes with a king post set above the straining beam.

Hawksmoor used a combination of king and queen post forms for his roof of St Alphege, Greenwich, in 1714 (Figure 5.16). When Hardwick came to replace the roof of St Paul's, Covent Garden (Figure 5.23) after its destruction by fire, he used queen post trusses to accommodate the wide overhangs rather than the awkward combination of king post forms that Inigo Jones had used. During the eighteenth century a number of Gothic cathedrals were re-roofed and the queen post truss proved a more effective solution than the king post for their steep pitches because it made it easier to strut the principal rafters. However, in spite of these advantages the queen post truss did not become popular until the nineteenth century, by which time other changes were taking place in roof truss design.

Although metalwork had been used in trusses for some time its use increased in the nineteenth century, both at the joints where it was used to supplement or possibly replace carpentry details, and as an integral part of the truss framing when metal tie rods were used to replace timber tension members. An early example of

the former was in the eighteenth-century roof of the Porter Tun room at the Whitbread brewery in London (Figure 5.24). In this the 20.7 m span trusses have metal caps bolted to the heads of the king posts to receive the principal rafters instead of the normal joggles in the timber. This innovation was not carried through into the other joints which still relied upon the carpentry. In later structures cast-iron shoes were to be used at the ends of tie beams to receive the feet of principal rafters and in a few cases at the feet of the king posts to carry the struts. Fastening of the tie beams to king posts was improved by better straps that were tightened by gibbs and folding wedges rather than relying upon the rather passive bolting previously used.

Metal tie rods could easily be used to replace the king posts or queen posts of trusses. Such tie rods would either be passed through the timber members and fastened with washers or spreader plates or they could be fixed to cast-iron connectors. A common method was to use simple spreader plates under the tie beam and iron connectors at the head of the rods. This arrangement was used by Soane in 1830 when he replaced the roof of the Banqueting House, Whitehall, using queen post trusses. Although the queen post of the trusses is timber there are central tie rods to assist the tie beam. An iron casting is bolted to the centre of each straining beam and held in position by timber struts from the bottom of the queen posts while suspended from this casting are pairs of tie rods (Figure 5.25).

The open roofs required for warehouses, workshops or railway stations, having no ceilings to support, could

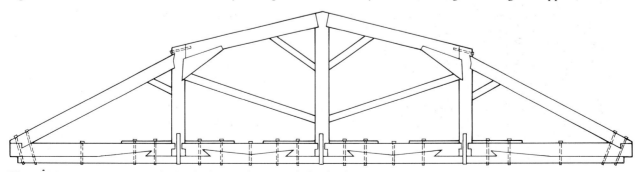

Figure 5.20 *Wren's truss design for the Sheldonian Theatre, Oxford. After drawing in* Parentalia.

Figure 5.21 *Roof over the hall at Chelsea Hospital.* Photograph: Jewell Harrison.

Figure 5.22 *Roof of All Saints Church, Oxford; now Lincoln College library.* Photograph: Jewell Harrison.

Figure 5.23 *Hardwick's replacement roof for St Paul's, Covent Garden.* Photograph: Jewell Harrison.

Figure 5.24 *Roof of the Porter Tun Room, Whitbread Brewery, Chiswell St., London.* Photograph: Julian Harrap, Architects.

Figure 5.25 *Soane's replacement roof for the Banqueting House, Whitehall.* Photograph: Jewell Harrison.

be built with iron tie rods replacing the timber tie beam. There was now no need for the tie beam to be straight and there might be an advantage in improved headroom if it were raised. Variations in the form of roof truss were designed along these lines which combined timber compression members with iron tension rods and so clearly articulated the direction of the forces within the structure. Some fine examples of these were used by Brunel for buildings on the Great Western Railway (Figure 5.26). These roofs were often similar in form to the cast- and wrought-iron roofs of the same period. Indeed we probably associate this period and these industrial and commercial buildings with a growth of iron structures at the expense of timber.

Nothing has been said so far about timber arches which had been used in bridge construction. During the eighteenth century both permanent timber bridges and the temporary centres for masonry structures were built in the form of arches. These comprised a number of straight pieces of timber jointed together to form a framework with the shape of that framework forming an arch. However arch bridges had been built in other countries that comprised curved planks of timber fastened together to form an arch; in effect laminated timber. In Britain in the nineteenth century timber bridges

Figure 5.26 *Engine House, Swindon. Drawing from* Bourne's Great Western Railway.

80

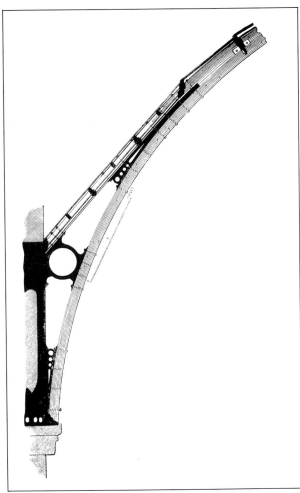

Figure 5.27 *Laminated arches at King's Cross Station, London.*
Reproduced from The Builder *2 October 1852.* Photograph: RIBA Library.

were built by the railway companies and while many of these were truss or trestle forms, some used laminated timber arches. When King's Cross Station, the third of the major London termini, was built, it also had roofs of laminated timber arches (Figure 5.27).

Laminated timber of this kind was a fairly recent development for roofs although it was used elsewhere in Britain. At King's Cross 38 mm boards were bolted together to form arch ribs 600 mm deep which were carried by masonry corbels set into the wall of the station building. These spanned over 30.5 mm across the tracks and were echoed in the semi-circular glazing of the station facade. The form and spacing of these arches can still be seen in the replacement iron roof which stands on the original supports. Unfortunately steam from the engines standing at the arrival platforms caused deterioration of the timbers which led to the need for their replacement, but a similar structure built only a few years afterwards survives in a building close to the station. The German Gymnasium, built in 1866, had laminated timber arches of a similar form (Figure 5.28) and although it has been suggested that they might have been made with timbers salvaged from the station, there is no evidence to substantiate this. In the Gymnasium iron castings bolted to the top of the arches carry rafters to form a pitched roof with clerestory glazing down the centre. The building is no longer used as a gymnasium and now serves as offices with an inserted upper floor but the arches remain in service and one can still see the hooks from which climbing ropes were once suspended.

The most intriguing railway station roof is Brunel's Temple Meads Station, Bristol (Figure 5.29), where he used hammerbeams. Like the earlier hammerbeams this

Figure 5.28 *The German Gymnasium; now used as offices.*
Photograph: Jewell Harrison.

Figure 5.29 *Brunel's hammerbeam roof at Temple Meads Station, Bristol. Drawing from* Bourne's Great Western Railway.

Figure 5.30 *Pilkington's roof of Barclay Church, Edinburgh.*
Photograph: Jewell Harrison.

form was more decorative than structural and the roof relies upon metal strapping hidden above the rafters and tying them back into the masonry of the building. However this was in the spirit of much roof carpentry of the period because, while there were the structural developments that have been described, there was a lively interest in earlier decorative forms. The Brandons' book from which some of the illustrations here have been taken was one manifestation of this. While many Victorian churches had roofs based on medieval forms, the hammerbeam roof became popular in other countries as well as Britain. Not all these roofs relied upon direct copying. At Addiscombe, Surrey, Lamb devised a roof for St Mary Magdalene that was a rather free interpretation of the hammerbeam and scissor braced forms creating a dramatic crossing. Perhaps the most imaginative as well as dramatic roof was that designed by Pilkington for his Barclay Church, Edinburgh, where a complex plan is covered by a combination of tied arches incorporating suggested hammerbeams and all ornately decorated (Figure 5.30).

6 Development of modern timber structures

Phillip O Reece

Phillip O Reece OBE CEng MICE FIStructE MIMunE FIWSc, now retired, was director of TRADA from 1948–1960. He then worked for Phoenix Timber Ltd, Powell Duffryn Timber Ltd and was managing director of Hydro-Air International (UK) Ltd.

The structural use of timber is as old, or older, than civilization. Long before the invention of the mathematical sciences, early man was building rude shelters which, over the ages, by trial and no doubt considerable error, led to patterns of timber construction which left their permanent imprint on the stone and marble temples of classical Greece. In spite of its antiquity – or perhaps because of it – timber has suffered some neglect at the hands of general practitioners in materials science and engineering, with the result that most engineering textbooks tend to give the impression that the application of structural theory is limited to steel or other man-made materials. Yet, weight for weight, timber is as strong or stronger than steel and much stronger than most of its structural competitors.

The tree

In considering the structural use of any material it is convenient to distinguish between the material and the structure of which it is part, but the material itself is also a structure, either macroscopically or microscopically, and in timber we have a very complex internal structure which has evolved to fulfil its function in the tree. In a typical conifer the exposed area of its foliage may be comparable to the sail area of a contender for the America's Cup and may stand 60 m or more high. Exposed to the wind, rain, snow and ice of the northern latitudes the tree has, of necessity, developed the properties of strength, stiffness, resilience, toughness and durability which have made it the oldest and largest of living things on earth.

Research and development

The emergence of mild steel from cast iron was accompanied by and engendered a growth in materials science which ensured a fairly steady, continuous and orderly growth of design techniques. No such influence was brought to bear on timber which, by contrast, jumped forward in the fits and starts of economic and national exigency. In modern historical times such a jump occurred with the outbreak of the First World War when the need for a low-density material for the construction of aircraft led to research into the behaviour of timber at the Royal Aircraft Establishment at Farnborough on a scale never previously attempted in Britain. One eventual outstanding result of this was the Mosquito, a wooden aeroplane which is still regarded as one of the most successful aircraft of all time (Figure 6.1).

The second spasmodic upheaval occurred in the United States during the Second World War when, after Pearl Harbour, America needed all her steel for military purposes and used her ample supplies of timber for an amazingly wide range of constructional projects including bridges, floating docks, aircraft and dirigible hangars, ships and buildings of all kinds.

At the end of the Second World War the Timber Development Association – TDA (now the Timber Research and Development Association – TRADA) embarked on a deliberate policy of bringing British timber engineering up to date in line with the wartime achievements of the USA and Canada. The work which had been initiated by the Royal Aircraft Establishment had already been largely transferred and extended by the Forest Products Research Laboratory set up in Princes Risborough in the early 1920s, from which time timber research in Britain became a continuing process. The TDA contribution in the decade to about 1960 was concerned not so much with research as with design and, in the fits and starts which have characterized British timber engineering, may reasonably be described as the third significant jump since 1914. This would not have been possible without considerable reliance on results of work carried out elsewhere, results freely given by the laboratories at Princes Risborough, the United States, Canada and the Scandinavian countries. It should perhaps be borne in mind that research and development are not quite the same thing, the scientist and the engineer starting from opposite ends of what may be a long and difficult road, with a common meeting place at the point where Codes of Practice, British Standards and Building Regulations are framed.

Bones and muscles

The net result of structural research and development in the last 70 years has been the virtual abandonment of the structural techniques established so slowly and painfully in the preceding millennia. The break with the past is nearly complete, the contemporary timber structure being different from its predecessor in both kind and degree. The raw material is the same but our understanding and control of its strengths and weaknesses are very different.

From the purely structural point of view, if one had to pick out a single factor which, more than any other, is responsible for this change, it has to be the development of efficient tension joints. The pre-scientific age of timber construction had no effective means of utilizing the very high tensile strength of timber. Traditional carpentry aimed therefore at putting all joints into compression which meant that the missing tensile forces had to be compensated with heavy masonry walls, buttresses and foundations. The development of modern glues and timber connectors has enabled a wide range of structures to contain both tensile and compression forces within themselves, with consequent economy in their supporting elements.

Every pull in a structure must be balanced with a corresponding push or, as Newton put it more succinctly, action and reaction are equal and opposite. Man, like a framed girder, is a self-contained structure, his bones being in compression, his muscles in tension. This is one of the reasons he can walk about without falling apart. Arches, suspension bridges, hammerbeam roof trusses and jellyfish have to be externally restrained.

Strength and stiffness

All materials will deform and break if pushed, pulled, bent or twisted hard enough, but some will deform and break sooner than others. Deformation is due to the application of external forces to the internal chemical bonds which hold the atoms and molecules of the material together, bonds which act like springs and may be compressed, extended or broken by compression, tension or shear. Material under test will display strength values lower than those which might be predicted from the strength of their atomic or molecular bonds. This is due to discontinuities in the atomic or molecular structure which may even appear as minute cracks as in glass. When loaded, these discontinuities will become points of stress concentration which, if stressed sufficiently, will propagate cracks in the material leading to its ultimate fracture and failure. This may be illustrated by trying to extract a piece of cheese from its plastic wrapper – surely one of the most frustrating facets of modern life. If one cuts a tiny nip in a folded corner of the plastic and concentrates one's strain-energy on it, the resulting crack propagation is most satisfactory, the piece of cheese becomes, as it were, a piece of cake. Timber is an extraordinarily strong and tough material but it is still not as strong as the cellulose chains which make up about 60 per cent of wood substance. It does not behave in quite the same way as the crystalline metals since, although some 30 to 40 per cent of the cellulose in wood is in crystalline form, considerable extra work must be done to untangle its very complicated structure. Weight for weight, the total work required to fracture it is roughly the same as in commercial mild steel.

The strength of a structural member, as distinct from

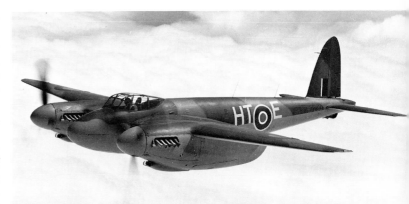

Figure 6.1 *Mosquito aircraft.* Photograph: British Aerospace Aircraft Group.

the strength of its material, may be defined as the load it will carry before failure. Such failure may be due to the rupture of the material as described above, or the deformation of the member beyond the limits of acceptability. We are concerned therefore with both strength and stiffness, each of which is determined by multiplying together a factor of unit strength (f or E) and a geometrical property of the cross-section of the member (A, Z or I). Once a particular material is selected, not very much can be done about its strength property, but a great deal can be done with its geometry. Fold a piece of paper into a V-section and you can safely light your pipe with it, leave it in its pristine form and it will flop about and burn your fingers – yet the strength of the paper as a material is unchanged.

Geometry on the whole is more important than mechanical strength and the value of the low-density materials in general, and timber in particular, is that you get more geometrical property per pound weight than with the heavier materials. This means that although timber is very much weaker than steel when measured per square inch of cross-section, this may be more than compensated by the greater cross-section A, the greater modulus of section Z and the greater moment of inertia I, for sections of equal weight. We may determine from considerations such as these that, for members of equal weight, timber may be superior to steel in tension, bending and stiffness, but inferior in direct crushing and shear. Clearly, if we restrict timber to those uses in which it is superior, we should obtain more efficient structures.

Optimum structures

Considerations such as the foregoing lead to the conclusion that timber should be used for all structural members which are liable to fail through elastic instability by buckling, bending or wrinkling at comparatively low loads rather than through the direct crushing of the material. Such members are the slender, lightly-loaded columns of solid, hollow or built-up section; long, lightly-loaded beams such as the floor joists of houses in which the design may be governed by deflection rather than stress; the so-called 'stressed-skin' construction in which the space-covering material is used as a load-bearing element as in flush doors, plywood covered wall and roof units, gliders and boats, furniture and, in general, all structures which are lightly loaded in relation to their

Figure 6.2 *Transport of large glulam beams by road can impose limitations on size.* Photograph: Laminated Wood Ltd.

size. By this definition we should also include most roof structures, masts, telegraph poles, pylons, towers, hangars, footbridges and lightly-loaded floors and platforms.

Size and scale

With the solid stone lintels of antiquity there was a limit to the maximum spans which could be achieved due to the low strength/weight ratio of stone in tension and the fact that, while the weight of a solid beam varies as its cube, its strength varies only as the square of its depth. In practice, a point is reached when the lintel can barely sustain its own weight, let alone support a superimposed load. With a low density, high strength material and the wide range of structural forms avail-

able, the question whether it is possible to assign any upper limit to the possible size of a timber structure is much more complex.

In the past there was a limit to the dimensions of timber available and this is no doubt one of the reasons why the cedar of Lebanon was so highly prized in biblical times – it grew to a great age, a great height and a great width. Today the dimensional limitations imposed by the size of a tree are no more, the use of strong and durable adhesives, plywood, glued lamination and end or finger jointing means that timber from comparatively small trees can be obtained in almost any width, depth or length required; the only limitation arising from the means to be made available for transport and handling. Very large structures may be assembled on site from prefabricated parts, when the problem resolves itself into limiting the size of the largest part according to the mode of transport and erection to be adopted (Figures 6.2, 6.3 and 6.4).

Some megastructures

About AD 530–537 the Emperor Justinian, or perhaps more accurately his architects Anthemius of Tralles and Isidore of Miletus, rebuilt the church of Hagia Sophia at what used to be called Constantinople, with a dome of 32.5 m in diameter built with pumice-stone bricks, supported by four great arches, in turn buttressed with half-domes, all together combining to give an unobstructed floor area 60 × 30 m. Professor Gordon in his book *Structures* has suggested that this was probably the greatest unobstructed area achieved until the advent of the modern railway station.

What was described as 'the absolute climax of the railway roof in Britain' was the roof of St Pancras station in London, built 13 centuries later, in 1868, with

Figure 6.3 *The prefabricated sections of the Thames Flood Barrier roofs were floated on barges for erection by crane onto the concrete piers.*
Photograph: Tysons (Contractors) Ltd.

tied steel arches and a clear span of 73 m – then the world's largest span.

The largest timber structures built in the USA during the Second World War were the blimp hangars for the US Navy with spans of about 73 m. At the time these hangars were the largest timber structures in the world; they were constructed with bolted and connectored framed arches, transported in relatively small parts and erected with mobile scaffolding (Figure 6.5).

In the fits and starts of timber engineering such records do not necessarily last as long as Hagia Sophia's. In 1977 the Northern Arizona University built a timber-framed dome to cover a playing field and spectator stands to seat 15,000 people with an ice-hockey rink, a 400-metre running track, tennis courts, basketball courts and facilities for a host of other sports and civic activities. The dome is about 153 m in diameter and 28 m high (Figure 6.42). This is currently the largest timber structure on record.

Deflection and creep

All materials and structures deflect under load and large structures deflect more than small ones. Anyone who has dined at the top of an American skyscraper must have watched with some horror while the chandeliers swayed back and forth as plumb-bobs measuring the lateral deflection of the building – a vertical unpropped cantilever perhaps 400 m high.

BS 5268 Part 2 recommends that deflections be restricted within limits appropriate to the type of structure and gives, as a very general guide, a deflection limit of 0.003 of the span of a fully loaded beam. This is about 27 mm in 9 m which, with a slight camber, would be scarcely noticeable and would do no harm. In a span of 153 m it would be about 460 mm which might not be

so acceptable. Fortunately domes do not deflect as much as beams and this would in any case be less noticeable. In an unpropped cantilever 400 m long, as in the skyscraper, the deflection would be 2.4 m which would give an amplitude of oscillation of 4.8 m – surely too much for even the most hardened New Yorker.

The problem of deflection is made more difficult as Hooke's Law, that strain is proportional to stress, is only approximately true. It is generally true for low loads and short periods of time but under high stress, and for long periods, strain may increase in all materials without any increase in stress. Owing to the practical difficulties of testing materials over periods corresponding to the life expectancy of structures, which may be 50 to 100 years, we get around this problem by referring to deformation due to stress as 'deflection' and deformation due to time as 'creep'. This is not very satisfactory as strain is a three-dimensional and not a two-dimensional problem. Creep is not merely the product of time but of the combined effects of time and stress; if the stress is below a critical level there may be little if any creep, but if the stress is high the effect of creep may be very great. As an illustration of this, two pairs of domestic roof trusses were maintained under full design load, including snow load, at the Princes Risborough Laboratory for a period of ten years. At the end of this period the initial deflections had increased by an average of 164 per cent. When the load was removed 43 per cent of this deflection was recovered and, when tested to destruction, there was no significant difference from the required strength and stiffness of new trusses.

It would be doing less than justice to nature to regard creep merely as an unmitigated nuisance. In steelwork, for instance, advantage has been taken of it in the plastic theory of bending which, in many applications, is of outstanding merit in securing economy not only in material but in the drawing office also, by eliminating some of the more tiresome consequences of the theory of elasticity. In timber the beneficial aspects of creep arise from the fact that the most highly stressed parts creep the most, thereby relieving stress concentrations which might otherwise initiate failure.

Figure 6.4 *The laminated sections for a bridge at Tintagel were floated by sea and then lifted into place by helicopter.* Photograph: Julia Brooks.

Figure 6.5 _US Navy blimp hangars under construction during the 1930s. The arches span about 73 m and were constructed using mobile scaffolding._ Photograph: US Navy Department.

In timber, stress concentrations are not perhaps as damaging as in steel but nevertheless need to be taken into account. All joints, sharp re-entrant angles at holes and openings, the inner side of the haunches of portal frames of built-up (as distinct from laminated) construction, abrupt changes of cross-section, lap joints – all are liable to induce stress concentrations of greater or lesser magnitude, against which creep may be the final safeguard.

Long-term performance

The price we pay for beneficial creep is increased deflection, but it is better to bend than bust. It should be remembered that all structures are erected in defiance of the law of gravity and they react by doing what comes naturally; they sag or, more elegantly, they act in such a way as to reduce their potential energy by getting their centres of gravity as close to the ground as possible. This is what happens to a length of chain suspended from its two ends; it does not form an arc of a circle or even a parabola; its shape is that of a catenary which gives it the lowest possible centre of gravity.

Soils creep as other materials, and the man who builds

a large house on sand is likely to suffer even more tribulation than the man who builds a small one. It is perhaps worth recalling that 20 years after its construction the great dome of Hagia Sophia collapsed and great was the fall of it. It was replaced by the existing structure. The collapse was probably due to creep and the lack of any adequate means of developing ring tension at the base of the dome.

If the megastructures of the future are to be built of timber (which seems quite likely) we will have to take a much harder look at permissible deflection limits at the end of a projected life-span. This is not perhaps quite as difficult as it may sound; it is possible to plot strain against the logarithm of time, as was in fact done with the Princes Risborough roof trusses, from which it was projected that the average deflection after 50 years would be 0.0035 of the span.

Classification of structure

We normally classify structures according to their purpose, e.g. bridge, warehouse, hangar, etc. This takes no account of the fact that the purpose may be the only thing two structures have in common, as for instance the two bridges over the Forth, one a cantilever and beam, the other a suspension bridge, differing from each other in both concept and appearance. From an engineering point of view a better classification would take into account the means adopted to transmit the loads to the foundations, joining pieces together for this purpose being what structural engineering is all about.

The introduction of tension joints has made a radical difference to timber structures, making them lighter and apparently more fragile – the difference between a termite hill and a spider's web. Except in very short lengths, all metals and timber are stronger in tension than in compression and in comparing modern structures with the massive buildings of the past it is perhaps salutary to give some thought to all the temples, churches and cathedrals which fell down to pay the price of those still standing.

Joints

The first essential step towards the development of timber as a modern engineering material was to establish means of assigning permissible working stresses to commercially available timber. This is the function of stress grading (see Chapter 4). The second logical step was to standardize the means of joining pieces of timber together in such a way as would enable positive strength values to be assigned to joints in compression, tension and shear.

Mechanical connectors

The development of nails, screws, coach-screws and bolts has lain chiefly in standardization and the evaluation of their performance to the point where joints could be designed in the same way as riveted joints in steel. Pre-boring holes to pattern, by making possible the closer spacing of nails without splitting, has brought nailed joints into the practical field of structural connections and with or without glue, characterized the evo-

Figure 6.6 *Diagonal web beam.*

lution of the diagonal web plate girder (Figure 6.6).

A significant development has been the bolted metal connector. There are two main types in use: the toothed plate (Figure 6.7) and the split ring (Figure 6.8). The

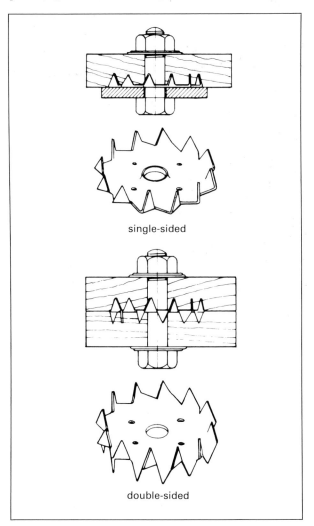

single-sided

double-sided

Figure 6.7 *Toothed plate connectors.*

former is a thin plate of galvanized steel with triangular teeth projecting on one side (single-sided) or alternately on both sides (double-sided). The plates are placed concentrically on the bolt connecting the members to be joined, the teeth being embedded in the timber under mechanical pressure. The purpose of the single-sided connector is to facilitate the use of steel gusset or fish plates for the connection on site of prefabricated parts.

The split ring is rather like a piston ring. It is a heavy duty connector transmitting shear in much the same way as the toothed plate, being placed in a pre-cut circular groove in the contact faces of the timbers to be joined (Figure 6.9). Corresponding to the single-sided toothed plate connector, the shear plate (Figure 6.10) is used to transmit the load to the connecting bolt and thence to the steel gusset or fish plate.

The latest recruit to the ranks of the mechanical connectors is the integral nail-plate (Figure 6.11) which so far has found its greatest use in the trussed rafter. The nails are short, slender and closely spaced; they are punched out from the parent plate by a stamping process and embedded, normally with hydraulic presses, on each side of the timbers to be joined together. The effect of the parent plate is to enable the nails to act like miniature cantilevers and to counteract the splitting which might otherwise occur with such a close nail spacing. Experience with their use over the last 20 years in Britain (and longer in the USA) has proved very satisfactory.

All lap joints, whether nailed or glued, tend to create stress concentrations at their ends. This tends to put more load on the end nails of a plate than on the nails at the middle, but in the course of time the joint is likely to become stronger, the end nails deflecting slightly and transferring load more evenly throughout the plate.

Glue

The significant advances which have been made in mechanical connectors are at least matched by the achievements in the field of synthetic resin glues of the urea-formaldehyde, phenol-formaldehyde and resorci-

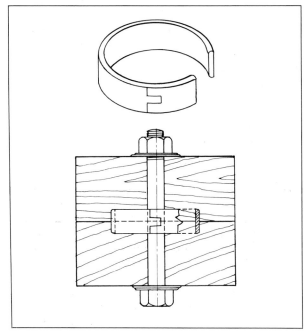

Figure 6.8 *Split ring connector.*

Figure 6.9 *Split ring connectors are placed in a pre-cut groove in the timber.*

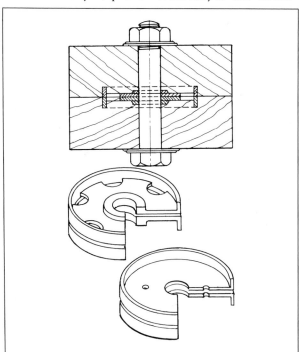

Figure 6.10 *Pressed steel and malleable iron shear plate connectors.*

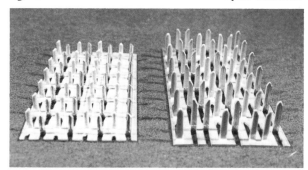

Figure 6.11 *Types of nail plates.*

nol types. These do for timber what welding does for steel – producing effective continuity at a joint which is just as strong as the wood itself. A comparison of joint efficiency achieved by different methods is difficult and may be misleading, but there need be no equivocation about the possibility, with good workmanship under controlled conditions, of securing 100 per cent efficiency in a glued joint. In such conditions some of these glues may be virtually indestructible by weather, micro-organisms, cold and boiling water, low temperature, and heat. They inevitably are part of the future of structural timber.

Glued lamination

Owing to the variability of strength properties within the same tree, let alone the same species, it was always necessary to employ working stresses much lower than the average to allow for the weaker pieces. It followed that the greater the variation, the greater the sacrifice in the interests of safety and the smaller the range of variation the closer the minimum strength value would be to the average. The introduction of mechanical stress grading not only ensured the more systematic evaluation of strength properties but also facilitated the separation of pieces into different strength grades, in each of which the range of variation would be reduced, with consequent increases in their individual strength values. In theory this means that the greater the number of strength grades the more efficient the utilization of available timber.

Glued lamination introduces yet a further increase in the efficiency of utilization. The range of variation of strength which occurs even in the same grade is such that if two pieces of timber be glued together and subjected to the same strain, the stresses to which they are individually subjected may be very different owing to differences in E, the modulus of elasticity. This is a case where the effect of variability works in reverse and advantage may be taken of the higher strength of one piece to compensate for the lower strength of the other. In a horizontally laminated beam, for instance, of LB grade and consisting of ten laminations, the SS grade value of the timber in bending may be increased by more than 40 per cent.

In modern commercial practice the individual pieces of a laminated member may be end scarfed (Figure 6.12) or finger jointed (see Chapter 4) with no great loss in strength so that, in theory, a member may be of infinite length (Figures 6.13 and 6.14). The laminations may be of such thickness as will enable them to be bent around a curved frame or jig and glued together to produce almost any desired shape.

A cross-section may be built up to any required dimension and form, high and low strength timber may be used at points of high and low stress, different species may be mixed to exploit their different properties. In the last 40 years or so glued lamination has been used on an increasing scale for the construction of long members, closed rings, bents or portal frames and arches. Its main advantage over rolled or extruded metal sections lies in greater freedom to vary its section along its length; its advantage over reinforced concrete arising from its high strength-to-weight ratio and its appearance.

Figure 6.12 *Scarf joints cut in timber before gluing.*

Beams

A thin piece of wood may easily be bent or broken by hand but it cannot easily be stretched or shortened. Timber is much stronger in direct stress parallel to the grain than in bending. Although the solid beam is one of the most useful maids-of-all-work in building, large structures are designed to avoid bending as much as possible and put the material in direct compression or tension. A solid piece of timber may still make the most economical beam in the sizes commercially available but, as the depth required becomes greater, the beam becomes less efficient as the maximum stresses can be attained only at the top and bottom edges. A point will arise when it is cheaper to do away with the middle under-stressed material near the neutral axis and replace it with a thinner web, as in a plate girder or a triangulated lattice in which all the forces are resolved into direct compression and tension in the flange and web members.

Exceptions may sometimes be made to this general rule in favour of the laminated beam. Occasions may arise when the advantages of a long continuous beam may outweigh the merits of other forms of construction. Laminated beams have been manufactured in lengths of over 30 m, their cross-sections are easily changed along the length and they have very high fire endurance.

Plate girders

The development of the plate girder took place along two main lines; in North America by the use of plywood webs in beams of box or I section (Figures 6.15 and 6.16), in Europe with webs diagonally cross-banded with softwood boards nailed together in two or more layers, usually in beams of I section (Figure 6.6). Plywood webs are now most commonly used in Europe.

A standard width for plywood sheets is 1200 mm and this sets practical beam depths of 300, 400 and 600 mm to avoid waste. If we assume a span/depth ratio of 12 to 18 depending on the intensity of loading, then suitable

Figure 6.13 *Laminated timber can be made in very long lengths. This illustration shows the laminated beams being manufactured for the Festival of Britain arch.*

spans may be considered to be from 3.6 m to 10.8 m for these sizes, the use of 1200 mm depths being fairly uncommon as the lattice type of beam becomes more economical.

A novel variation of the box and I section plywood beam is a proprietary system in which a single web snakes sinusoidally from side to side of the flange. It is machine produced, the web being glued in pre-cut grooves in the flanges increasing both its stiffness and the shear resistance between web and flange (Figure 6.17).

Lattice girders

Highly competitive with glued plywood beams in the range of spans about 7.5 m is a proprietary system of nailed lattice girder, the typical web member consisting of a strip of thin galvanized steel sandwiched in between twin timber members and projecting between twin timber flanges, the whole being nailed together through both wood and steel, the effect of this being to bulge out the steel plate locally around the nail, effectively increasing its diameter at the interface (Figure 6.18).

A later development from the integral nail plate (Figure 6.11) is the combined plate and pre-formed web member. With this component metal-web beams are formed by pressing the ends of the web members into the sides of timber flanges (Figure 6.19).

One of the few legacies of the nineteenth century was the Belfast truss (Figure 6.20). This was a remarkably economical truss for spans up to about 36 m. It was remarkable in its ingenious use of short lengths and small sections to produce large assemblies, but compared with its modern counterpart it is lacking in lateral stability and does not lend itself to the passage of pipes and ducts, while its criss-cross pattern of small members presents a greater fire hazard.

The modern timber framed girder has employed all the framing patterns common to structural steelwork which were in turn inherited from (and are still known

Figure 6.14 *Glulam beams can be manufactured in complex shapes and curves. These beams are of double curvature to form the helmet shaped roofs of the Thames Flood Barrier.* Photograph: Tysons (Contractors) Ltd.

Figure 6.15 *Plywood box beams in a swimming pool at Yate, Bristol.*

Figure 6.16 *Plywood I beams, used here in association with glulam beams to provide a large clear span structure.*

Figure 6.17 *Sinusoidal plyweb beam.* Photograph: Rainham Timber Engineering Co. Ltd.

Figure 6.18 *Proprietary lattice girder.* Photograph: Rainham Timber Engineering Co. Ltd.

by the names of) the pioneers of the American railroads, who supposedly invented them – Fink, Howe, Pratt and Warren. Of these the Fink (Figure 6.21), the Pratt (Figure 6.22) and the Warren (Figure 6.23) are the most common. The Fink is now almost exclusively employed for domestic pitched roofing while the Pratt and Warren are associated with flat or near-flat industrial roofs. For large spans or heavy loads the Pratt should be more economical than the Warren, owing to the shorter length of its compression members, but both have been used successfully for spans of 36 m and more with span/depth ratios of from eight to ten. The most efficient type of girder for spans over 36 m is probably the bowstring girder (Figure 6.29). This is in essence a tied arch and will be discussed later.

Arches

In spite of the great corbelled vaults of Mycenae, built more than 3000 years ago and still extant, classical Greece never discovered the arch or, alternatively, preferred not to know about it. It was left to the Romans to develop this form of structure and their success in embodying it in bridges, aqueducts and buildings was probably the reason why engineers became – all too briefly as it transpired – such privileged members of Roman society.

Under a uniformly distributed vertical load the parabolic arch is in direct compression and is a very efficient structure, provided its foundations are adequate to resist horizontal thrust. In timber, arches have been built from nearly all the methods of construction described for beams and girders. The simplest (and probably the most satisfying aesthetically) is the glued laminated arch which has been used for spans of more than 90 m (Figures 6.24, 6.25 and Plates 6 and 7). The best known examples in the United Kingdom were probably those constructed for the Waterloo entrance to the Festival of Britain site (Figure 6.26). These were 30 m span and 18 m high. They were a landmark for some years but were removed in 1957 to make room for new building development.

Figure 6.19 *Proprietary metal web girder.* Photograph: Hydro-Air International (UK) Ltd.

Figure 6.21 *Fink truss: these are largely used for house roof construction.*

The bowstring girder

As has already been mentioned, the parabolic arch is a most efficient structure under uniformly distributed vertical loading and with unyielding supports; it is not necessarily efficient, however, under point or lateral wind loading or with supports which are liable to creep. The bowstring girder (Figure 6.28) is a tied laminated arch with a framed and braced web designed to meet these contingencies and is probably the most efficient form of girder for very large spans. The framing is normally a combination of Pratt and Warren – the vertical compression members being introduced to reduce the distance between the node points of the arch. Economically it probably becomes viable at spans over 24 m and spans of up to 55 m are fairly common.

The rigid frame

Bent, portal or rigid frames (Figures 6.29, 6.30 and 6.31) may be classed as arches as the bending moments induced by loading are resisted by reverse moments due to the horizontal reactions at the foundations. They may be built in any of the ways described for beams and girders, care in detailing at the haunches being critical. Aesthetically, glued lamination probably offers the most satisfactory solution and has the structural advantage of smoothing away possible stress-concentrations at the haunches. Spans of this type of construction normally range between 12 and 30 m. Unlike the parabolic arch, there is a marked concentration of bending moment at the haunches and in large spans, particularly in nailed construction, special care must be given to the effect of creep.

Folded plates

Folded plates are generally variations on the theme of the strip of paper folded in a V-section as referred to earlier. If plate girders be laid with what are normally their vertical axes inclined at an angle to the horizontal, their top and bottom edges will form the ridges and furrows of a concertina-like structure, but if provided with suitable transverse diaphragms, will be prevented from acting like one.

As industrial roofs they are commoner on the Continent than in Britain, generally of boarded and nailed construction. Special precautions must be taken with

Figure 6.20 *Belfast trusses at the Royal Air Force Museum, Hendon, before renovation.* Photograph: Royal Air Force Museum.

A notable achievement of the 1920s was the Lamella roof (Figure 6.27). This consists of intersecting systems of closely spaced diagonal arches bolted together forming diamond patterns of thin, deep members. It is built up of relatively short pieces and appeared to be economical, light and fairly easily erected, but suffered some neglect from independent designers – the not uncommon fate of proprietary systems.

Figure 6.22 *Pratt truss used for timber storage building in Scotland. Span almost 33.5 m.*

Figure 6.23 *Warren girder used in a shed for the Mersey Docks and Harbour Board. Span almost 27 m.*

Figure 6.24 *Glulam arches were used in the David Lloyd Tennis Centre near London airport. Each arch spans over 35 m.*

Figure 6.25 *Cranked glulam arches were used for ICI at Cleveland.* Photograph: Rainham Timber Engineering Co. Ltd.

Figure 6.26 *Glulam arches at the Waterloo entrance of the Festival of Britain.* Photograph: The Design Council.

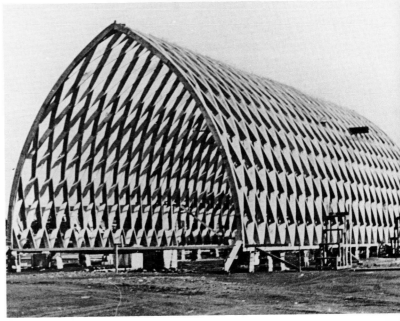

Figure 6.27 *Lamella roof.* Photograph: Architectural Press.

Figure 6.28 *Bowstring truss of almost 55 m span at Garston Docks, Liverpool.* Photograph: Rainham Timber Engineering Co. Ltd.

Figure 6.29 *Portal frames are used for a wide range of buildings. This basic laminated portal frame is at a church in Selsey.*

Figure 6.30 *The basic portal frame with nailed plywood gussets can be adapted to more complex building designs as in this school in Hampshire.*

large structures of this kind as drifting snow may cause overloading. In Britain they are more frequently plywood structures employed for architectural effect and in configurations designed to minimize the effect of snow (Figure 6.32).

Membrane shells

With shell roofs timber made its first tentative steps into the space age of the twentieth century – three-dimensional space structures as distinct from the plane or two-dimensional structures so far discussed. The pattern of evolution of the timber shell after the first 30 years or so is perhaps now becoming discernible and the following discussion is intended to highlight what are thought to be the salient points of progress.

Shells were initially seen as thin membranes relying on their curvature for their stiffness, the ratio of shell thickness to radius of curvature being critical. Under uniformly distributed loading the shell is a very economical structure and theory might suggest a very thin membrane indeed, even with a large radius of curvature. Apart from being too flexible, a shell in such circumstances might be in neutral equilibrium when a slight eccentricity of loading could cause it to snap into reverse curvature like the bottom of a tin can, or the alternative shapes of the classical textbook illustrations of the Euler column.

The small radius of curvature of the fuselage of the Mosquito aircraft made plywood construction feasible and satisfactory but as the technique was applied to larger and larger roof structures it became clear that considerable care was needed to avoid local instability. Maintaining a small radius of curvature could result in heights of structures more spectacular than useful, and remedies were found in increasing the thickness of membranes and introducing double curvature as in the turtle-back and the hyperbolic paraboloid.

A landmark in the development of large timber shells was the completion in 1956 of the roof for the assembly hall of the College of Engineering in Rangoon (Figure 6.33). This was an elongated turtle-back 46.6 m long and 28.3 m wide, made up of five layers of teak, each at an angle of 45° to the next, glued together forming a shell 85 mm thick.

Perhaps the most exciting use of double curvature is the hyperbolic paraboloid. In spite of its saddle-back shape it is generated by straight lines running from side to side of a rectangular area to boundary members inclined at an angle to one another. Its efficiency is due to it being a direct stress structure, diagonal lines running

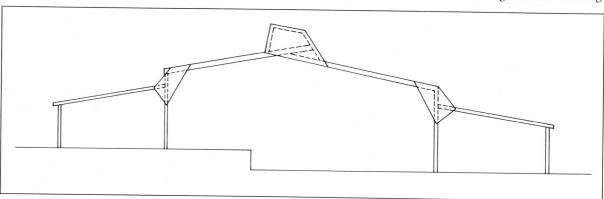

98

Figure 6.31 *Proprietary nailed portal frame system, Gatwick airport.*

Figure 6.32 *Folded plate plywood roof for the lecture theatre at the BRE Princes Risborough Laboratory.* Photograph: Crown Copyright.

Figure 6.33 *Turtle back roof for the assembly hall at the College of Engineering, Rangoon.* Photograph: Raglan Squire and Partners.

from high point to high point being in tension like the cables of a suspension bridge, those running from low point to low point forming an arch, in compression (Figure 6.34).

The first tangible result of research into this form of structure was the construction of a roof for the Wilton Royal Carpet Company in 1957 (Figure 6.35). This roof is 35 m square on plan and consists of four panels of hyperbolic paraboloid shells each 17.5 m square. It is supported at four points, on concrete columns at the mid-points of each side. The shells are 45 mm thick and consist of three layers of 15 mm softwood boarding nailed together, a 1.8 m strip around the edges of each panel being glued in addition to nailing, the outward thrust being restrained by mild steel tie rods running diagonally across each panel. A significant factor is that the cost of the building at the time was only about half that of traditional construction.

Stiffened shells

The next stage of development emerged from two of the disadvantages of the thin membrane: firstly, it required a fairly substantial falsework structure to support the layers of timber boarding before they could be glued and nailed or screwed; secondly, site gluing is very much at the mercy of the weather, yet it is a critical and time-consuming operation in the building process. Clearly, if some part of the falsework could be incorporated in the permanent structure then a thinner membrane could be treated as a stressed-skin and applied as and when convenient without holding up the ordered progress of other construction.

This involved the consideration of a membrane stiffened with ribs and stringers, forming a supplementary framework which could be erected independently by crane and mobile scaffolding. In the construction of

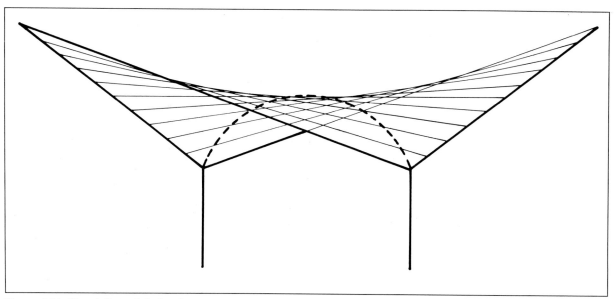

Figure 6.34 *Hyperbolic paraboloid roof.*

Figure 6.35 *Hyperbolic paraboloid roof at the Wilton Royal Carpet factory.*

domes, the first attempt to solve this problem was logically made by using laminated arches as ribs radiating from the centre of the dome and connected laterally by stringers. Aesthetically this is very satisfying as may be seen from Figure 6.36, but there are limits to the size of a laminated member which can conveniently be transported and it may be shown that the final structure is not the best fitted to resist the unbalanced lateral forces of wind and snow.

The mathematical treatment of shell structures leads naturally to the kind of paper engineers love to write but will never read if they can possibly help it. Fortunately, we may be a little more discursive and, with any luck, more comprehensible. If a lattice girder be regarded as a solid beam with triangular holes in it, then it may be thought of as a structure in which the lines of internal force have been dragooned into predetermined lanes of web members and flanges instead of being allowed to wander all over the place. We may do the

same thing with, say, a hemispherical dome. We may make it as thick as we like and then assume there are holes on it. If we decide to dragoon the lines of force along lines of longitude and latitude we have the truly geodesic (or geodetic) structure of Figure 6.36. Unfortunately the holes we are left with are four-sided trapezoids – a bad shape structurally as they can be distorted or racked without meeting any resistance from their boundary members. A better shape of hole would of course be the triangle as it cannot be distorted without straining at least two of its three boundary members.

This is not to say the geodesic approach is wrong. London and Liverpool are both located in space by their longitude and latitude but, in moving from one place to the other, it is not necessary to go via either Grimsby or Cardiff, which is what we do with the forces in Figure 6.36. Longitude and latitude may be regarded as the co-ordinate axes by which we may accurately locate the node points in a triangulated space structure, the

Figure 6.36 *Laminated timber dome at the Lightfoot Sports Centre, Newcastle upon Tyne.*

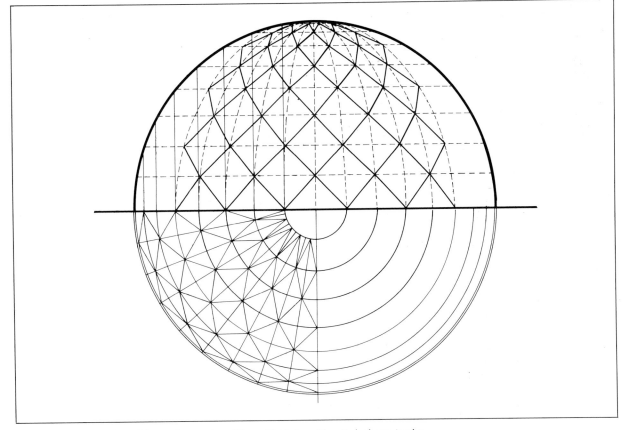

Figure 6.37 *Hemispherical domes. Intersection of lines of latitude and longitude shown in plan.*

Figure 6.38 *Transport of prefabricated shell roof components.*

Figure 6.39 *Shell roofs can also be made on site from individual pieces.*

surface of which may be curved or in flat plates between the frames. Figure 6.37 illustrates this approach, defining a diamond pattern which may then be triangulated with vertical or horizontal members, or both, running across each diamond.

This form of structure has been termed 'reticulated' which means 'network' but of course it is more than a network, it is a triangulated network. Such a structure may be transported and erected in small prefabricated panels (Figure 6.38) or in separate pieces (Figures 6.39, 6.40), the method to be adopted in a particular case being decided at the design stage. The example given was of course for a hemispherical dome but applies to any other shape; in the case of a structure rectangular on plan the lines of longitude would be parallel to one another as in Figure 6.41.

The Ensphere

The largest reticulated dome in existence is believed to be the 'Ensphere' – the sports arena built for the Northern Arizona University as referred to earlier (Figure 6.42). It covers about 1.8 hectares, the total design load is about 2000 tonnes and its main lattice members are of laminated Southern Yellow Pine about 125 mm by 685 mm in section.

A careful cost analysis was made by the architects, Messrs Rossman and Partners of Phoenix, Arizona. Taking the cost of the present timber structure as 1, the comparative costs of other systems analysed were: non-rigid fabric 1.2, two concrete systems 1.5 and 1.6, a suspension system 2, steel 2.2, aluminium 3.

A point which emerges from Dr Rossman's paper on the 'Ensphere' may be of particular significance to a future energy-conscious world:

> Energy consumption to heat the arena is far less than anticipated. This is due to ground heat-emission created by the highly insulative cover over a rather large disc.

In his paper Dr Rossman refers to a projected dome 260 m in diameter. This would cover an area of about 5.25 hectares. There is no obvious limit to the size of structure which might be built in this way. The mathematics are easily handled by computer. Fortunately for some of us there is no need to know how the computer works. What is important is to understand how the structure works, what holds it together and prevents it falling apart.

We need a better understanding of fracture mechanics and we should un-Hooke ourselves from concepts of stress and strain which have outlived their undoubted usefulness in the past. This is perhaps all we need to enable us to take the next leap forward and establish timber firmly in the space age of the twentieth century, with unlimited possibilities for the timber structures of the future.

Choice of Structure

Changing patterns of structural form have evolved partly from improvements in the techniques of jointing, assembly, transport and erection, partly from the introduction of new materials, and partly from changing ideas about the aesthetic and functional requirements of modern buildings. In the result timber offers a very wide range of different structural forms, any one of which may be suited to a particular situation. Probably the easiest way of arranging the different options in some sort of systematic order is by reference to the spans for which experience has shown the different forms to be suitable. Figure 6.43 is a formalized presentation of different spans which have been successfully employed by different systems, the upper and lower limits of which are indicated, on a logarithmic scale, by the horizontal intercepts between the diagonal dotted lines. It will be seen that apart from the extremes of very short and very long spans there are relatively few mutually-exclusive categories; over a wide range of spans one form of construction may be as acceptable as two or three others. The choice of a particular system will generally be de-

Figure 6.40 *Shell roof at a school in Woodbridge, Suffolk.*

Figure 6.41 *Shell roof under construction at a school in Bury St Edmunds.*

103

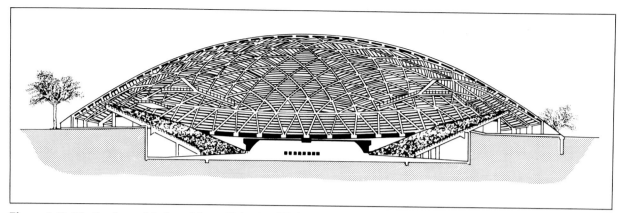

Figure 6.42 *The Ensphere at Northern Arizona University, USA.*

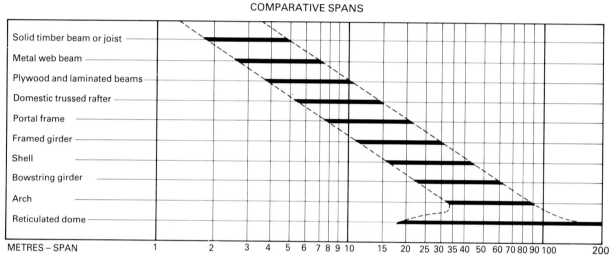

Figure 6.43 *Comparative spans of various types of timber structures.*

termined by the criteria of cost and fitness-for-purpose, the former being evaluated in consultation with the manufacturer, the latter by a number of considerations which may be unique to a particular situation, e.g. intensity of loading, permissible deflection, available headroom, provision or otherwise of false ceilings, continuity at supports, fire resistance, space for cables or ducts and last, but not least, the architectural concept.

7 Timber frame construction

Peter Grimsdale

Peter Grimsdale AIWSc is a director of the Swedish Finnish Timber Council and is chairman of the BSI committee currently preparing a Code of Practice for the design of timber frame walls. He moved to SFTC from TRADA where he was head of advisory services and was also involved in setting up the timber frame house appraisals service. He was previously with a national timber engineering manufacturer.

Timber has been used for building houses for centuries and there are many historic timber houses still in use today. Towards the end of the seventeenth century, British craft skills were taken to the New World, where traditional timber houses continued to be built until well into the nineteenth century.

In North America, at this time, the population was expanding and there was an urgent need to rationalize the way houses were built if demand was to be satisfied. This demand coincided with several other developments. Sawmills had now become mechanized and could saw to accurate and small sizes with ease. Wire nails were being produced which meant that small section timber could be jointed without the need for intricate, hand-crafted joints, and so the skeletal framework was born not just in North America but in the other major softwood producing countries of the world.

Since then the method of timber frame construction has evolved to a point where there are more timber framed dwellings built in the world each year than houses of any other form of construction.

Although it is not difficult to find examples of the modern type of timber framed house in the UK dating back 100 years or so, the main stimulus for timber frame came in the early 1960s and since then growth has been steady. The method of timber framing which has developed in the UK is based mainly on partial or complete factory prefabrication. Hardly any houses built in the UK at present are built on site from loose timber – 'stick built' as it is called. Normally, prefabrication entails the factory manufacture of stud wall panels of, say, anything up to five metres in length with the exterior sheathing (plywood, fibreboard, etc) pre-fixed. In most cases the linings, claddings, insulation etc are fixed on site.

Two principal methods have developed in this country for framing a timber house. 'Platform framing' is the method whereby wall panels are constructed in storey heights and the intermediate floor is constructed on top of these panels to form a permanent platform and a staging for the erection of subsequent storey wall panels (Figure 7.1). The other method of construction which has been tried over the years is so-called 'balloon framing'. With this method the external wall panels are produced two storeys in height so that two storeys are erected in one operation and the intermediate floor suspended between them (Figure 7.2).

Some companies have experimented with completely prefabricated volumetric units which are delivered to site in complete sections and off loaded and lifted into position by crane. The design limitations and the special purpose equipment needed to produce such units have meant that they have been used only on very specialized projects. Over the years balloon framing has become less popular than platform frame and almost all dwellings currently built in the UK use the platform frame technique in one form or another. It is for this reason that the remainder of this chapter will concentrate on this method of construction.

TIMBER FRAME DESIGN REQUIREMENTS

There are many regulations which control the way that houses are built but some have special significance to the timber frame designer and these are summarized below. Under UK Building Regulations timber frame can be used readily in houses and flats up to three storeys in height. The principal control documents are of course the national Building Regulations but these are supplemented, for houses built under the National House Building Council warranty scheme, by their requirements, the main points of which are also summarized on page 114.

MANUFACTURE AND ERECTION

Timber is an ideal material for the fabrication of building components whether on site or in the factory. Timber is light in weight and it is easy to handle the finished components in the factory and on site. Transport of completed components is simplified and once on site there is no other material which is easier to cut and joint. Timber frame wall panels can be made in a factory to almost any size, the method of erection determining how large the panels are to be. Unless cranes are available on site it is unlikely that a builder would order

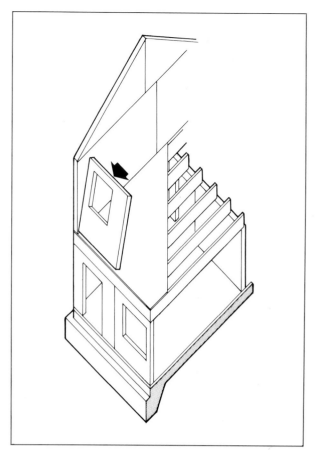

Figure 7.1 *Platform frame construction.*

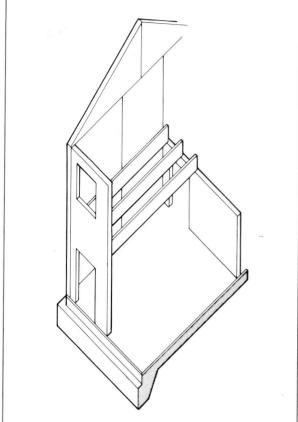

Figure 7.2 *Balloon frame construction.*

panels much in excess of 3.6 metres wide and they could be as small as 0.6 m wide.

In this country so far, the level of prefabrication has been limited to stud wall panels sheathed with plywood or other sheet materials, and sometimes the breather membrane is pre-fixed. As timber framing develops there may be a demand for greater levels of prefabrication with a possibility of insulation, vapour checks and internal linings being pre-fixed in the factory.

The manufacture of timber framed wall panels is really a rather simple operation. Repetition demands that some form of assembly jig is used although this can be as rudimentary or as sophisticated as production expectations require. A very simple jig is shown in Figure 7.3. Even with the most sophisticated of assembly processes the most common form of connection is nailing. Nowadays nails are most commonly inserted with pneumatic nailing equipment. Nails will be used at butt joints in framing members and in all probability they will be used to fix the sheathing in position. Panels are normally made with a minus tolerance. With panels of up to 2.4 m high and up to 3.6 m wide it is normal to manu-

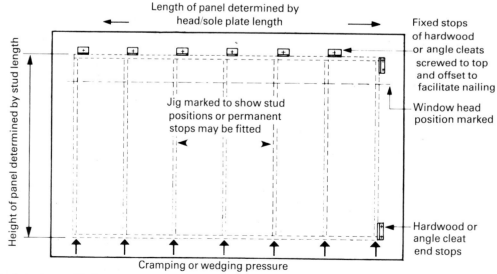

Figure 7.3 *A simple assembly jig.*

106

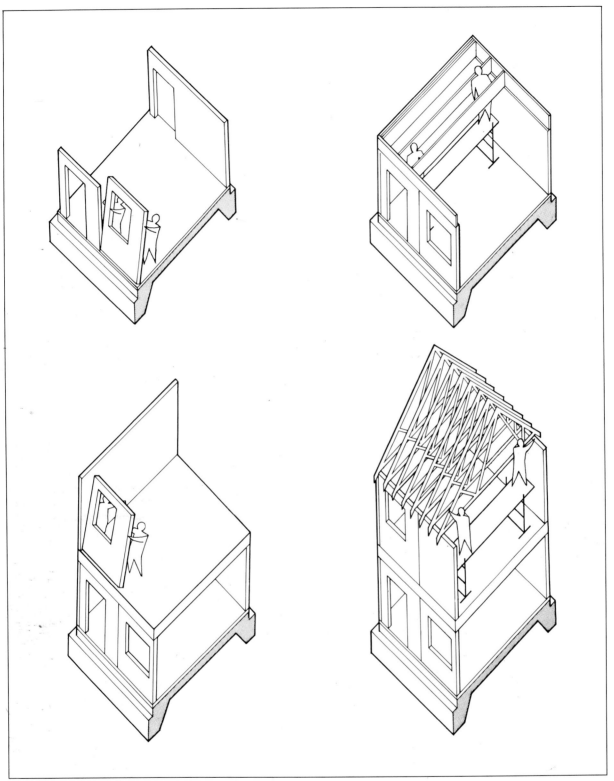

Figure 7.4 *Sequence of erection.*

facture with a tolerance of $+0\text{--}3\,\text{mm}$ in both directions. This minus variation is essential if a build-up of tolerances is to be avoided on site.

Timber framed houses can be erected using small man-handleable panels or large panels lifted into position using mechanical plant. It is important that the method of erection is decided at the design stage. The indications are that crane erection can be justified only on sites where the continuity of work can ensure that the crane does not stand idle for long periods of time.

Whichever method is chosen the erection will follow roughly the sequence shown in Figure 7.4. Only the size of individual panels will change and some builders who crane-erect also pre-assemble the floor and roof construction.

FOUNDATIONS AND GROUND FLOORS

Timber framed walls can be considerably lighter than their traditional counterparts, and although this means

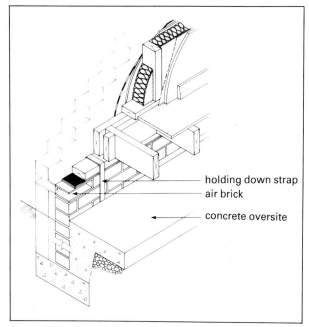

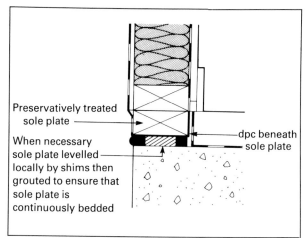

Figure 7.6 _Levelling the sole plate._

Figure 7.5 _Suspended timber floor with timber framed wall construction. When there is an external cladding of brick or blockwork, the cavity formed between this and the timber frame should be vented to the external wall by open perpends. Air bricks to ventilate the underfloor space should bridge through to the outside air._

that timber frame has often been used to solve building problems on sites with low soil bearing pressure, for the most part little advantage has been taken of this reduction in weight and timber framed houses have been built on what are essentially traditional foundations.

Although solid concrete ground floors are as common in timber framed houses as they are in other houses there is something very logical about using a suspended timber ground floor beneath a timber framed house (Figure 7.5). It fits in well with the construction sequence, it lends itself to the incorporation of high levels of thermal insulation and is generally more compatible with the concept of a timber framed house.

Whichever method is chosen it is imperative that the timber sole plate is accurately positioned and levelled. The sole plate forms the basis for the erection of the rest of the timber framed shell and a little extra time taken to ensure that the substructure is as level as possible and that the sole plate is accurately positioned and shimmed for level will pay dividends at every other stage of erection (Figure 7.6).

EXTERNAL WALL CONSTRUCTION

Figure 7.7 shows the typical construction of a timber framed external wall. The external wall of any dwelling has certain vital functions:

a) To carry the weight of the building, its contents and other occasional loads.
b) To act as a barrier to the elements during the life of the building.
c) To provide resistance to fire so that the wall continues to perform its structural function during and after a fire.
d) A modern day consideration is that it should provide a degree of resistance to the loss of heat.

The various elements of the timber frame external wall are incorporated to ensure that it can perform these functions.

The framework

The timber framed wall is designed to carry all the vertical loads imposed by the building and transmit them to the foundation. Sheathing on the outside of the framework not only provides lateral rigidity to the building but it also ensures a stable background for the fixing of the breather membrane and flashings within the external wall cavity.

Studs and sheathing materials

The sizes of the studs and other members in the timber framework may vary slightly between individual suppliers. Those using material of North American origin will almost certainly supply timber surfaced to the CLS/ALS 89 mm × 38 mm finished size. Timber of European origin may be typically 100 × 50 mm or 75 × 50 mm basic size, and planing will reduce these sizes to 97 × 47 mm and 72 × 47 mm. Increasingly, Nordic suppliers are producing the surfaced 89 × 38 mm size for the UK industry and this now forms a significant proportion of the framing material used in timber frame wall panel construction.

Since the timber frame is an 'engineered' structure the structural timbers must of course be stress graded and since 1983 it has been a requirement of the NHBC that the external wall timber framing be preservatively treated.

The most commonly used sheathing in Britain is sheathing grade plywood, usually of 8–10 mm thickness, alternatively bitumen impregnated fibreboard or medium board may be used provided these comply with the necessary standards.

Vapour check membrane

A vapour resistant sheet, usually polyethylene film, is fixed on the inside face of the studs and on the 'warm' side of the insulation. The purpose of the vapour check is to minimize the quantity of water vapour, generated within the house, that can permeate into the external

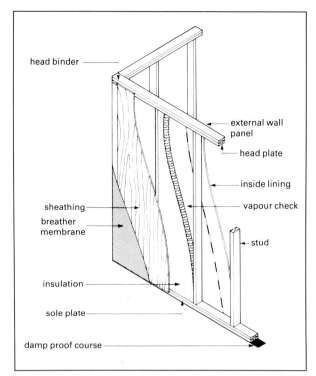

Figure 7.7 *Timber frame external wall. Cladding not shown for clarity.*

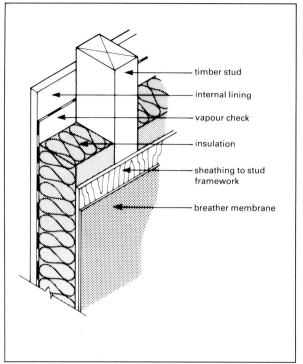

Figure 7.8 *Vapour control in external wall.*

wall (Figure 7.8). Vapour checks when installed should be as imperforate as possible, any unavoidable tears should be repaired with a suitable adhesive tape. Minimal perforations in the vapour check to permit installation of services will not substantially affect the performance of the vapour check but these should be kept to a minimum.

Breather membrane

The external sheathing material is normally covered with a protective breather membrane. This protects the structure during erection and backs up the cladding when complete. Since internal vapour checks are seldom perfect and because the structure can get wet during construction, it is imperative that the membrane is permeable enough to prevent moisture being trapped in the external wall construction. Hence the name 'breather' membrane.

Thermal insulation

Insulation is fixed between the studs and outside the line of the vapour check. Insulation quilts are available in varying thicknesses but the mineral fibre quilts in common use today for the insulation of timber frame external walls are usually 80 mm in thickness.

UK Building Regulations require that the thermal transmittance coefficient (U value) for external walls should not exceed 0.6 W/m² °C. Characteristically, a timber framed wall as shown in Figure 7.8 with 80 mm of insulation would give a U value of about 0.35 W/m² °C.

Internal linings

The majority of timber framed houses built in the UK

are lined internally with plasterboard. Modern dry-lining techniques ensure smooth joints between sheets of plasterboard which are practically undetectable. Other linings may be used but wood based sheet materials must be treated with a flame retardant to meet the Class 1 surface spread of flame category required by Building Regulations.

Fire resistance

The fire resistance requirements for external walls of houses, flats and maisonettes up to three storeys in height are as follows:

Houses up to three storeys and flats or maisonettes of two storeys	$\frac{1}{2}$ hour
Three storey flats or maisonettes	1 hour

The half-hour requirement is normally satisfied by an internal lining of 12.7 mm plasterboard with the joints taped and filled. One hour fire resistance is achieved by two layers of 12.7 mm plasterboard fixed with joints staggered and the face joints taped and filled.

There are other rules in the Building Regulations concerning proximity of boundaries and internal surface characteristics but these are common to other forms of construction.

INTERNAL WALLS

Timber stud wall construction, which forms the basis of the timber framed external wall, has also tended to predominate in the construction of internal partitions.

There are basically two types of internal walls. First, non-load-bearing walls which are required entirely for space separation purposes and as such are not required to carry load or provide fire resistance. Second, load-

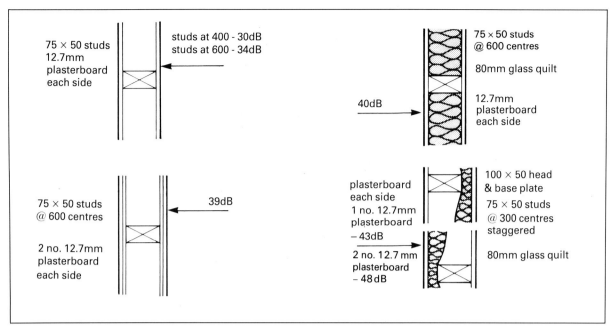

Figure 7.9 *Sound reduction performance of some stud partitions.*

bearing internal walls (usually restricted to the ground floor storey) which may be required to support upper floors and as a result must be structural and provide the same fire resistance as the floor they support.

Generally speaking stud partitions incorporating studs of the same sizes or slightly smaller than the external wall studs are capable of carrying the loads which are likely to be encountered in up to three-storey dwellings. Half-hour or one hour fire resistance is imparted to the partition by the lining materials in a similar manner to the external walls.

It is unusual for sound insulation to be required for internal partitions (except the 35 dB NHBC requirement around wc's) but Figure 7.9 shows the normal performance of a plasterboard lined partition and how this may be upgraded.

INTERMEDIATE FLOORS

The structural requirements for floors in timber frame dwellings are identical to those for other dwelling types. The same design consideration should be given to the incidence of partitions which are supported by the floor and allowance made within the floor for nailing timber stud partitions.

One of the major factors which influences the use of timber framed construction is the simplicity of erection without the necessity for any special-purpose handling equipment. The introduction of a heavy steel beam trimmer into a floor zone to support joists will not only make fixing difficult, it will slow down erection and demand some form of heavy lifting gear. If at all possible it is advisable, and usually cheaper in the long run, to use multiple joists as trimmers or even to consider a glulam or box beam.

In normal platform frame construction the floor decking is laid over the extent of the floor in advance of upper floor panels being fixed as shown in Figure 7.10. However, if the floor decking is one that is vul-

nerable to damage during erection then it may be preferable to insert a packing strip under the wall panels so that erection can proceed without the floor deck having to be laid (Figure 7.11).

Compartment floors are required between flats and maisonettes which must provide the necessary half-hour or one hour fire resistance and also adequate sound insulation. There are a number of ways of satisfying the requirements for timber compartment floors and specialist advice should be sought.

TIMBER SEPARATING WALLS

The Building Regulations permit separating walls between houses and flats of up to three storeys in height to be constructed of timber frame construction. The specific requirements of the wall are that it should provide a fire resistance from either side of not less than one hour and that it should provide adequate resistance to the passage of sound from one dwelling to the other.

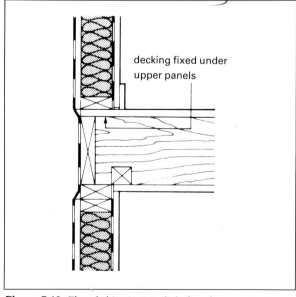

Figure 7.10 *Floor decking in typical platform frame construction.*

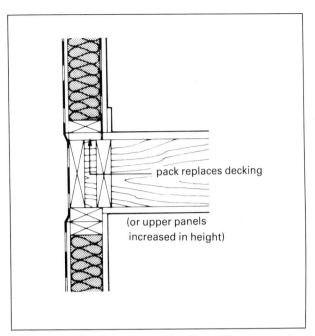

pack replaces decking

(or upper panels
increased in height)

Figure 7.11 *Floor decking in modified platform frame construction.*

The construction shown in Figure 7.12 has been shown by comprehensive testing to satisfy both of these requirements.

CAVITY BARRIERS AND FIRESTOPS

By definition cavity barriers and firestops have quite distinct functions in our Building Regulations even though, on occasions, they may appear to be fulfilling a similar role.

Cavity barriers

A cavity barrier is a device placed within the external cavity of timber frame and brick wall for example, or between connecting elements of structure with the specific purpose of limiting the open area of cavity through which flame and smoke may spread.

A summary of the mandatory requirements is given in Figure 7.13. A cavity barrier may be constructed of any material which is capable of providing fire resistance of at least half an hour, but usually comprises 38 mm wide timber battens (Figures 7.14 and 7.15) or 'sausages' of polyethylene covered mineral wool.

Firestops

Firestops are required to seal imperfections of fit between fire resisting building elements or where openings are made through such elements for services etc. The Regulations also require that where an external wall or roof cavity passes over the end of a separating wall then the junction must be firestopped (Figure 7.16).

Firestops must be constructed of non-combustible materials.

INSTALLATION OF SERVICES

One of the many advantages of timber framed construc-

tion is the simplicity of installing services. The space formed between the framing members in the wall panels, floors and roofs provides a safe and economical location to conceal the greater part of the heating, plumbing and electrical distribution systems.

Like any other form of construction there are rules which must be observed in installing appliances such as central heating boilers, etc and these requirements are much too specific to be incorporated within this chapter. There are a number of excellent handbooks available to help with this aspect of design.

The beauty of timber framed construction is that installation of the services can take place inside the weathered shell of the building whilst the framework is still exposed. With a little thought at the design stage the majority of pipes, wires, etc can be arranged to run parallel to framing members thus avoiding unnecessary cutting and drilling of structural members. Any cutting that is necessary should be approved by the building designer but in the absence of any more specific recommendations the suggestions given in Figures 8.17 and 8.18 may be assumed to be satisfactory.

EXTERNAL CLADDINGS

It is incumbent upon the timber frame designer to ensure that the timber framed shell of a dwelling is capable of carrying out all the necessary structural functions of the completed building. This means that any cladding which is added to the outer face of the timber frame has only to provide long-term weather resistance and, of course, has to be aesthetically pleasing. What this means is that with a little care almost any established durable cladding may be added to the timber framed construction.

There are two basic rules which should be followed when applying claddings to any type of building:

1 The cladding must in itself be capable of lasting the lifetime of the building. If not it must be capable of being maintained or if necessary replaced without affecting the structure of the building.
2 Whichever cladding is chosen it is essential that it is ventilated on both sides, i.e. it should have an adequate air space behind it.

The most common cladding in use with timber framed dwellings in the UK is brickwork. The brickwork, normally a 100 mm thick veneer, is constructed in the normal way but after the timber frame shell is complete. The brick veneer is attached to the timber frame via a 50 mm cavity with wall ties, specially designed to allow differential movement between the brick and timber walls. Figure 7.17 shows the general arrangement of a brick veneered timber frame wall. Timber weatherboarding, used extensively throughout Scandinavia and North America, is less commonly used in the UK where timber is more often used in combination with brickwork (Figures 7.18 and 7.19).

Other forms of cladding are available; two which are commonly used are hung tiling on horizontal battens (Figure 7.20) and cement render either on a brick or block substrate or on a galvanized or stainless steel mesh fixed on battens (Figure 7.21).

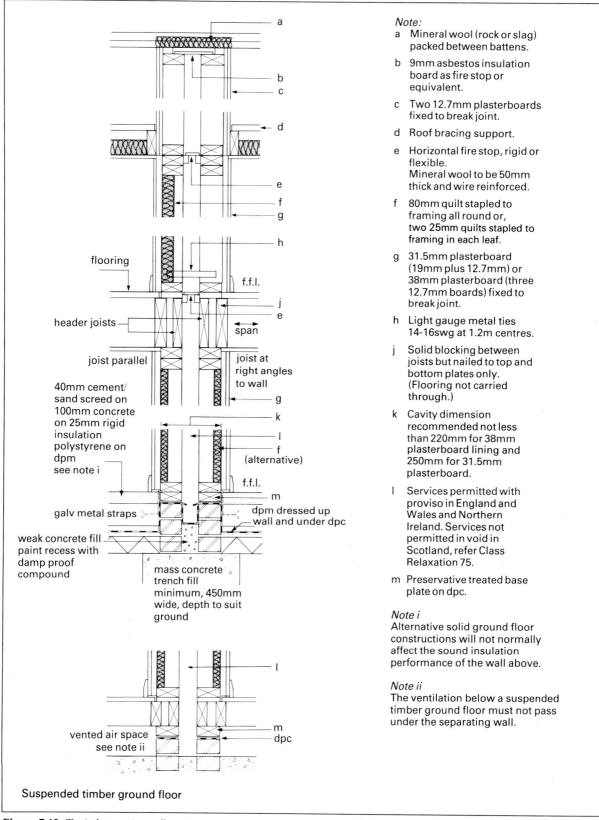

flooring

f.f.l.

header joists

span

joist parallel

joist at right angles to wall

40mm cement/ sand screed on 100mm concrete on 25mm rigid insulation polystyrene on dpm see note i

f.f.l.

galv metal straps

dpm dressed up wall and under dpc

weak concrete fill paint recess with damp proof compound

mass concrete trench fill minimum, 450mm wide, depth to suit ground

vented air space see note ii

m
dpc

Suspended timber ground floor

Note:

a Mineral wool (rock or slag) packed between battens.

b 9mm asbestos insulation board as fire stop or equivalent.

c Two 12.7mm plasterboards fixed to break joint.

d Roof bracing support.

e Horizontal fire stop, rigid or flexible. Mineral wool to be 50mm thick and wire reinforced.

f 80mm quilt stapled to framing all round or, two 25mm quilts stapled to framing in each leaf.

g 31.5mm plasterboard (19mm plus 12.7mm) or 38mm plasterboard (three 12.7mm boards) fixed to break joint.

h Light gauge metal ties 14-16swg at 1.2m centres.

j Solid blocking between joists but nailed to top and bottom plates only. (Flooring not carried through.)

k Cavity dimension recommended not less than 220mm for 38mm plasterboard lining and 250mm for 31.5mm plasterboard.

l Services permitted with proviso in England and Wales and Northern Ireland. Services not permitted in void in Scotland, refer Class Relaxation 75.

m Preservative treated base plate on dpc.

Note i
Alternative solid ground floor constructions will not normally affect the sound insulation performance of the wall above.

Note ii
The ventilation below a suspended timber ground floor must not pass under the separating wall.

Figure 7.12 *Typical separating wall construction.*

Timber frame construction should be considered as a method of building rather than a system. The designer is able to develop his own details, or in consultation with the proprietary timber frame fabricators develop his own design using their structural designs. It enables the architect to have considerable freedom since there are few limitations on the method other than those related to a sensible site sequence.

Since the change in the Building Regulations thermal insulation requirements in 1982, timber frame offers one of the simplest and proven methods of compliance and makes the task of developing energy efficient construction both economic and straightforward.

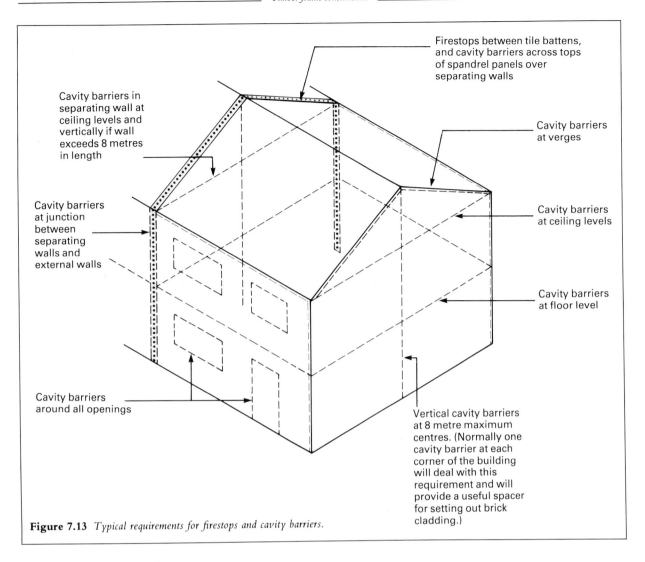

Firestops between tile battens, and cavity barriers across tops of spandrel panels over separating walls

Cavity barriers in separating wall at ceiling levels and vertically if wall exceeds 8 metres in length

Cavity barriers at verges

Cavity barriers at junction between separating walls and external walls

Cavity barriers at ceiling levels

Cavity barriers at floor level

Cavity barriers around all openings

Vertical cavity barriers at 8 metre maximum centres. (Normally one cavity barrier at each corner of the building will deal with this requirement and will provide a useful spacer for setting out brick cladding.)

Figure 7.13 *Typical requirements for firestops and cavity barriers.*

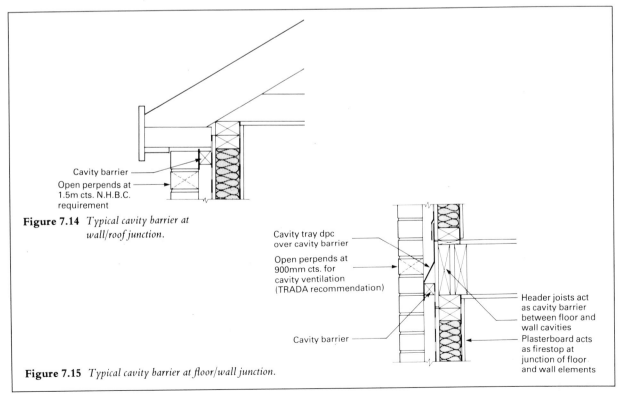

Cavity barrier

Open perpends at 1.5m cts. N.H.B.C. requirement

Figure 7.14 *Typical cavity barrier at wall/roof junction.*

Cavity tray dpc over cavity barrier

Open perpends at 900mm cts. for cavity ventilation (TRADA recommendation)

Cavity barrier

Header joists act as cavity barrier between floor and wall cavities

Plasterboard acts as firestop at junction of floor and wall elements

Figure 7.15 *Typical cavity barrier at floor/wall junction.*

Function	Building Regulations*	NHBC	Function	Building Regulations*	NHBC
Fire resistance	Periods of minimum fire resistance are given in the Regulations. a) External walls and load-bearing partitions in houses up to three storeys and flats up to two storeys are required to have at least half-hour fire resistance. b) Intermediate floors in two-storey houses must have at least a modified half-hour fire resistance. c) Houses of three storeys and flats of two storeys must have full half-hour fire resistance to intermediate floors. Except in Scotland where two-storey flats must have one hour fire-resisting compartment floors. d) Three-storey flats must have at least one hour fire-resisting external walls, load-bearing partitions and compartment floors. e) Separating walls between all dwellings up to three storeys in height must provide one hour fire resistance from either side.	As Building Regulations	Firestopping and cavity barriers	This is dealt with separately on page 111	
			Thermal insulation	Minimum requirements include: External walls – 0.6 W/m² °C Roof – 0.35 W/m² °C	
			Sound insulation	Regulations give general requirements for separating walls and compartment walls and compartment floors. Regulations do not apply to external walls, partitions or floors (unless compartment floors)	Partitions around wc's to have sound reduction of 35 dB
			Moisture	Regulations lay down fundamental requirements for protection against moisture for all house constructions	Practice Note 5 lays down quite specific requirements for vapour checks, breather membranes, preservation of timber, flashing and dpc details, etc.
			Structural design	Regulations lay down general requirement for structural stability and are satisfied by calculations in accordance with CP112: Part 2: 1971 or BS 5268: Part 2: 1984	Designs to be in accordance with CP112: Part 2 or BS 5268: Part 2 but in addition NHBC requires each and every house to be certified by a qualified designer

* See note on Building Regulations (page 12)

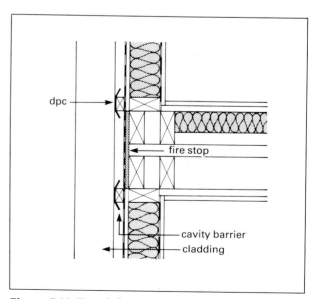

Figure 7.16 _Typical firestops and cavity barriers at separating walls._

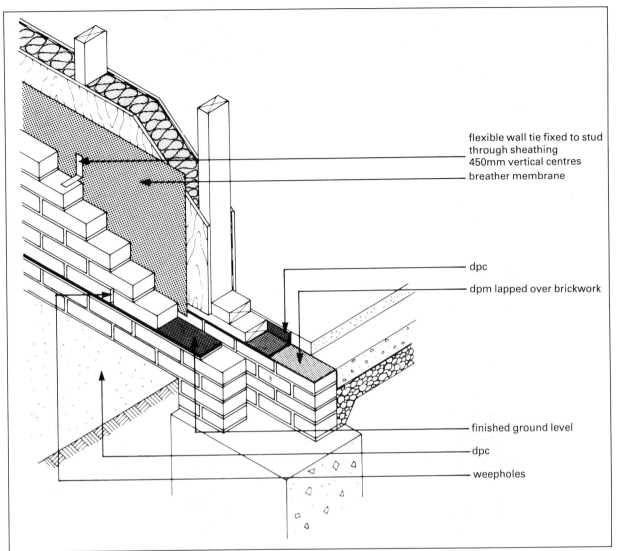

flexible wall tie fixed to stud
through sheathing
450mm vertical centres
breather membrane

dpc
dpm lapped over brickwork

finished ground level
dpc
weepholes

Figure 7.17 *Typical external wall with brick veneer.*

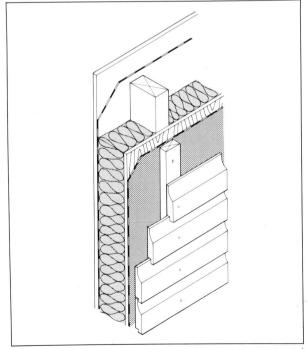

Figure 7.18 *Typical construction – rebated shiplap horizontal boarding.*

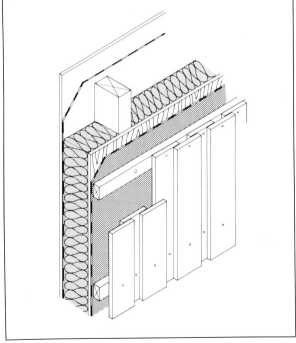

Figure 7.19 *Typical construction – board on board cladding.*

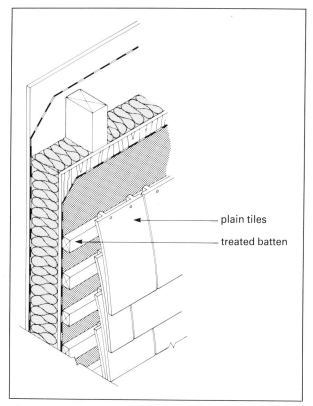

Figure 7.20 *Typical construction – tile hanging.*

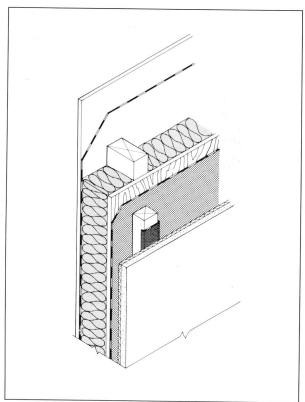

Figure 7.21 *Typical construction – cement render on steel mesh.*

In Figure 7.20:
- plain tiles
- treated batten

Figure 7.22 *Pages 116–18 show some examples of timber frame housing*

Photograph: Walker Timber Ltd.

Photograph: Housing Systems Design.

Photograph: James Riley and Associates Ltd.

Photograph: Swedish Finnish Timber Council.

Photograph: Purpose Built Ltd.

Photograph: Purpose Built Ltd.

Figure 7.22 (*continued*)

Photograph: Frame Form Ltd.

Photograph: Hill Leigh (Timber Frame) Ltd.

Photograph: Guildway Ltd.

Photograph: Nordic Building Components Ltd.

Photograph: Prestoplan Homes Ltd.

Photograph: Transline Group Ltd.

Figure 7.22 (*continued*)

8 Domestic carpentry

George E. Mitchell

George E. Mitchell FIOC LCG AIWSc MRSH is lecturer in wood trades at the South East London College and is regional examiner for the Institute of Carpenters. Following his apprenticeship he worked as a setter out and as a contracts manager before going into teaching.

Timber has long been the traditional material for domestic floors and roofs. Its advantages of high strength to weight ratio, ease of cutting and fixing on site, plus more modern developments in grading, jointing methods and sheet materials ensure that timber retains its place as the most economic method of fulfilling the structural requirements in these situations.

FIXINGS AND FASTENINGS

Nails

There are very many varieties of both shape and material. Round wire nails are by far the most commonly used fasteners for timber, others include clout nails which have large heads and are often specified under end use names such as slate nails, plasterboard nails etc. Lost head nails are used in situations where appearance is important. Wire nails are available with corrosion resistant coatings; usually these are zinc based including sherardizing and hot dip zinc galvanizing. Machine driven nails have heads shaped to assist packaging and magazine loading; coated nails are available but in less variety than round wire nails. Specially hard-

ened and tempered nails allow timber to be fixed directly to dense materials like brick and stone by shot firing or by hand.

Improved nails, with better withdrawal characteristics, include ring shanked, annular grooved and helically threaded; they may be round or square and are available as bright galvanized, sherardized or untreated. Improved nails are commonly used for attaching plywood gussets and for fixing sheet materials for floors where they resist 'nail popping' better than plain shank nails. Figure 8.1 shows a variety of nail types and Table 8.1 gives the sizes included in BS 1202 Part 1 'Steel nails'.

Staples

Staples (Figure 8.2) are used in some situations as an alternative to nails; they are usually pneumatically driven although hand 'tackers' for smaller sizes are available. Due to their limited shank length they are normally used for attaching sheet materials to solid sections, for example plywood gusseted joints, sheathing for timber frame panels. Staples are normally stainless or mild steel; mild steel staples are available with a rust-proofing treatment. There is currently no British Standard for staples; they are available in a range of sizes: the crown width varying from 5 to 11 mm and the lengths from 9 to 63 mm approximately.

Screws

Screws are available in mild steel, stainless steel, brass etc in an extremely wide range of sizes with various designs of head depending on their purpose (Figure 8.3). Tables 8.2 and 8.3 give sizes of mild steel and stainless steel screws included in BS 1210 'Wood screws'.

Coach screws are of similar form but have a square or hexagonal head and are tightened using an appropriate spanner. They are usually of mild steel and are available in diameters from approximately 6 to 13 mm and lengths of 25 up to 153 mm.

Bolts

Ordinary mild steel bolts with hexagonal heads and nuts

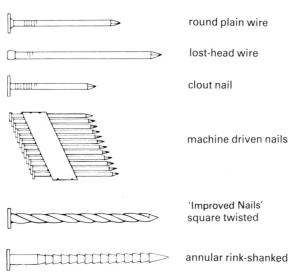

round plain wire

lost-head wire

clout nail

machine driven nails

'Improved Nails' square twisted

annular rink-shanked

Figure 8.1 *Types of nails.*

are now generally used. Coach bolts (Figure 8.4) require two different sized washers for each bolt, and for use with timber joints, washers larger than those normally supplied are required. Essentially the higher loading values for bolts, compared with nails or screws are due only to the increase in diameter. The use of bolts in timber construction is often associated with the use of timber connectors – these are described in Chapter 6. Bolts are available in low or medium carbon steel, the heavier ranges in black, bright, high tensile or high strength steel. Larger bolts for external use may be elec-

Table 8.1 *Nail sizes*

Length mm	Shank mm	Round, plain head	Annular, flat head	Round, lost head	Clout
200	8.0	★	★		
180	6.70	★	★		
150	6.0	★	★		
150	5.60	★			
125	5.60	★	★		
125	5.00	★			
115	5.00	★	★		
100	5.00	★	★		
100	4.50	★			★
100	4.00	★			
100	3.75	★			
90	4.50	★			★
90	4.00	★	★		
90	3.75	★	★		
90	3.35	★	★		
75	4.00	★	★		
75	3.75	★	★	★	★
75	3.35	★	★		
75	3.00	★			
65	3.75	★	★		★
65	3.35	★	★	★	
65	3.00	★	★	★	
65	2.65	★			
60	3.35	★	★	★	
60	3.00	★	★	★	
60	2.65	★	★		
50	3.75				★
50	3.35	★	★		★
50	3.00	★	★	★	★
50	2.65	★	★	★	★
50	2.36	★			
45	3.35				
45	2.65	★	★		★
45	2.36	★	★		
45	2.00	★			
40	3.35				★
40	2.65	★	★		★
40	2.36	★	★	★	★
40	2.00	★			
30	3.00				★
30	2.65				★
30	2.36	★	★		★
30	2.00	★	★	★	
30	1.80	★			
25	2.65				★
25	2.00	★	★		
25	1.80	★			
25	1.60	★			
25	1.00			★	
20	2.65				★
20	1.60	★	★		
20	1.40	★			
20	1.00			★	
15	2.36				★
15	2.00				★
15	1.40				
15	1.00			★	

Table 8.2 *Sizes of mild steel screws*

countersunk★   round head ^

Length mm	0	1	2	3	4	5	6	7	8	9	10	12	14	16	18	20
152.4											★	★	★	★		
127.0											★	★	★	★		★
114.3											★	★	★	★		★
101.6									★		★	★^	★	★	★	★
88.9									★		★	★^	★	★		
82.6											★	★	★			
76.2							★^	★	★^	★	★^	★^	★	★	★	★
69.9								★	★		★	★				
63.5							★	★	★^	★	★^	★^	★^	★	★^	
57.2							★^	★	★^	★	★^	★^	★			
50.8					★	★	★^	★^	★^	★	★^	★^	★^	★		★^
44.5					★	★	★^	★	★^	★^	★	★	★			
38.1				★^	★^	★^	★^	★	★^	★^	★	★^	★^	★^		
31.8				★^	★^	★^	★	★^	★^	★^	★^	★				
25.4		★	★	★^	★^	★^	★^	★^	★					^		
22.2			★	★^	★^	★^	★^	★^	★^		★^					
19.1		★	★^	★^	★^	★	★^	★^	★^	★^	★^					
15.9	★	★^	★^	★^	★^	★^	★^	★^	★^		★^					
12.7	★	★	★^	★^	★^	★^	★^	★^	★^	★^	★^					
11.1					★		★									
9.5	★^	★^	★^	★^	★^	★^		★^	★^							
7.9		★^	★^	★^	★^	★	★^									
6.4	★^	★^	★^	★^	★^	★^		^		^						
4.8		★^		^												

Table 8.3 *Sizes of stainless steel screws*

countersunk★   round head ^

Length mm	0	1	2	3	4	5	6	7	8	10	12	14	16	18
101.6												★		★
88.9											★			
76.2										★^	★^	★	★	★
63.5									★^	★^	★	★		
50.8									★^	★	★^	★		
44.5									★	★	★			
38.1							★^		★^	★^	★^	★^		
31.8							★^		★^	★^	★	★		
25.4				★^	★	★^	★	★^	★^	★				
19.1				★^	★	★^	★	★^	★					
15.9					★^	★^	★^	★	★^					
12.7		★^	★^	★^	★^	★^			★^					
9.5		★^	★^	★^			★							
6.4		★^												

Table 8.4 *Sizes of black bolts*

Length mm	Diameter mm						
	6	8	10	12	16	20	24
180				★			
160							★
150				★	★	★	
140					★	★	★
130				★	★	★	
120			★	★	★	★	★
100			★	★	★	★	★
90			★	★	★	★	★
80			★	★	★	★	★
70		★	★	★	★	★	★
65					★	★	
60	★	★	★	★	★	★	
50	★	★	★	★	★		
45				★			
40	★	★	★	★			
35	★	★	★				
30	★	★					
25	★						

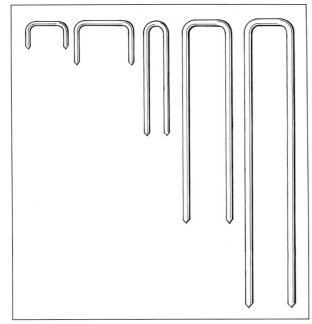

Figure 8.2 *Staples.*

troplated or spun galvanized or stainless steel. Table 8.4 gives the range of sizes for black bolts.

Design of timber joints

The Code of Practice for the structural use of timber, BS 5268 Part 2, gives details of the design requirements for joints in timber and wood based sheet materials. This covers most nailed, screwed, bolted, connectored and glued joints.

Timber connectors of sheet metal

The punched metal plates (Figure 8.5) which are used in vast numbers for trussed rafters and other manufactured components are suitable only for installation by special machinery in a factory under controlled conditions by fabricators who normally hold manufacturers' licences for the use of a particular make of plate. Hand nail plates (Figure 8.5) are available for use on site using a hammer or mechanical hand gun. The Code of Practice for trussed rafter roofs covers joints made using both types of connector plate.

Joist hangers

Joist hangers and framing anchors of many types are now available (Figures 8.6 and 8.7) and are being used in rapidly increasing numbers. They may be thin pressed and/or folded metal sheet or thicker welded steel plate. BS 5268 does not give guidance on the use of joist hangers and it is therefore necessary to specify a type which is supported by published material or to have tests carried out.

FLOORS

Ground floors

The increasing demand for high levels of insulation in buildings has led to a resurgence of interest in timber ground floors due to the ease with which thermal insulation can be incorporated.

The Building Regulations require that any part of the building next to the ground shall have a floor which is constructed to prevent the passage of moisture from the ground to the upper surface of the floor. This requirement is commonly satisfied in England and Wales by covering the ground beneath a timber floor with a 100 mm thick layer of concrete. In Scotland a similar requirement is satisfied by blinding the ground with suitable fine material and covering the surface with a continuous layer of bituminous damp resisting material to BS 2832 'Hot applied damp resisting coatings for solums'.

However, there are other ways in which the requirements of the Building Regulations can be satisfied. These include overlaying the ground with weighted down polyethylene sheeting. The National House-Building Council currently require the polyethylene sheet to be protected by a 50 mm layer of weak concrete. The protection afforded against ground moisture by the use of polyethylene sheet is better than that provided by oversite concrete laid directly on hardcore.

Damp-proof courses in cavity walls must be placed at least 150 mm above the external ground level. The upper surface of the oversite concrete must always be above the external ground level. The minimum distance between the top of the concrete ground cover and the underside of any wall plate is required to be 75 mm by

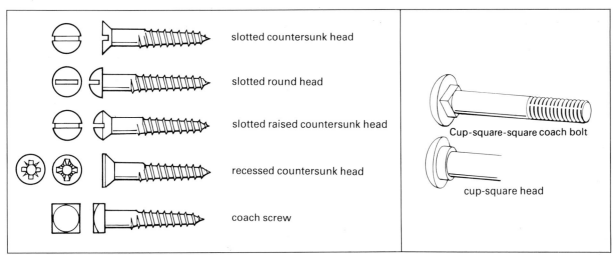

Figure 8.3 *Types of wood screws.*

slotted countersunk head

slotted round head

slotted raised countersunk head

recessed countersunk head

coach screw

Cup-square-square coach bolt

cup-square head

Figure 8.4 *Types of bolts.*

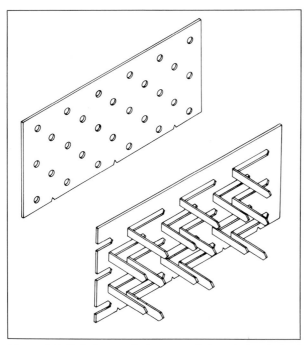

Figure 8.5 *Nail plates: nail plate or punched metal plate for hand nailing (left); punched metal plate (right).*

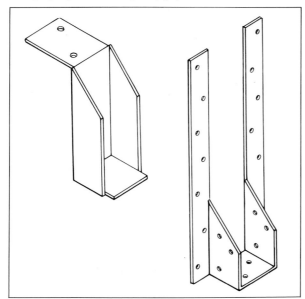

Figure 8.6 *Joist hangers.*

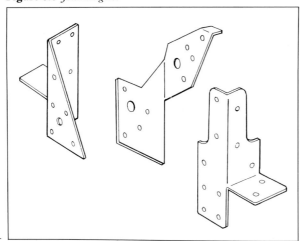

Figure 8.7 *Framing anchors. All are made handed and reversed.*

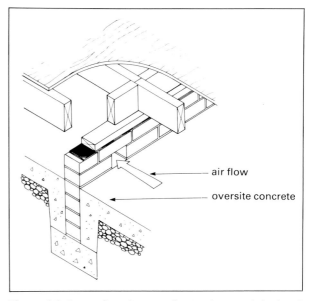

Figure 8.8 *Intermediate sleeper wall using honeycomb brickwork for cross ventilation.*

the England and Wales Building Regulations and 150 mm by the Scottish Regulations and by NHBC. The England and Wales Regulations also require the minimum distance from the top of the ground cover to the underside of any joist to be 125 mm whereas the Scottish Regulations and the NHBC call for a minimum of 150 mm.

Ventilation beneath a suspended timber floor is essential. The Building Regulations (E & W) call for 'adequate' ventilation but the Scottish Regulations stipulate an open area of 1500 mm² per metre run of external wall. Sleeper walls providing intermediate support to joists are usually one brick thick and may be built in honeycomb brickwork (Figure 8.8) or floor noggings can be offset or reduced in depth to permit the circulation of air (Figure 8.9).

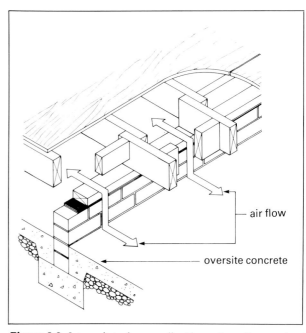

Figure 8.9 *Intermediate sleeper wall with noggings offset or reduced in depth to permit cross ventilation.*

Ground floor joists

Timber wall plates supporting floor joists must be laid on damp-proof courses and should be treated with preservative in accordance with BS 5268 Part 5 'Preservative treatments for constructional timber'. This allows ground floor joists of timber which is non-durable or better (see Appendix) to be used without preservative treatment. Provided that the sub floor ventilation and the protection against ground moisture is adequate, preservation can be considered as a matter of insurance against possible risks of future replacement work. However, in view of the consequences of decay of ground floor joists and the cost and complexity of remedial work, TRADA recommends that such use should be regarded as category C of BS 5268 Part 5 in which the specification of effective preservative treatment for non-durable timbers is desirable rather than optional. This advice is independent of the type of ground cover employed.

Floor joists may be fixed by skew nailing with galvanized or sherardized wire nails onto wall plates or supported on joist hangers (Figure 8.10). Joists may be of sawn or regularized softwood (see Chapter 4). Joist spans and sizes may be taken from published tables or calculated in accordance with BS 5268: Part 2. Table 8.5 shows typical spans for domestic floor joists.

Traditionally it was common practice to have sleeper walls at relatively close centres (less than 2 m). However the designer must decide whether this is the most economic approach or whether larger section joists of longer span would be preferable. Where the end of the floor joist is unprotected it should be stopped slightly short of the external wall to reduce the possibility of moisture being transferred into the end grain of the timber.

Where a fireplace is incorporated into the building, a fender wall of brickwork or concrete must be provided in the underfloor area around the hearth. Timbers should not be fixed nearer than 150 mm to the inside of the brickwork jambs of the fire opening or nearer than 500 mm from the face of the brickwork forming the fire breast in accordance with the Building Regulations (Figure 8.11).

At the present time the Building Regulations have no insulation requirements for normal timber, suspended

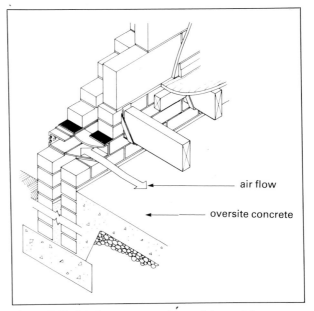

Figure 8.10 *Joist hanger support of suspended ground floor.*

timber or for solid ground floors. However, added insulation should be considered for all ground floors both to improve the energy efficiency of the building and to reduce the risk of condensation occurring at skirting level due to cold bridging. In suspended timber floors insulation in the form of glass or mineral wool can be incorporated supported on galvanized wire or plastic mesh. This can be draped over the joists (Figure 8.12) or, where access is available, the mesh may be fixed to the underside of the joists.

Intermediate floor joists

The spans for intermediate floor joists may be greater than those required for suspended ground floors due to the need to span the full width of the rooms below. Spans of 4 to 4.5 m can be provided from normally available softwood timber; for spans greater than this some form of intermediate support will be required or the use of structural hardwood or laminated beams considered. Like those for ground floor joists, sizes and spans may be taken from published span tables (Table 8.5) or calculated in accordance with BS 5268 Part 2.

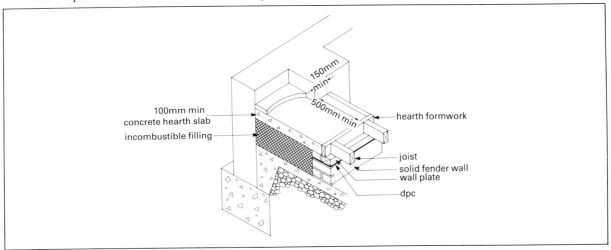

Figure 8.11 *Typical hearth construction at ground floor level.*

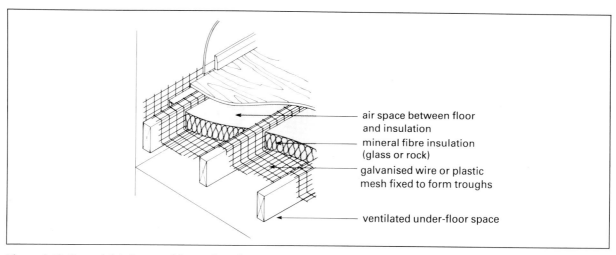

air space between floor and insulation

mineral fibre insulation (glass or rock)

galvanised wire or plastic mesh fixed to form troughs

ventilated under-floor space

Figure 8.12 *Suspended timber ground floor with insulation supported by galvanized wire or plastic mesh.*

Table 8.5 *Permissible clear spans for floor joists:* **SC 3★**: *regularized sizes†*

Size of joist	Dead load (in kN/m²) supported by joist, excluding the self weight of the joist								
	Not more than 0.25 (25.5 kg/m²)			More than 0.25 but not more than 0.50 (51 kg/m²)			More than 0.50 but not more than 1.25 (127.5 kg/m²)		
	Spacing of joists (in mm)								
	400	450	600	400	450	600	400	450	600
	Permissible clear span								
mm	m	m	m	m	m	m	m	m	m
38 × 72	1.132	1.014	0.770	1.064	0.957	0.735	0.923	0.838	0.656
97	1.831	1.695	1.307	1.719	1.559	1.218	1.427	1.305	1.042
122	2.485	2.388	1.929	2.371	2.218	1.759	1.951	1.795	1.453
147	2.987	2.872	2.514	2.857	2.711	2.336	2.457	2.294	1.877
170	3.446	3.311	2.878	3.285	3.103	2.695	2.813	2.655	2.273
195	2.944	3.757	3.269	3.729	3.523	3.062	3.195	3.016	2.616
220	4.439	4.198	3.655	4.167	3.938	3.425	3.573	3.374	2.928
44 × 72	1.283	1.163	0.887	1.209	1.091	0.842	1.038	0.944	0.744
97	1.964	1.857	1.494	1.865	1.761	1.384	1.590	1.458	1.170
122	2.609	2.509	2.190	2.495	2.399	1.983	2.160	1.991	1.621
147	3.135	3.015	2.701	3.000	2.884	2.530	2.641	2.492	2.082
170	3.616	3.479	3.092	3.461	3.329	2.896	3.022	2.853	2.476
195	4.136	3.981	3.510	3.961	3.781	3.290	3.432	3.241	2.813
220	4.653	4.481	3.923	4.458	4.224	3.678	3.836	3.624	3.148
47 × 72	1.326	1.236	0.945	1.275	1.156	0.894	1.093	0.996	0.787
97	2.027	1.916	1.586	1.922	1.820	1.464	1.668	1.531	1.232
122	2.666	2.564	2.305	2.551	2.453	2.090	2.259	2.084	1.700
147	3.203	3.082	2.790	3.066	2.948	2.614	2.727	2.574	2.179
170	3.694	3.555	3.192	3.537	3.403	2.991	3.121	2.947	2.558
195	4.225	4.068	3.624	4.047	3.894	3.397	3.543	3.346	2.907
220	4.727	4.577	4.050	4.554	4.359	3.798	3.960	3.741	3.252
50 × 72	1.367	1.289	1.002	1.313	1.220	0.946	1.147	1.046	0.828
97	2.086	1.974	1.676	1.977	1.873	1.542	1.743	1.602	1.292
122	2.721	2.617	2.373	2.604	2.504	2.195	2.330	2.175	1.778
147	3.268	3.145	2.859	3.129	3.010	2.694	2.811	2.654	2.274
170	3.769	3.628	3.289	3.609	3.473	3.083	3.216	3.037	2.637
195	4.310	4.150	3.733	4.129	3.974	3.500	3.651	3.449	2.997
220	4.797	4.664	4.172	4.646	4.472	3.913	4.080	3.855	3.352
63 × 147	3.521	3.390	3.087	3.373	3.247	2.954	3.040	2.924	2.581
170	4.058	3.909	3.561	3.889	3.744	3.409	3.508	3.374	2.954
195	4.637	4.468	4.075	4.446	4.282	3.901	4.013	3.855	3.355
220	5.065	4.928	4.585	4.909	4.774	4.370	4.517	4.307	3.751
75 × 195	4.833	4.703	4.310	4.686	4.526	4.129	4.246	4.088	3.651
220	5.272	5.131	4.797	5.113	4.975	4.646	4.745	4.600	4.080

* For species/grade combinations in this strength class, see Chapter 4 and BS 5268: Part 2: 1984, tables 3 to 7.
† Regularized sizes are given in Chapter 4 and BS 4471: Part 1.

Joist supports

The traditional way of supporting the ends of the joists was to build them straight into the internal leaf of the external wall as the work progressed. The joist should have a minimum bearing of 75 mm (90 mm is preferable) and is supported on a wall plate if an offset wall is used (Figure 8.13), or on joist hangers. This avoids the timber penetrating the wall element.

In the past trimmer or trimming joists around openings for chimney breasts, stairwells etc were supported by a tusk tenon. However, today these are usually fixed and supported by a hanger or framing anchor (Figure 8.14).

The NHBC recommend the following guidelines for trimmer joist sizes where joist centres are at a maximum of 600 mm:

Trimmer carrying 1 joist nearer to end than span/5	No extra width
Trimmer carrying 1–4 joists	Minimum 12 mm wider than joists
Trimmer carrying 5–8 joists	Minimum 25 mm wider than joists
Trimmer carrying more than 8 joists	Design in accordance with BS 5268 Part 2

Joists can be given extra rigidity by means of strutting which is cut and fixed between them, the line of struts being equally placed. Two common methods are used. Solid bridging (Figure 8.15) is cut from material similar to the joists. Herringbone strutting (Figure 8.16) is a series of criss-cross timber pieces approximately 25 × 50 mm fixed at the top and bottom of each joist. Proprietary mild steel components are also available to form

Table 8.5 (cont) *Permissible clear spans for floor joists:* **SC 4★**: *regularized sizes*†

Size of joist	Dead load (in kN/m²) supported by joist, excluding the self weight of the joist								
	Not more than 0.25 (25.5 kg/m²)			More than 0.25 but not more than 0.50 (51 kg/m²)			More than 0.50 but not more than 1.25 (127.5 kg/m²)		
	Spacing of joists (in mm)								
	400	450	600	400	450	600	400	450	600
	Permissible clear span								
mm	m	m	m	m	m	m	m	m	m
38 × 72	1.264	1.191	1.026	1.217	1.148	0.992	1.111	1.051	0.878
97	1.938	1.831	1.589	1.840	1.742	1.517	1.638	1.555	1.363
122	2.584	2.485	2.203	2.472	2.372	2.079	2.183	2.076	1.831
147	3.106	2.987	2.713	2.972	2.857	2.593	2.671	2.566	2.310
170	3.584	3.447	3.132	3.430	3.298	2.994	3.084	2.963	2.684
195	4.100	3.945	3.587	3.925	3.776	3.429	3.531	3.393	3.075
220	4.614	4.441	4.039	4.418	4.251	3.863	3.977	3.823	3.465
44 × 72	1.360	1.283	1.108	1.307	1.234	1.070	1.189	1.126	0.981
97	2.077	1.965	1.709	1.968	1.865	1.629	1.747	1.659	1.458
122	2.713	2.609	2.363	2.596	2.496	2.225	2.321	2.210	1.953
147	3.259	3.136	2.850	3.119	3.000	2.725	2.806	2.697	2.444
170	3.759	3.671	3.290	3.599	3.462	3.146	3.239	3.114	2.823
195	4.299	4.138	3.766	4.117	3.962	3.602	3.708	3.565	3.234
220	4.788	4.655	4.240	4.633	4.460	4.057	4.176	4.016	3.644
47 × 72	1.405	1.326	1.146	1.349	1.275	1.106	1.226	1.161	1.013
97	2.142	2.027	1.766	2.028	1.922	1.681	1.797	1.708	1.503
122	2.772	2.667	2.423	2.653	2.551	2.293	2.385	2.272	2.010
147	3.330	3.204	2.914	3.188	3.067	2.786	2.869	2.757	2.500
170	3.839	3.696	3.363	3.677	3.538	3.217	3.311	3.184	2.888
195	4.390	4.228	3.849	4.206	4.049	3.683	3.790	3.645	3.308
220	4.864	4,729	4.333	4.712	4.557	4.147	4.268	4.105	3.727
50 × 72	1.448	1.367	1.183	1.390	1.313	1.141	1.261	1.195	1.044
97	2.205	2.087	1.820	2.085	1.977	1.731	1.846	1.755	1.545
122	2.829	2.722	2.474	2.708	2.604	2.358	2.436	2.331	2.065
147	3.397	3.270	2.974	3.253	3.130	2.845	2.929	2.185	2.554
170	3.916	3.771	3.432	3.752	3.611	3.284	3.380	3.250	2.950
195	4.478	4.313	3.928	4.291	4.131	3.759	3.869	3.721	3.378
220	4.935	4.800	4.422	4.782	4.648	4.233	4.355	4.190	3.806
63 × 147	3.657	3.523	3.210	3.505	3.375	3.072	3.161	3.041	2.762
170	4.214	4.060	3.702	4.040	3.891	3.544	3.647	3.509	3.189
195	4.773	4.640	4.235	4.618	4.449	4.056	4.172	4.015	3.651
220	5.208	5.068	4.735	5.049	4.912	4.564	4.683	4.519	4.112
75 × 195	4.968	4.836	4.478	4.819	4.689	4.291	4.412	4.249	3.869
220	5.418	5.275	4.935	5.257	5.116	4.782	4.882	4.747	4.355

* For species/grade combinations in this strength class, see Chapter 4 and BS 5268: Part 2: 1984, tables 3 to 7.
† Regularized sizes are given in Chapter 4 and BS 4471: Part 1.

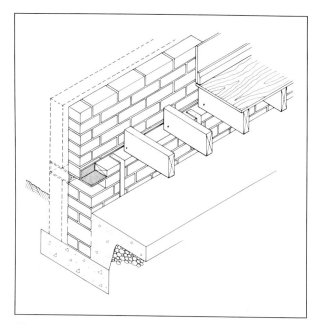

Figure 8.13 _Offset wall support for suspended timber ground floors._

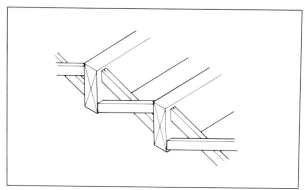

Figure 8.15 _Herringbone strutting._

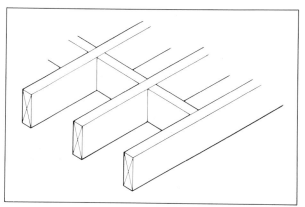

Figure 8.16 _Solid bridging._

Table 8.6 _NHBC recommendations for strutting_

Joist span m	Rows of strutting
up to 2.5	none
2.5–4.5	1
over 4.5	2

adjacent to bearings off steelwork or similar supports
Herringbone strutting should be at least 38 × 38 mm and shall be located clear of the top and bottom edges of the joists
Solid strutting should be at least 38 mm thick
The depth of solid strutting is normally at least three-quarters of the depth of the joists

FLOORING AND DECKING

Softwood boarding

For many years softwood was the most commonly used floor decking, originally with plain edged boards until the development of tongued and grooved boards allowed thinner sections to be used whilst still providing an adequately stiff floor. It is especially suitable where small areas of floor are required or where easy access is required to services in the floor construction. It is not suitable where thin sheet or tile finishes are to be laid due to the number of joints and the potential for movement during the initial reduction in moisture content which can show through the finished surface.

Unless specific protection is provided, softwood flooring should not be fixed until the building is waterproof. In a normally heated building the boards will eventually attain a moisture content of around 10 per cent, however it is not normally practicable to specify

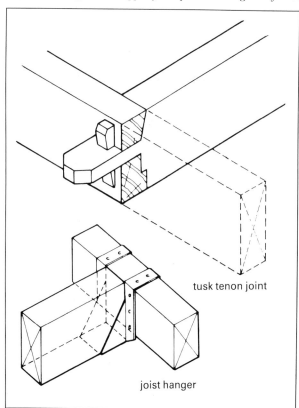

Figure 8.14 _Supports for trimmed joists._

herringbone strutting. The recommendations laid down by the NHBC for the positioning of strutting are shown in Table 8.6. At both ends of the line of strutting, the gap between the last joist and the adjacent wall is closed by means of folding wedges positioned in the line of thrust. The efficiency of solid bridging can be affected by slight shrinkage of the joists; herringbone strutting is not affected in this way.

Notching and drilling of joists for services should be approved by the building designer but in the absence of specific recommendations the details shown in Figures 8.17 and 8.18 should be satisfactory.

tusk tenon joint

joist hanger

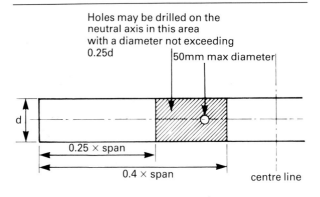

Figure 8.17 *Service holes in joists.*

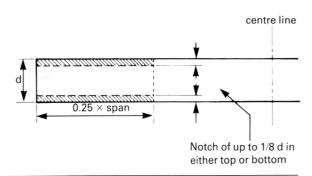

Figure 8.18 *Service notches in joists.*

and install boarding at this moisture content in a building under construction and a figure of 16 to 18 per cent is more realistic. BS 1297 'Grading and sizing of softwood flooring' refers to a moisture content of 16 to 22 per cent for normal use.

It is not normally necessary to specify the timber species for softwood floorboards. BS 1297 includes Canadian spruce, Douglas fir, European redwood and whitewood and Western hemlock, all of which are suitable for the purpose. It is not usually necessary to specify preservative treatment for floorboards.

The finished face widths of tongued and grooved boards normally correspond to the board thickness e.g. a 16 mm thick board usually has a face width of 65 mm; a 19 mm board a face width of 90 mm; and a 21 mm board a face width of 113 mm. These combinations reduce any tendency to cup in the width of the board. Board lengths should average 3 m and should not generally be less than 1.8 m. Table 8.7 gives normal maximum joist centres for normal domestic floor loadings of 1.3 kN/m².

Table 8.7 *Joist centres for t and g boarded floors*

Finished board thickness mm	Max. span (centre to centre) mm
16	505
19	600
21	635

Softwood boards should be tightly cramped together before fixing. Header (butt) joints should occur over joists and should be staggered so that they are at least two board widths apart. Boards are usually face nailed to the joists using either oval or lost head nails, cut brads or improved nails; two nails per intersection.

Wood chipboard flooring

Flooring grade chipboard complying with BS 5669 'Specification for wood chipboard and methods of test for particleboard' Type II or Type II/III are suitable for domestic use and form a good subfloor for most finishes. Type II designates flooring grade and Type III moisture resistant chipboard. The appropriate grades and other identifying marks should be printed on one face of the board; this face should be laid to the underside of the floor to give a clean finished surface.

Flooring grades of chipboard are available with tongued and grooved edges, on all four sides, on the long edges only or as square edged boards. Square edged boards must have all edges supported, the long edges on joists and the short edges supported by noggings between the joists. Tongued and grooved boards are laid with the long edges across the joists with the board edges falling centrally on the joists; support is not necessary to the long edges except at perimeters and to cut edges. Boards are normally available 18 or 22 mm thick and in the following sizes; 2400 × 600, 610, 1200, 1220 mm.

When laid over joists or battens the maximum recommended span for domestic floors is shown in Table 8.8.

Table 8.8 *Maximum spans for chipboard in domestic floors*

Thickness mm	Max. imposed load kN/m²	Max. span (centre to centre) mm
18	1.5	450 (400 in GLC area)
22	1.5	600
22	2.0	450

Boards should be conditioned on site by laying them in place for 24 hours before fixing. They should not be fixed to joists or battens with a high moisture content as this can cause localized swelling in the chipboard. Board joints should be pulled tightly together and fixed with screws or nails at 200 to 300 mm centres along all supports. Board joints may be glued with a PVA, or similar adhesive which produces a rigid floor and is recommended where thin sheet or tile finishes are to be applied. A gap should be left around the perimeter of each floor area to allow for possible expansion of the boards at a later stage. This should be approximately 2 mm each end per metre run of board with a minimum of approximately 10 mm per end. This gap is usually covered by the skirting.

Plywood flooring

There are three distinct categories from which to select plywood for domestic floorings:

1   Douglas fir plywood

Finnish birch plywood
Southern pine plywood

2 Douglas fir faced plywood
Finnish birch faced plywood
Southern pine faced plywood

3 Softwood plywood (pine, spruce or fir species)

Plywoods in category 1 are generally confined to specialized performance requirements; categories 2 and 3 are more commonly specified for domestic floors.

Plywood for flooring should be bonded with WBP type adhesives (see Chapter 2); it can withstand site wetting better than other types but, like all timber flooring, should be protected from excessive moisture on site. Plywood which will form the finished surface must be sanded and have a better visual surface appearance than that which will be covered. Where carpets, thin tiles or sheets are to be used, touch sanded tight faced plywood should be specified, but where wood blocks or strips or other tiled surfaces are to be used an unsanded surface with lower face grades can be accepted (see Chapter 2). When specifying sanded plywood it is important to check that the reduction in thickness does not fall below the recommended spans given by the manufacturers.

BS 5268 Part 2 accepts that the quality and grading of plywood is controlled by the country of origin and refers to the following standards:

USA   US Product Standard PS1-83
Canada   CSA 0121 and 0151
Finland   SFS 2412-2417 and 4091-4093
Sweden   SBN 1975:5

The appropriate standard reference should always be included in specifications for flooring plywood.

The face grain of plywood affects its strength and stiffness and the face grain should always be positioned

Table 8.9 *Typical spans for simply supported American and Canadian plywood flooring*

American plywoods
Southern pine (SP) and Douglas fir (DFP)

Thickness mm	Max. span: Multi support mm
15 or 16	510 SP or DFP
18 or 19	610 SP or DFP
28	1220 SP or DFP

Canadian plywoods
Canadian softwood plywood (CSP) and Douglas fir (DFP)

Thickness mm	Max. span: Multi support mm
12.5	300 CSP or DFP
15.5	480 CSP or DFP
18.5	600 CSP or DFP
20.5	800 CSP or DFP

Table 8.10 *Typical spans for simply supported Finnish plywood (sanded) flooring*

Birch throughout (B), birch faced (BF) and conifer (C)

Thickness mm	Single support mm		Multi support mm	
12	500 B BF	400 C	600 B BF	500 C
15	600 B BF	500 C	600 B BF	600 C
18	800 B BF	600 C	800 B BF	600 C

running at right angles to the joists. Some plywood is manufactured with the face grain parallel with the shortest side but most is parallel with the longest side. This will determine whether the plywood long edge runs at right angles to, or parallel with, the joists.

Plywood for flooring is available as square edged or tongued and grooved, usually only along the long edges. Square edges must be fully supported on joists or noggings, tongued and grooved edges only need support at the room perimeter and at cut edges. A gap should always be left at the room edges; this will be covered by the skirting. Typical spans for simply supported plywood flooring are shown in Tables 8.9 and 8.10.

Where narrow sheets of plywood are used which span between one pair of joists, the allowable span is less than that for sheets which span three or more joists. This is indicated in Tables 8.9 and 8.10 by figures for single and multi support.

Plywood flooring is normally fixed with common or annular grooved nails at 150 mm centres at edges and 300 mm at intermediate supports.

DECORATIVE FLOORING

Decorative timber flooring can take many forms from softwood boards, plywood or chipboard finished to provide a decorative surface, to hardwood blocks, strips, parquet or mosaic. Hardwood species of sufficiently high density and hardness will provide a hard wearing and long lasting decorative surface. The Appendix gives details of those timbers which are suitable as flooring.

In general, flooring in an intermittently heated room will not exceed 14 per cent moisture content in use; with continuous heating the moisture content will not exceed 11 per cent, and with underfloor heating the moisture content could be as low as six per cent. All hardwood flooring is kiln dried to a suitable moisture content and it is essential that the conditions of temperature and humidity in the building are favourable before, during and after laying. The heating system should be installed and working for at least ten days before the flooring is installed with adequate ventilation to allow moisture from the construction to escape.

Timber overlays to solid floors

Timber overlays to solid floors are most often used to provide a decorative wearing surface in the form of wood blocks or strips, usually hardwood. Such floor construction is often associated with extensions to existing buildings. Where this is the case, and the original building has a suspended timber floor, the ventilation to the existing floor must be fully maintained by the inclusion of ducts through the new solid floor to air bricks on the external wall of the extension.

When wood block or strip floors are laid over screeded concrete slabs it is essential that the sand/cement screed is adequately dry before the floor finish is laid. A damp-proof membrane must be incorporated between the main slab and the screed and the relative humidity over the screed should be 75 per cent or less when tested. Wood flooring should never be laid before the glazing and plastering are completed. Storage of wood flooring on site for long periods is not recommended; short term storage should be clear of the floor in a dry, well ventilated area.

Wood blocks are fixed using a suitable adhesive; bitumen emulsions mixed with latex have been widely used. The advice of the specialist flooring contractor or supplier should be sought on the specification of suitable substrates and adhesives. All blocks should be manufactured with an interlocking system, most often in the form of tongued and grooved blocks but alternative proprietary systems are available.

Strip floors are laid on preservative treated battens which are fixed to the concrete slab by proprietary shoes or clips. The spaces between the battens should either be adequately ventilated or filled with sand/cement screed. Alternatively, dovetail section treated battens may be cast into the screed which should finish flush with the top of the batten to avoid an air space beneath the flooring. Strip flooring is normally fixed to the battens by secret nailing just above the tongue.

Wood mosaic flooring is usually supplied in panels which are bonded to a felt or paper base. The panels are bonded to the dry, flat concrete slab or sand/cement screed using a bituminous adhesive.

Decorative floors on joists

Decorative hardwood strip flooring can be laid directly onto joists, end matched flooring with tongued and grooved board ends allows joints to be made at any point rather than having to cut boards so that joints occur over joists.

All types of timber decorative flooring can be laid directly onto plywood or chipboard floors but parquet and wood block floors require a thin plywood or hardboard underlay when used over a boarded floor.

ROOF CONSTRUCTION

Pitched roofs of timber construction can be designed and constructed in a number of ways. Traditionally they were constructed on site with each piece cut and fitted to its neighbours. This type of construction requires considerable constructional skill and tends to use more material. In order to simplify the geometry and speed of construction, various forms of prefabricated truss were developed with the intermediate rafters and purlins cut and fitted on site. More recently the highly engineered trussed rafter where the rafters and ceiling joists are triangulated to form a lightweight prefabricated truss has become the most widely used form of domestic roof construction. However, trusses, of whatever kind, do not constitute roofs – they have to be integrated with the roof structure in its entirety.

Site constructed roofs

The simplest form of pitched roof construction is the couple roof (Figure 8.19) which consists of rafters bearing against each other at the ridge board with the load and the thrust at the eaves being resisted by the lateral strength of the wall. Except for the very smallest spans,

modern lightweight (cavity type) wall construction is unlikely to be adequate and this form is therefore little used now.

Collar roofs

By adding a collar to the roof construction (Figure 8.20) it is possible to relieve the walls of thrust; the nearer the collar is to the bearing point the greater will be the effect. However, the collar imposes a bending moment on the rafter; the higher the collar the greater the bending moment. Rafter sizes may have to be increased to handle the stresses, for example, a small roof, tied at the supporting wall plate level requiring 38×100 mm rafters will require 50×150 mm rafters when the collar is located at the mid height of the rafters.

Hangers and binders (Figure 8.21) are normally added when the span exceeds about 2.5 metres in order to prevent the ceiling joist increasing to an uneconomic size. The ceiling joists are in tension when they tie the

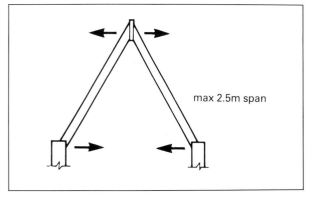

Figure 8.19 *Couple roof.*

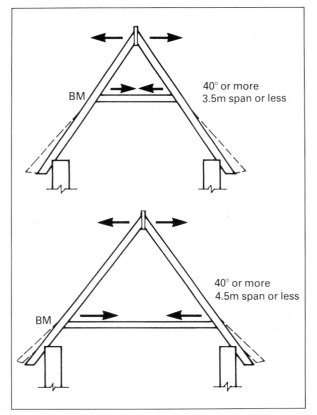

Figure 8.20 *Collar roof/raised tie roof.*

rafter feet to prevent spreading and they relieve the wall of all horizontal thrust. This simple, three-member form of a close couple roof can be used for spans up to approximately 5.5 metres. Rafter sizes can be calculated or, depending upon the roof dead load, be ascertained from tables.

In cut-roof construction the common rafters are, traditionally, birdsmouthed over the wall plate at eaves level and fixed to a ridge board at the apex of the roof. The ridge board is wider than the common rafter to enable it to rise to a plane on the upper roof surface in common with the tile battens. The accurate cutting of

the birdsmouth over the wall plate, and the plumb cut against the ridge at the top of a rafter, contribute significantly to the ability of the roof to contain the imposed load. Inaccurate cutting or assembly will reduce stability and may induce undesirable stresses.

Purlin roofs

For roofs with a span in excess of 6 m, additional support for the rafters will be necessary in order to keep the rafters to an economic size. This can be achieved by fixing purlins to the underside of the rafters midway

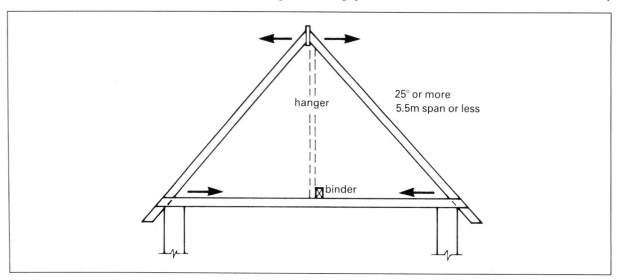

Figure 8.21 *Close couple roof.*

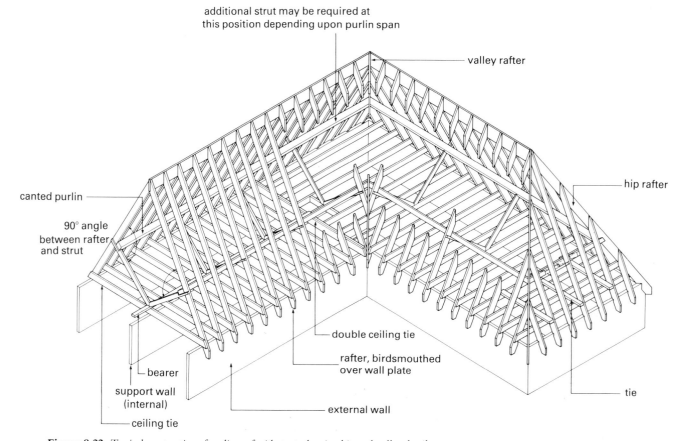

Figure 8.22 *Typical construction of purlin roof with strut, showing hip and valley details.*

through their length and supporting them by means of struts spaced approximately 1.5 m apart and bearing upon load-bearing partitions or beams. Purlins are of relatively substantial size and should be set at 90 degrees to the roof pitch. Purlin struts should be notched to the purlin to give maximum support. Ceiling joists will need to be given extra support by binders supported by hangers as mentioned earlier.

A strut, in the form of a collar, is often used placed above the purlin to minimize the deflection that may take place in the rafters and purlins. A section through a roof of this type, suitable for a span of up to approximately 8 m, is shown in Figure 8.22.

Hipped ends and valleys in purlin roofs

It may be assumed that hip rafters in roofs pitched lower than about 30 degrees are subject to bending stress and need to be propped or designed to resist such bending. However hipped ends are less common on low pitched roofs than on steeper ones. When the roof pitch is over 30 degrees the hip rafter is virtually unloaded, being unable to attract load from the jack rafters attached to it. The hip and valley rafters have a number of constructional uses. They make convenient jointing pieces enabling the jack rafters to be fixed together in pairs. Similarly they facilitate the location and jointing of purlins. They support the ends of tile battens and the hip tiles or valley construction.

The rafter thickness should provide for nail holding and is usually the same as the common rafter thickness. The depth should normally be at least 50 mm greater than the common rafter depth to make full contact with the cut end of the jack rafter and deeper where it is required as the jointing member between the mitred ends of purlins. Figure 8.22 shows typical details of hips and valleys.

Bolted and connectored trusses

In order to economize on the amount of timber used and, in some situations, the time spent in fabricating a roof on site, various designs of truss were produced in the years following the Second World War. These were predominantly based upon the use of bolted connections using double sided tooth plate connectors at the timber interface, although other designs using nailed plywood gussets were also developed. The designs were (and in many cases still are) available as detail drawings for use in specification and construction.

TRADA (then known as the Timber Development Association, TDA) produced a range of designs for roof structures of this type which continue to be used. The construction uses trusses at 1.8 metre spacing with common rafters carried on purlins between the trusses. Traditionally a roof truss is a triangulated framework, in the structural sense, with principal rafters larger than those in the rest of the associated roof. These principal rafters normally appear in a lower plane than the common rafters and have the purlin over the top. The

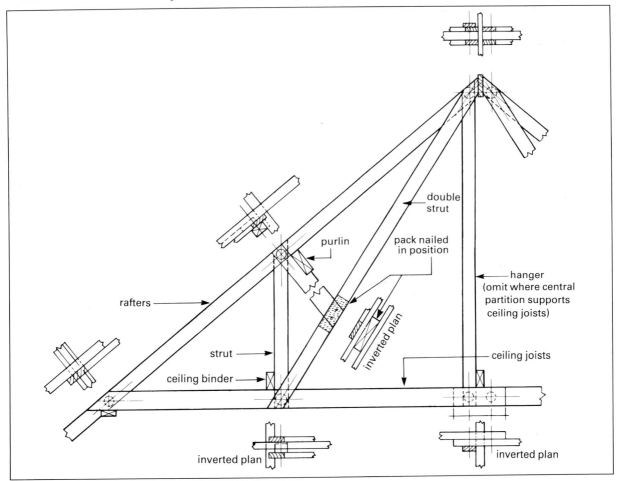

Figure 8.23 *Typical TRADA truss.*

TRADA roof truss is, by this definition, nearer to being a trussed rafter because the principal rafters are mostly the same section size as the commons and occur in the same plane, not lower. Many of the principal rafters are made up of two common rafter-sized members used together.

Designs are available from TRADA for trusses up to 12 metres span and pitches between 15 degrees and 40 degrees (Figure 8.23). Standard details for forming hips and valleys are also available. A similar range of designs was produced by one of the major concrete roofing tile manufacturers.

Figure 8.24 illustrates a roof construction of this type. The main advantage compared with a trussed rafter roof is that the internal framing occurs at 1.8 metre centres rather than the 600 mm (maximum) centres of a trussed rafter roof. This allows more free space within the roof and also provides flexibility for building designs where the repetitive requirement needed to use trussed rafters most efficiently is absent. The fact that the trusses are usually made by the contractor enables variants to deal with changes of building form to be easily handled.

In any roof design using standard design trusses care is essential to ensure that additional loads from water tanks etc are adequately supported. The design criteria should be checked to ascertain what allowance has been made, or support should be provided from partitions or walls below.

The allowable design load for the roof tiles should also be established since designs produced to support some types of concrete tiles may be inadequate to carry the dead load from clay tiles.

Any roof structure which has principal rafters, purlins and intermediate common rafters will have hard lines up the slope at intervals along the length (at purlin supports). This can display phenomena not unlike those associated with masonry party walls, occasioning humping in the tiles on walls of terraced houses, due to the brickwork not being correctly set with compressible material above. Therefore the type of tile ought to be considered during the roof design and if large flat shapes are proposed, consideration should be given to stiffening the purlins to prevent them deflecting. This can be done by increasing their depth, or by adding struts (Figure 8.25) or propping, if supports are available.

Trussed rafter roofs

The introduction of this type of roof from the United States in the early 1960s has effectively revolutionized the construction of roofs. Each trussed rafter consists of the sloping rafter members plus a ceiling member and the necessary intermediate framework (web members), the individual timbers being jointed with punched metal plate fasteners. The designs are produced by the manufacturers of the metal plates who give licences for use by fabricators through franchise agreements. Design criteria are established by prototype testing of many different types and sizes of each truss. The criteria are then applied to produce further designs intermediately among the tested range of standard designs. In some cases the fabricating company has a design team who will also use the plate supplier's design criteria under the licence agreement. Plate 8 shows a typical trussed rafter roof.

Trussed rafters are fabricated from stress graded timber which is normally regularized to a constant thickness of 35 mm although thicker sections can be used if specified. The connector plates are punched from pregalvanized steel plate or stainless steel plate (the former

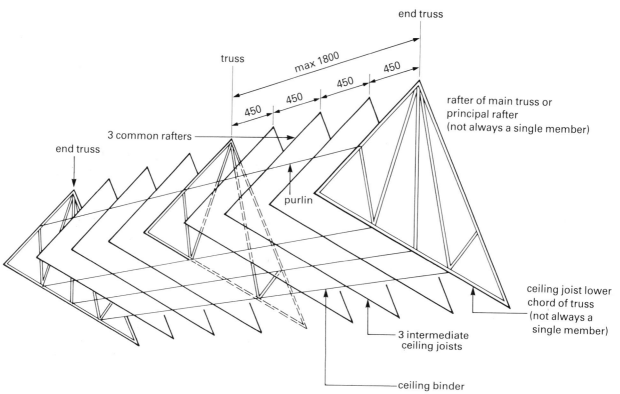

Figure 8.24 *Typical TRADA standard roof design.*

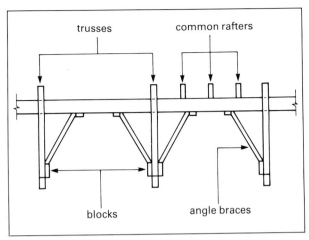

Figure 8.25 *Stiffening of purlins.*

being more common) of approximately 1.0 mm thickness (Figure 8.5). The timber members can be preservative treated if required and organic solvent double vacuum treatment is normally used.

The largest normal span for trussed rafters is 16–18 metres although larger spans have been produced, the limitation being as much controlled by transportation and handling difficulties as by the structural requirements.

All that is normally required of the specifier is to provide details of the required span, the pitch, the tile load and details of tanks or other loads to be carried. If it is desired to have adjacent roofs of differing spans but with a common roof plane it is important to ensure that the fabricator is aware of this since otherwise he will use the most economic timber sections for each span which can result in a change of plane at the junction line. Trussed rafters are normally spaced at either 450 or 600 mm centres and this requirement should be provided.

Symmetrical, asymmetrical, monopitched and many other shapes of truss are produced and manufacturers' catalogues should be examined to find the 'normal' range (Figure 8.26). When special shapes are needed the specifier should provide a drawing giving the fabricator the relevant dimensions.

Trussed rafters are factory fabricated on accurate jigs with the plates pressed home by hydraulic presses. Due to the time required for setting up, they are most economic if a production run can be made. The resulting truss is comparatively flimsy until it is fixed in place and has its requisite bracing. Handling and storage must be correctly done in order to avoid damage to the joints by distortion. Recommendations for correct site storage are shown in Figure 8.27.

Fixing and bracing

Trussed rafters may be fixed with either proprietary truss clips or by skew nailing from both sides into the wall plate. If nails are used these should avoid the connector plates since these can be broken away from the timber by the skew nails. It is essential that correct roof bracing is specified and correctly fixed in position. Full details are given in BS 5268 Part 3. Figure 8.28 shows the bracing required in the roof plane. BS 5268 also requires diagonal bracing in the ceiling plane.

Loads from water storage tanks must be spread over a series of trussed rafters. Recommendations are given in BS 5268 Part 3 and by the ITPA.

Hips and valleys in trussed rafter roofs

The various proprietary designs have slightly varying methods for dealing with these. Two methods are commonly used; either using truncated trusses to form the hip or by the use of multiple trusses to form a girder truss from which jack rafters and site cut common rafters are supported. Valleys are usually formed by running one set of trusses through, and either supporting diminishing trusses from these to the second roof structure or by using a valley lay-board, a ridge purlin and site cut common rafter to form the second roof. The roof truss fabricator's advice should be sought to establish the most economic solution using his components. Figures 8.29 and 8.30 show typical solutions.

Trussed rafters must never be cut or adjusted on site without the approval of the fabricator or designer. Openings for access hatches, chimney stacks, etc should

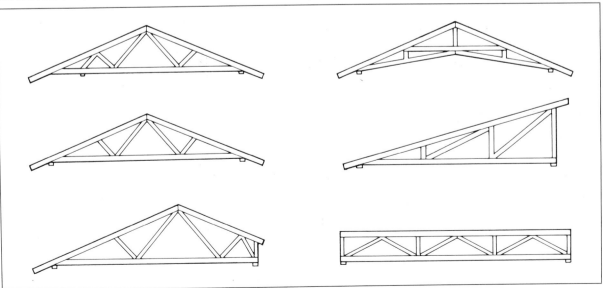

Figure 8.26 *Some trussed rafter designs.*

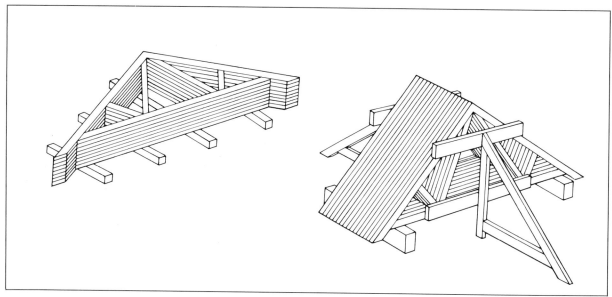

Figure 8.27 *Site storage of trussed rafters, before covering, stacked horizontally (left) and vertically (right).*

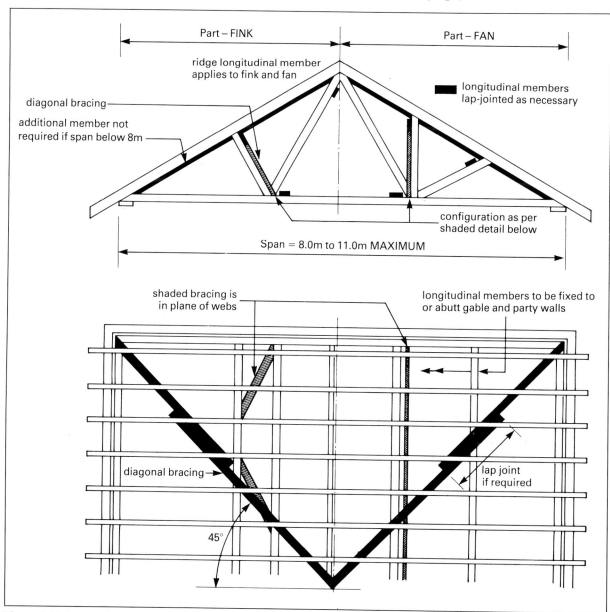

Figure 8.28 *Bracing of trussed rafter roofs.*

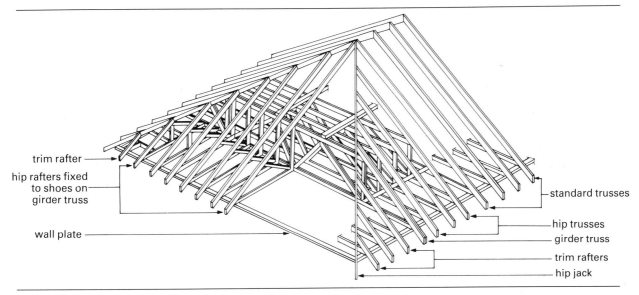

trim rafter

hip rafters fixed
to shoes on
girder truss

wall plate

standard trusses

hip trusses

girder truss

trim rafters

hip jack

Figure 8.29 *Typical hip construction in trussed rafter roofs.*

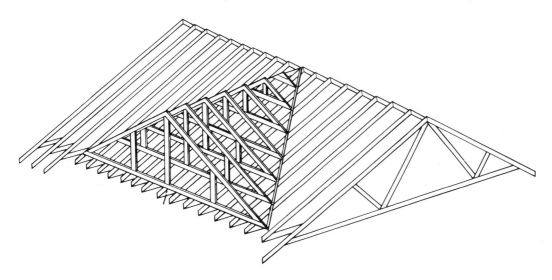

Figure 8.30 *Valley set of diminishing trussed rafters.*

be allowed for in the initial design and the correct framing method used. A typical detail for a chimney stack opening is shown in Figure 8.31.

ROOF SPACE VENTILATION

In order to avoid high moisture contents and condensation caused by excess water vapour in pitched roof spaces it is essential to provide adequate ventilation of the roof space. The following minimum allowances should be made:

For roofs above 15 degrees pitch ventilation openings equivalent to a continuous opening of 10 mm should be provided along two opposite sides of the roof.
For roofs of 15 degrees pitch or below the ventilation should be increased to the equivalent of 25 mm continuous opening (n.b. mesh is required to prevent entry of birds and insects).
Eaves or gable vents may be used to equal effect and, in many cases, ridge vents in addition to the normal

provisions may be useful as air flow can distribute more evenly throughout the roof. Further, with ridge vents some ventilation is possible even in still air conditions due to the stack effect.

Great care must be taken with the positioning of insulation in loft spaces (Figure 8.32). Insulation which is pushed too far into the eaves can block the air flow possibly resulting in loft space condensation. Insulation left short of the inner wall line can result in a 'cold bridge' at the ceiling/wall junction and possible mould growth at the edge of the ceiling.

ROOM IN THE ROOF CONSTRUCTION

The Building Regulation requirements for the height of habitable rooms define the floor areas related to the ceiling areas at defined heights. These requirements will determine the room size.

Rooms in the roof can be provided in traditional cut-roof construction using either canted or vertical purlins. Other methods of construction include prefabricated attic trusses or the use of stressed skin panels.

135

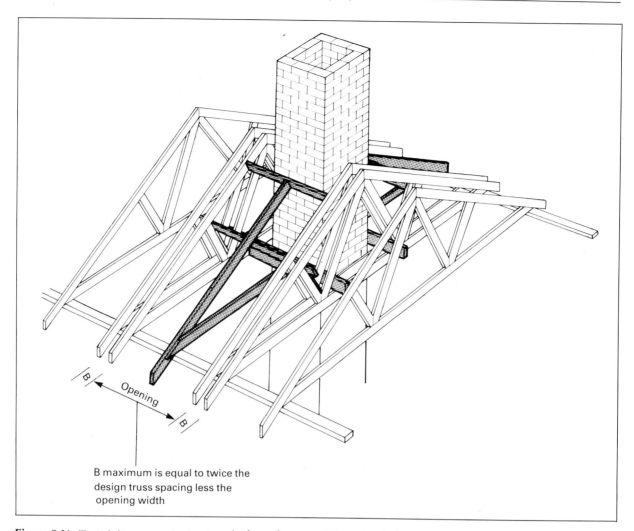

B maximum is equal to twice the design truss spacing less the opening width

Figure 8.31 *Typical chimney opening in a trussed rafter roof.*

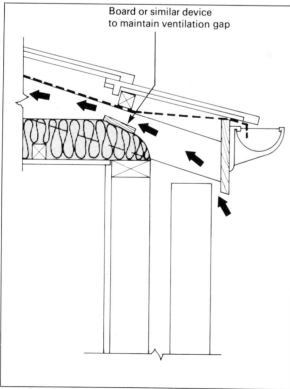

Board or similar device to maintain ventilation gap

Figure 8.32 *Insulation in pitched roof spaces.*

Where insulation is located between the rafters, a clear path of 50 mm minimum depth must be provided above the insulation to allow a flow of air. In roofs with habitable rooms it is essential that high level ventilation openings are provided in addition to those at eaves level.

Cut rafters and canted purlins

The canted purlin roof relies on the majority of the internal partitions being load bearing. The purlin loads are transmitted to the load-bearing walls or beams through struts fixed at 90 degrees to the jack rafters (Figure 8.33). The struts must be positioned according to the permissible span of the purlins, which for solid timber will usually be at a maximum of about 3 to 3.5 m. Timber sizes can be calculated or taken from published span tables. This form of construction is suitable for small buildings only and imposes severe restraint on internal floor planning at all levels. Gable windows and rooflights can easily be incorporated but the height and support of the purlins can affect the construction of dormer windows.

Cut rafters and vertical purlins

A cut rafter and vertical purlin roof relies on the provision of load-bearing cross walls or vertical posts for the support of purlins (Figure 8.34). The purlins may be solid timber, laminated or plybox beams, or lattice

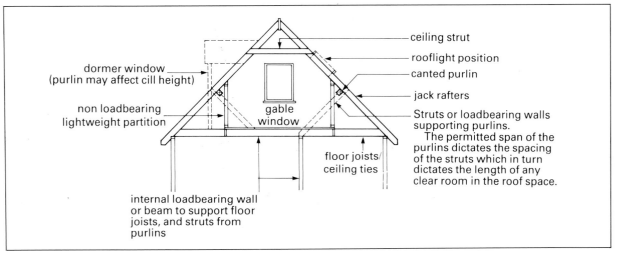

Figure 8.33 *Room in cut rafter and canted purlin roof.*

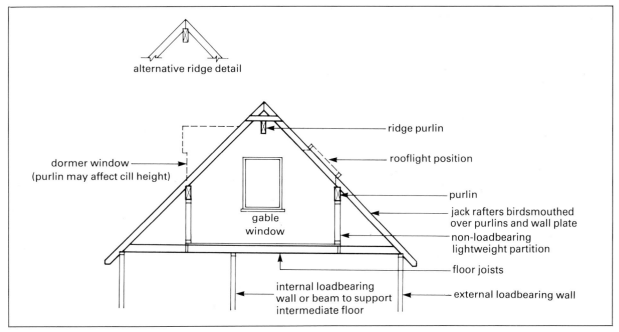

Figure 8.34 *Room in cut rafter and vertical purlin roof.*

trusses. This allows much larger clear spans, the limiting factor being the span of intermediate floor joists. The ridge can be constructed using either a ridge purlin or

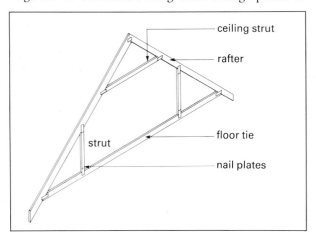

Figure 8.35 *Typical prefabricated attic truss.*

a ridge board with ceiling ties. Gable windows, rooflights and dormers are easily constructed in this form.

Attic trusses

Prefabricated attic trusses are now produced by many of the trussed rafter manufacturers (Figure 8.35). They may be produced as a single unit or broken down into several sections. The fabricators should be consulted if hips or complex structures are proposed using attic trussed rafters. All bracings and ties should be designed by the fabricators for the particular roof in question. Dormers and rooflights are easily formed so long as they do not have openings in excess of 1800 mm. Stairs should be arranged to run parallel to the trusses in order to minimize the number of trusses with truncated bottom chords.

Stressed skin panels

This form of construction provides a clear triangular roof space free from struts, ties and bracing (Figure

8.36). The panels would normally be fabricated off site and either manhandled or craned into position, depending upon their size and weight. The plywood skin may be fixed either to the top or bottom of the ribs, depending on the particular requirements for insulation, condensation control and internal finish. If placed on the bottom with 150 mm deep ribs, then 100 mm insulation can be installed from above leaving a 50 mm air space for roof ventilation. If the plywood is placed on the top of the ribs and 100 mm insulation is installed from below, care must be taken and a suitable detailing method devised to prevent it blocking the passage of ventilating air. Floor decking is extended to the outer walls to assist the restraint of the horizontal forces imposed on the floor structure by the panels.

Rooflight openings can be incorporated in panels but a solid panel must be located on each side of window panels. Dormers should be formed in opposite pairs in order to avoid the problem of eccentric loading. Details of panel construction for spans up to 9 m are available from TRADA.

FLAT ROOFS

The structural design of flat roofs is fairly straightforward and follows a similar pattern to floor design. The loading requirements need to be determined at an early stage and the detailed design of the roof will influence these. Once the loading requirements are known the joist sizes can be calculated or obtained from published tables. When the required spans exceed those economically obtainable with conventional timber joists in available sizes, alternative forms such as glulam, plybox beams or proprietary lattice beams should be considered.

Decking materials

Since it is not possible to guarantee that the roof structure will not get wet during construction or during its life span as a result of failure of the waterproof layer, the decking should be of a moisture resistant material. The most commonly used are sheathing quality plywood or moisture resistant chipboard (see Chapter 2).

Falls to facilitate roof drainage can be achieved either by adjusting the bearing heights of the roof structure if it is acceptable to have an independent suspended ceiling or a non-horizontal directly fixed ceiling. Alternatively firrings can be used and the joists maintained in a horizontal plane. Firrings placed parallel with the roof joists can reduce to zero, or a nominal dimension. Firrings placed at right angles to the joists must have sufficient minimum depth to span the joists without deflection. BRE Digest 221 'Flat roof design: the technical options' recommends a minimum fall of 1:40, subject to this being acceptable for the waterproof layer.

Insulation methods

Cold deck roofs
A cold roof deck (Figure 8.37) incorporates insulation immediately above the ceiling. The ceiling must incorporate an effective vapour check and there must be adequate ventilation of the air space between the insulation and the roof deck. Ventilation apertures must be provided at least at each end of every cavity, equal in total to 0.4 per cent of the roof plan area. The air space

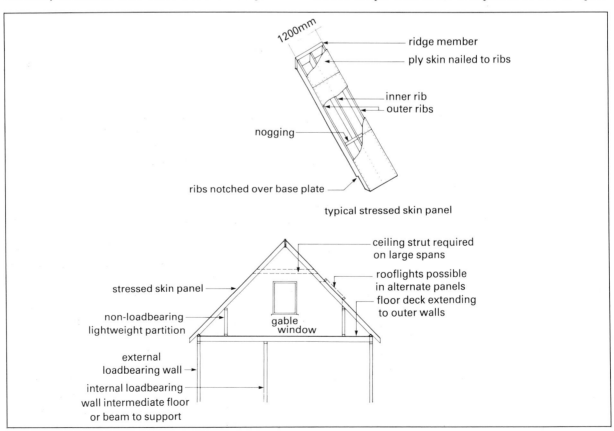

Figure 8.36 *Typical stressed skin panel roof.*

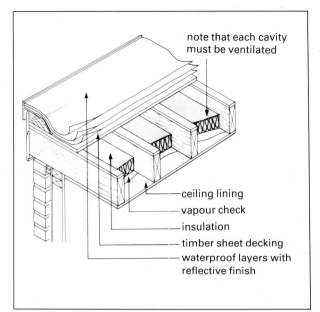

note that each cavity
must be ventilated

———ceiling lining
———vapour check
———insulation
———timber sheet decking
———waterproof layers with
reflective finish

Figure 8.37 *Cold roof deck.*

———ceiling lining
———timber sheet decking
———vapour check
———rigid insulation
———waterproof layers
(with reflective finish)

Figure 8.38 *Warm deck sandwich construction.*

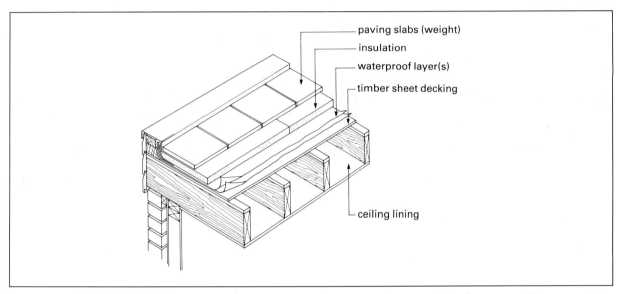

———paving slabs (weight)
———insulation
———waterproof layer(s)
———timber sheet decking

———ceiling lining

Figure 8.39 *'Upside down' construction.*

should be at least 50 mm deep above the insulation. In situations where through ventilation openings are not possible along the joist span, firrings of sufficient depth, fixed at right angles to the joists, can be used. In roofs spanning more than about 9 m consideration should be given to intermediate ventilators through the roof deck or to multi-directional ventilation (or to the use of a warm deck unventilated roof).

The main advantages of cold roof decks are the independence of the waterproof layer, allowing this to be replaced during the life of the building without disruption to the other elements, and the comparative simplicity of the construction. The main disadvantages are the need to seal the vapour check around service entries, and that leaks or faults in the vapour check/ventilation provision may not be apparent prior to serious damage being caused.

Warm deck roofs
By placing the vapour check and the insulation above

the joists and structural deck it is possible to avoid the ventilation requirements of the cold deck roof. Two types of roof are used; warm deck sandwich construction (Figure 8.38) and 'upside down' construction (Figure 8.39).

Sandwich deck construction incorporates a vapour check above the deck and beneath the insulation and has a separate weatherproof membrane on top of the insulation, which must be a rigid type. The main advantage of this type of roof is its ability to accommodate services beneath the structural deck without risk to the vapour check, and the fact that the structural elements are contained within the heated envelope of the building. Its main disadvantages are that leakage of the waterproof membrane may allow water to become trapped in the sandwich construction, possibly causing damage to the insulation or the structural deck, and the possibility of early deterioration of the waterproof membrane due to thermal stresses resulting from the location of the insulation. Specific provision may have to be made for maintenance traffic on the finished roof to avoid damage to the waterproof membrane.

Warm deck 'upside down' construction places the insulation on top of the waterproof layer so that no separate vapour check is required. It therefore requires insulation material which will withstand external conditions and which can be held securely in place against wind forces either by adhesives or by weighting down with ballast or paving slabs. This type of roof has the advantage that the waterproof membrane is protected from the elements and from maintenance traffic and that services can be easily accommodated. The disadvantages are that weighting down can impose increased roof loadings and that the insulation layer must be removed to trace any leakage in the waterproof membrane.

9 Specifying joinery

Sylvester Bone

Sylvester Bone BA AADip RIBA DipTP is a private practice architect and freelance journalist.

This chapter discusses the specification of joinery in broad terms with guidance on relevant British Standards and the strategies to follow to ensure that the finished joinery will be to the anticipated standard. Emphasis is placed on the importance of correct moisture content since a lack of understanding of the behaviour of timber in various conditions of temperature and humidity can lead to problems which can be avoided by careful design and specification.

The term joinery has not always been very clearly defined and covers a very wide range of products and components. BS 6100 'Glossary of building and civil engineering terms' Section 1.0 'General and miscellaneous' defines joinery as the 'assembly of worked timber components and panel products rather than structural timber or cladding'. The revised edition of BS 1186 'Quality of timber and workmanship in joinery' Part 1 'Specification for selection of timber species; moisture content; classification of timber' (scheduled for publication in 1985) specifically excludes softwood flooring, cladding, profiled boards and wood trim. Previous glossaries and earlier editions of the joinery Standard were not so specific as to the items excluded and this led to the requirements in the Standard being used to specify items for which they were not intended and often not suited. Figures 9.1 to 9.7 and Plates 9 to 12 illustrate various items of joinery.

The number of components encompassed within the term joinery is matched by the diversity of materials e.g. timber species, panel products, adhesives, finishes, fixings and ironmongery which go to make up the components. This diversity, coupled with the variations in processing and workmanship can make joinery an area where it is apparently difficult to ensure that the specification will provide the quality of product anticipated by the specifier and his client.

It is necessary at an early stage to decide whether it is possible to specify components available 'off the shelf' or whether some form of non-standard product is required. Manufacturers' 'Standard' ranges (discussed in Chapter 10) include a wide range of designs, sizes and finishes for the most commonly used components. Where 'Standard' components are not available, or not suitable, there are two broad approaches to solving the problem:

- by agreement with a large scale manufacturer to obtain non-standard sizes, finishes etc
- by having the components purpose made by a specialist joinery company to a specific design

The cost of made to order items may be greater than that of standard components but the requirements may dictate the use of non-standard items or the difference may be offset by the convenient arrangement of a design which solves a particular problem. However, the detailed design of joinery is a specialized field and is best undertaken in consultation with a manufacturer. Standard components will often have been developed and tested over a period of years. There is increasing reference to performance standards, and components such as fire resisting doorsets and high performance exterior joinery should have the backing of test evidence of their performance before being offered for sale. It is very unlikely therefore that a 'one off' item, designed without the benefit of such experience, would be as successful in economically meeting the requirements demanded of such items.

The requirements for many items of joinery are laid down in British Standards; these can be divided into three categories covering:

materials
manufacturing and workmanship
performance

Standards should be the specifier's basic tool in ensuring that he obtains the goods required. The specification should refer to the appropriate Standard and to the appropriate clauses within that Standard.

MATERIALS

Timber

BS 1186: Part 1 separates timber into four quality classes by itemizing the allowable size of knots and other characteristics within any piece (described in Chapter 4). The

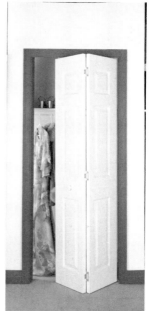 

Figure 9.1 *Doors available ex stock from joinery manufacturers can be used with appropriate ironmongery to satisfy specialist purposes, such as folding doors for wardrobes.* Photograph: Magnet and Southerns Ltd.

appropriate class of timber should always be specified, though the Standard does not require the species to be named. The requirements of the Standard relate to the quality of timber in joinery at the time of handover to the first purchaser. The Standard should not be used to specify general purpose timber. It is the responsibility of the manufacturer to ensure that the timber in the joinery is in accordance with the specification.

Where it is desirable or necessary to specify a species, the standard names given in BS 881 and 589 'Nomenclature of commercial timbers, including sources of supply', should be used. Some common names are used for more than one species or for groups of species, giving rise to the possibility of confusion. The Standard includes those species likely to be available in the UK although trading fluctuations mean that not all timbers included in the Standard will necessarily be available at any one time.

Board materials

Board materials are widely used in joinery, particularly for interior fittings. Many are covered by British or overseas standards; these are outlined in Chapter 2. BS 1186: Part 1 refers to other Standards for board materials (i.e. to BS 1142 Parts 1, 2 and 3 for various types of fibre building board and to BS 5669 for all types of wood chipboard). British made plywood is required to comply with the Association of British Plywood and Veneer Manufacturers Association specification BP 101 1965. Overseas plywood should comply with BS 1455 'Plywood manufactured from tropical hardwood', BS 3444 'Blockboard and laminboard' or with the national standards of the country of origin or to overseas grading rules recognized by the importer.

A new comprehensive Standard for plywood, BS 6566 is due for publication in 1985. This will replace BS 1455 and BS 1186: Part 1 will be amended to refer to the relevant parts of the new Standard.

Figure 9.2 *Entrance doors are available in a wide range of types and timber species ex stock. These hardwood doors are delivered complete and ready for finishing. External doors are often subject to extreme conditions with freezing rain on one side and central heating on the other. The species of timber and its quality should take into account the likely conditions of use.* Photograph: Magnet and Southerns Ltd.

Moisture content

Moisture content is one of the most important aspects of joinery specification. BS 1186: Part 1 gives five levels of moisture content to approximate to the conditions to which joinery will be subjected in use (Table 9.1). However it is important to ensure not only that the joinery is supplied and stored at the correct moisture content but that it is installed into conditions which will maintain it at that level. Joinery installed at too high a moisture content will shrink as it dries out, possibly resulting in distortion and splitting. Joinery supplied at the correct moisture content for the running temperature of the building but installed before the building has been allowed to dry out will first absorb moisture and then, as the building dries, lose it, possibly resulting in distortion. This situation is compounded, when in an effort to remove the moisture in a newly completed building, the heating system is turned on at a high level.

Adhesives

Four British Standards on adhesives are mentioned in BS 1186 'Quality of timber and workmanship in joinery' Part 2 'Quality of workmanship'. These are:

BS 745   Animal glue for wood (joiner's glue), (dry glue: jelly or liquid glue)

BS 1203   Synthetic resin adhesives (phenolic and aminoplastic) for plywood

BS 1204   Synthetic resin adhesives (phenolic and aminoplastic) for wood

Table 9.1 *Moisture content requirements from BS 1186: Part 1*

Position	Use	Average mc %	Max. individual mc reading %
External joinery	Floor level hardwood sills and thresholds	19 ± 3	hardwood 25
	Other external joinery	16 ± 3	softwood 23
Internal joinery	Buildings with intermittent heating	15 ± 2	
	Buildings with continuous heating room temperatures 12–19° C	12 ± 2	20
	Buildings with continuous heating room temperatures 20–24° C	10 ± 2	

Part 1   Gap filling adhesives
Part 2   Close contact adhesives
BS 1444   Cold setting casein adhesive powders for wood (now withdrawn)

The performance of adhesives is tested by destructive tests after immersing test specimens in water at various temperatures, including boiling for specified periods of time. Four categories are defined in BS 1203 'Synthetic resin adhesives for plywood' and BS 1204 'Synthetic resin adhesives for wood'. The categories are:

WBP – Weather and boil proof	joints highly resistant to weather, micro-organisms, cold and boiling water, steam and dry heat
BR – Boil resistant	joints with good resistance to weather and to the boiling water test but fail under very prolonged exposure which WBP types will withstand. Joints will withstand cold water for many years and are highly resistant to attack by micro-organisms
MR – Moisture resistant	joints will withstand full exposure to weather for only a few years, will withstand cold water for a long time, hot water for a limited time but fail in boiling water. Resistant to attack by micro-organisms
INT – Interior	resistant to cold water but not required to withstand attack by micro-organisms

These classifications refer to the performance of the adhesives only. For long term exterior use WBP adhesives should always be specified. When specifying plywood for exterior use it should be remembered that the durability of the timber should also be considered and a plywood manufactured from durable timber, or preservative treatment should be specified.

Since BS 1186: Part 2 was published in 1971, two British Standards on the classification of adhesives have been published. BS 5407 'Classification of adhesives' covers all types of adhesives for all purposes. BS 5442: Part 3 'Adhesives for use with wood' covers glues for wood and wood combinations. It gives specific guidance on glues for applying natural wood veneers, interior and exterior joinery and furniture. The Standard also covers gluing of wood or wood based products to other materials, such as laminated board manufacture and edge veneering on site.

The strength of glued joints depends on a number of factors in addition to the type of adhesive used. These include the moisture content of the timber, the condition and fit of the surfaces to be glued and the conditions for curing the adhesive. Some preservative and finishing treatments can react with adhesives; the manufacturer's

Figure 9.3 *Softwood stairs are available as stock items for standard floor-to-floor heights.* Photograph: Boulton and Paul Joinery Ltd.

Table 9.2 *Guidance on the selection of commonly used adhesives for wood*

BS 5442: Part 3 does not refer to the WBP, BR, MR, INT designations normally used for classifying adhesives for wood. This table gives the adhesive types suitable for use in various categories of exposure

Exposure category	Typical exposure conditions	Adhesive type	
Exterior high hazard	Full exposure to weather	Resorcinol-formaldehyde RF	WBP
		Phenol-formaldehyde PF	WBP
		Phenol/resorcinol formaldehyde PF/RF	WBP
Exterior low hazard	Protected from sun and rain e.g. inside roofs of open sheds and porches	Resorcinol-formaldehyde RF	WBP
		Phenol-formaldehyde PF	WBP
		Phenol/resorcinol formaldehyde PF/RF	WBP
		Melamine/urea formaldehyde MF/UF	BR
		other modified UF	BR
		Urea-formaldehyde UF	MR
		2 pack Poly vinyl acetate PVA*	MR
Interior high hazard	Building with warm and damp conditions where a moisture content of 18% is exceeded and where the glueline temperature can exceed 50° C e.g. laundries and unventilated roof spaces. Chemically polluted atmospheres e.g. chemical works, dye works and swimming pools	Resorcinol-formaldehyde	WBP
		Phenol-formaldehyde	WBP
		Phenol/resorcinol formaldehyde	WBP
		2 pack PVA*	MR
Interior low hazard	Heated and ventilated buildings where the moisture content of the wood will not exceed 18% and where the temperature of the glueline will remain below 50°C e.g. interiors of houses, buildings, halls and churches	Resorcinol-formaldehyde	WBP
		Phenol-formaldehyde	WBP
		Phenol/resorcinol-formaldehyde	WBP
		Melamine/urea-formaldehyde	BR
		other modified UF	BR
		Urea-formaldehyde	MR
		2 pack PVA	MR
		1 pack PVA	INT
		Casein	INT
		Animal†	INT

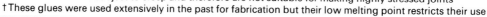

* PVA adhesives are subject to creep and therefore are not suitable for making highly stressed joints
†These glues were used extensively in the past for fabrication but their low melting point restricts their use

Figure 9.4 *Unusual shapes such as these windows require the use of purpose-made joinery. However manufacturers can often fabricate these using standard sections.*

advice should be sought regarding the suitability of various formulations.

In addition to situations where adhesives are used to bond two sections together, there are situations where, traditionally, they may be used as joint fillers. Materials such as white lead paste used to be used in such situations; today, PVA and other synthetic products may fulfil this role.

Preservatives

All external joinery should either be manufactured from durable timber or preservative treatment should be specified. If a durable timber is chosen then sapwood should be excluded in the specification. BS 1186 Part 1 gives details of common joinery timbers and states whether preservative treatment is required. The Appendix includes the durability classifications of some common timbers.

BS 5589 'Code of practice for the preservation of timber' defines the preservative treatments suitable for joinery. Most joinery timber is treated using organic solvent preservatives (see Chapter 3). Double vacuum treatment should be specified for maximum protection although the minimum treatment currently required by the NHBC is a three minute dip. Organic solvents are used because they provide the required degree of protection, but being spirit based do not increase the moisture content of the timber. The treated timber or components should be stored under cover to allow the solvent to evaporate before painting, gluing or similar processing is undertaken. Joinery can be treated with

Plates 30 – 32 This house and office at Danbury, Essex emphasizes the use of simple roof structures. The kitchen and dining area of double storey height leads up to the living area on the first floor. The collared roof is the predominant feature of this area.
The house is built in two sections with a glazed bridge over a stream linking the two halves.
Architect: **Robert Hutson**
Photographs: **Morley Von Sternberg.**

Plate 33 *(Above)* Clear finished Oregon pine structural timbers with tongued and grooved redwood boarding forming the ceiling of the vestibule of St. John Ogilvie Church, Bourtreehill, Irvine New Town. This part of the Church is of relatively conventional design.

Plate 34 *(Right)* However, on entering the church itself one is confronted with a complex assemblage of interconnecting timber girders. These are clear finished Oregon pine set off by poppy red stained tongued and grooved redwood boarding behind. All timber to timber and steel connections are bolted, with exposed 50mm diameter washers painted poppy red.

Plate 35 *(Opposite)* The church hall is connected to the main church and is of similar but less extrovert design. Here glulam beams form the hip rafters with a glulam ring beam supporting a glazed rooflight.

St. John Ogilvie Church, Bourtreehill, Irvine

Architect: Gerard Connolly Architects
Structural engineers: A M Sidey and associates
Quantity surveyors: Foote and McBride
Photographs: Keith Gibson.

Plate 36 *(Previous)* The Barbican Concert Hall features a Canadian hemlock stage lining and canopy. The acoustic boxes at the sides of the hall are veneered with aspen.

Plate 37 *(Above)* End grain European redwood blocks are used for the flooring in a number of foyer areas throughout the Barbican Centre.

Plate 38 *(Right)* Acoustic doors and wall linings in the theatre are manufactured from Peruvian Walnut veneers. The design of the Brazilian mahogany push plates and pull handles are reflected in the light fittings and loudspeaker covers housed in the columns between the doors.

Barbican Centre

Architects: Chamberlin Powell and Bon
Structural engineers: Ove Arup and Partners
Quantity surveyors: Davis Bellfield and Everest
Photographs: John Laing Construction Ltd.

Plates 39 – 40 An ingenious system of sliding cupboards screens the kitchen, cloakrooms and dining area, Shanghai Commercial Bank, London.

Plates 41 – 42 Non-coniferous trees represent about 165,000 million cubic metres of growing timber. The tropical forests provide much of the hardwood timber used today. With careful management and replanting, the supply is endless. The photographs show the Amazon forest in Brazil.

Photographs: United Nations 152, 683 + 4. George Love.

Plates 43 – 44 The Scandinavian forests are cultivated and harvested to provide a continuing supply of softwood timber to northern Europe. The photographs show forests in Finland.

Photographs: Swedish Finnish Timber Council.

Plate 45 *(Opposite)* Most of the softwood constructional timber used in the UK is imported, mainly from Scandinavia, Russia and North America.

Photograph: Mallinson-Denny (UK) Ltd.

Plates 46 – 47 Hardwoods in the UK may be British grown (plate 46) or imported (plate 47).

Photographs: Mallinson-Denny (UK) Ltd.

Plate 48 *(Right)* TRADA has undertaken work for UNIDO to encourage the construction of bridges using prefabricated modular wooden sections utilizing indigenous species.

Plate 49 *(Below)* The bridge components are manufactured locally and 'launched' into position without the need for cranes.

1 SYCAMORE

2 BIRCH, EUROPEAN

3 WHITEWOOD, EUROPEAN

4 AMERICAN ASH

5 KAUVULA

6 BEECH, UNSTEAMED

7 LIMBA

8 PAU MARFIM

9 REDWOOD, EUROPEAN

10 OAK, EUROPEAN-QUARTERED

11 IDIGBO

12 OBECHE

13 JELUTONG

14 MAPLE, ROCK

15 ASH, EUROPEAN

16 RAMIN

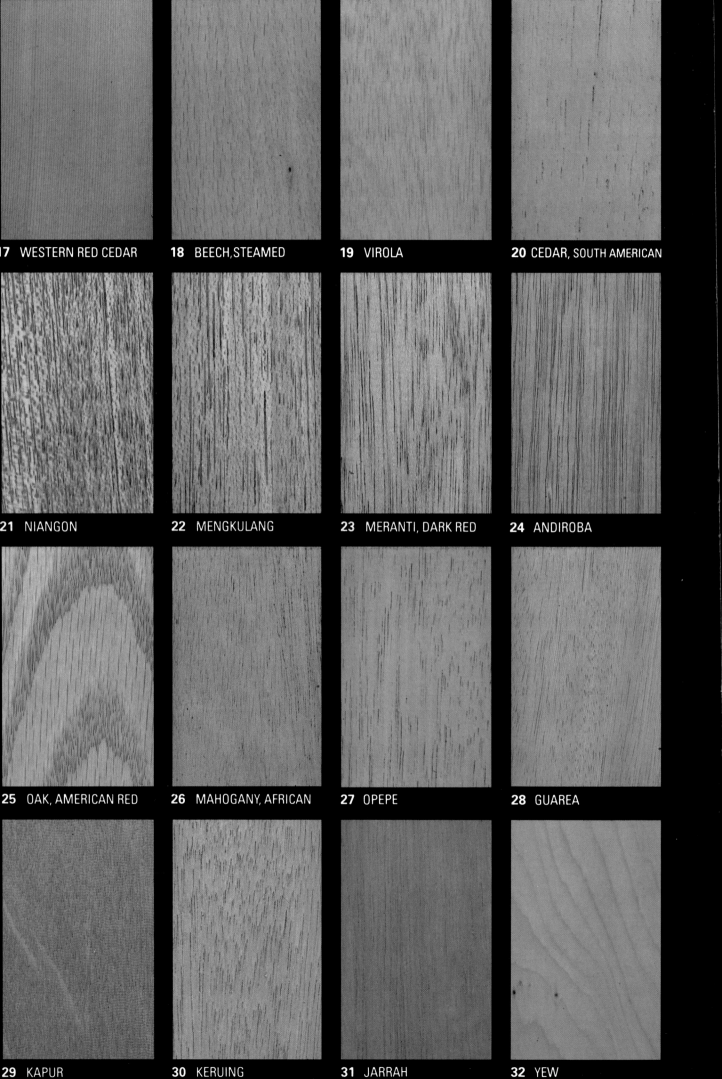

17 WESTERN RED CEDAR   **18** BEECH,STEAMED   **19** VIROLA   **20** CEDAR, SOUTH AMERICAN

21 NIANGON   **22** MENGKULANG   **23** MERANTI, DARK RED   **24** ANDIROBA

25 OAK, AMERICAN RED   **26** MAHOGANY, AFRICAN   **27** OPEPE   **28** GUAREA

29 KAPUR   **30** KERUING   **31** JARRAH   **32** YEW

33 AMERICAN CHERRY

34 DOUGLAS FIR

35 MAHOGANY, AMERICAN

36 ABURA

37 PARANA PINE

38 AFRORMOSIA

39 ELM, ENGLISH

40 MERANTI, LIGHT RED

41 HEMLOCK, WESTERN

42 CHESTNUT, SWEET

43 FREIJO

44 OAK, AMERICAN WHITE

45 GREENHEART

46 AGBA

47 WALNUT, AFRICAN

48 OAK, JAPANESE

49 IROKO

50 AFZELIA

51 WALNUT, EUROPEAN

52 WALNUT, AMERICAN

53 MERBAU

54 NYATOH

55 TEAK

56 UTILE

57 DANTA

58 GEDU NOHOR

59 MAKORE

60 SAPELE

61 KARRI

62 ROSEWOOD, INDIAN

63 EKKI

64 WENGE

Figure 9.5 *Kitchen units have developed in post-war years from basic joinery items for site finishing into highly finished factory-made components. They are available in a wide range of finishes.* Photograph: Boulton and Paul Joinery Ltd.

Figure 9.6 *Joinery includes specialist items, such as laboratory benches. The choice of timber species is particularly important; in this case the bench tops are iroko.* Photograph: Cygnet Joinery Ltd.

preservatives either after assembly or as component parts. Treating the individual parts has the advantage that the preservative can penetrate the end grain of joints which will later be hidden. However it is important to remember that preservative treatment provides a protective 'envelope' and that all machining must be carried out before treatment. Cutting or machining after treatment can expose untreated timber. Remedial application of preservative to cut areas is not as effective as a dip or pressure treatment and can downgrade the quality of the protection.

Waterborne preservative treatments are less suitable for joinery since the timber has to be re-dried after treatment. Some movement of the timber may occur during this process and precise components may need final machining after treatment. However such machining can breech the protective envelope of treated timber.

Finishes

The range of finishes available for timber is discussed in Chapter 3. BS 6150 'Code of practice for painting of buildings' includes not only information on conventional paints but also on natural finishes for wood – varnishes, decorative wood stains and exterior wood stains. The Standard includes guidance on preservative treatments and their compatibility with various types of finishes. This aspect should be checked with the manufacturers before preservative treatment and finishing systems are specified. The Standard includes tables on paint systems for wood including window joinery, external hardwood sills, doors and frames (interior and exterior), together with other items which are not usually classified as joinery. A table on natural finishing systems for wood includes varnishes and stain finishes for interior and exterior use with specific reference to exterior windows, doors and frames. Recommendations are also made on finishing systems for interior joinery, linings and fitments.

There are three British Standards which relate to primers of various types for wood; BS 4756 'Ready mixed priming paints for woodwork', BS 5082 'Water thinned priming paints for wood' and BS 5358 'Specification for low-lead solvent-thinned priming paints for woodwork'. External joinery components are usually supplied with a coat of primer for paint or with one coat of exterior wood stain for finishing on site. It should be borne in mind that exterior wood stains allow the moisture content of the timber to alter more rapidly than paint finishes. The design of the component should take this into account – it is not always satisfactory to alter the finishing specification for a component without taking into account other implications. For example, exterior wood stains do not provide sufficient protection to linseed oil putty and alternative glazing methods must be used e.g. proprietary dry glazing systems or non-setting mastic with beads.

The Building Regulations may require flame retardant treatments to be specified for internal timber panelling or lining. Flame retardant treatments are discussed in Chapter 3. They may be impregnation treatments, in which case the finishing treatment specified must be compatible with the flame retardant treatment and at the very least should not degrade the flame retardant properties imparted to the substrate. Alternatively flame retardant surface finishes may be specified. These are available in the form of paints and clear surface coatings which meet the requirements of Class 1 to BS 476 'Fire tests on building materials and structures' Part 7 'Surface spread of flame tests for materials' and Class O of the Building Regulations. Information on specific treatments which meet the performance requirements is available in the TRADA Wood Information Sheet series.

Glazing

When specifying glazed joinery items the method of glazing, type and thickness of glass and double glazed units and the type of finish to be applied to the joinery must be considered together. BS 6262 'Code of practice for glazing for buildings' includes information on glass types, glazing materials and the interaction between them. The size of glazed elements affects security, ease of cleaning and user safety. BS CP 153 'Windows and rooflights' Part 1 'Cleaning and safety' lays down recommendations for these components. The Glass and Glazing Federation or glass manufacturers can advise.

Ironmongery and fixings

The selection of ironmongery should take into account factors such as:

strength – hinges and fittings must be adequate to take the weight of and provide restraint to the timber elements. The ironmongery itself must be of sufficient strength and durability to meet the likely conditions of use and the safety and security requirements of the building.

dimensions – the ironmongery must be of suitable

Figure 9.7 *Ecclesiastical joinery is another specialist area. These pews at St Luke's Church, Cannock, are manufactured from English oak.*

dimensions to fit in or on the timber members without removing so much of the section that its strength is impaired. This is particularly relevant in the specification of mortices for locks where lock blocks are included in, for example, flush doors or the jambs of glazed doors.

compatibility – items such as door locks and knob sets must be compatible with each other. Fire resisting doorsets are tested with essential ironmongery installed, this should not be changed without reference to the manufacturer.

ergonomics – correct fixing heights and distance from e.g. walls and frames, must be considered in addition to aspects such as the forces required to operate.

In order for joinery components to perform satisfactorily they must be fixed on site in the correct way. The manufacturer's advice should be sought for proprietary components and the fixing of purpose made joinery should be considered as an intrinsic part of the overall design (Figure 9.8).

The fixings and ironmongery used can affect building operations. Lift-off doors, knock-down furniture, easily removed cover strips etc can simplify storage and decoration and can sometimes allow alternative building sequences. Large items of purpose made joinery may need to be prefabricated in the joinery shop and dismantled for re-erection on site. The design and choice of fixings must take this into account.

WORKMANSHIP AND MANUFACTURE

BS 1186 'Quality of timber and workmanship in joinery' Part 2 'Quality of workmanship' was first pub-

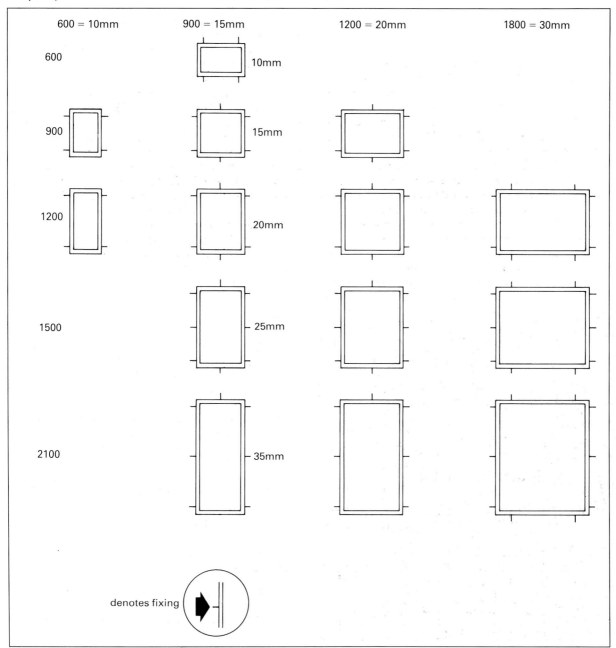

Figure 9.8 *Typical window fixings. (Doors and windows with hardwood sills up to 1200 mm wide are commonly not fixed through the sill.)*

lished in 1955 to provide a more precise alternative to phrases traditionally included in specifications such as 'in a workmanlike manner' or 'to the architect's satisfaction'. The present Standard was published in 1971 and is currently undergoing revision. The Standard in its present form defines the requirements for the fit of joints and the tolerances allowed. These apply at the time of manufacture and despatch from the factory when the parts are at the moisture contents defined in BS 1186: Part 1. The tolerances on joints which permit movement, such as those in various types of panelling, are defined in addition to allowable gaps between, for example, a door or sash and its surrounding frame.

Requirements for the gluing of joints and the production of laminated members and finger joints are covered but the Standard is not specific in relation to acceptable levels of surface finish for joinery components.

Mass produced joinery components are generally manufactured to comply with the requirements of BS 1186: Part 2. The approach to be adopted in procuring purpose made joinery where more specific requirements may be needed is discussed in the section on specification strategies. Standards relating to specific items of joinery may include details of manufacturing and workmanship requirements; some of these are discussed below.

Doors

The dimensional requirements for doors and doorsets are laid down in BS 4787 'Internal and external wood doorsets, door leaves and frames' Part 1 'Dimensional requirements'. This gives permissible deviations on the work sizes of components at the time of handover:

doorsets	± 2 mm on height	± 2 mm on width
door leaf	± 1.5 mm on height	± 1.5 mm on width
	$+1$ mm -2 mm on thickness	

Permissible deviations on rebate sizes, clearances etc are also included:

Deviations from plane:
bow in the length   4 mm
cup (horizontal bow)   2 mm
twist (deviation from plane)   6 mm

Deviation from squareness:
1.5 mm in 500 mm

Figure 9.9 *Performance testing of windows. The test rig can be used for air and water penetration tests.*

Windows

There are currently no British Standards on the dimensional tolerances for windows. However, the British Woodworking Federation in their performance standard for wood windows allows manufacturing tolerances of:

height and width ±3 mm

deviation from straight of jambs, sill, transoms, mullions:

      3 mm up to 1200 mm in length

      5 mm from 1200 to 2400 mm in length

difference in length of diagonals of outer frame:

    frame width plus height up to 1800 mm   3 mm

           over 1800, up to 3000 mm   5 mm

               over 3000 mm   15 mm

PERFORMANCE

There is an increasing trend for components to be specified and for British Standards to be drafted not in terms of the materials used in their manufacture and the standards of workmanship employed but for the component to reach a required level of performance. There are some performance standards published which relate to joinery and others are likely to follow. In some cases there may be test methods laid down for components but, as yet, no guidance on satisfactory performance levels related to test results.

Windows

Air and water penetration tests on windows are carried out to the requirements of BS 5368: Parts 1 and 2 and wind resistance tests to Part 3 (Figure 9.9). BS 6375: Part 1 'Classification for weathertightness' classifies windows according to the results of tests carried out. Windows should be specified by calculating the appropriate design wind pressure (to CP 3 Chapter 5: Part 2) for the location of the windows and selecting the appropriate test pressure class. The desired performance for water tightness and air permeability can then be selected. The BWF performance standard sets out three comparative performance levels for windows; high performance, energy saving and EJMA – based upon BS 6375 test criteria. Windows sold under the descriptions listed should conform to the levels shown. However descriptions such as

REQUIREMENT	ENVIRONMENT		MAXIMUM DEVIATION		
	Temp °C	RH%	Location	mm	
Temperature Humidity Differential	28 one 13 other	40 side 70 side	Leaf A D B C	7.5 7.5	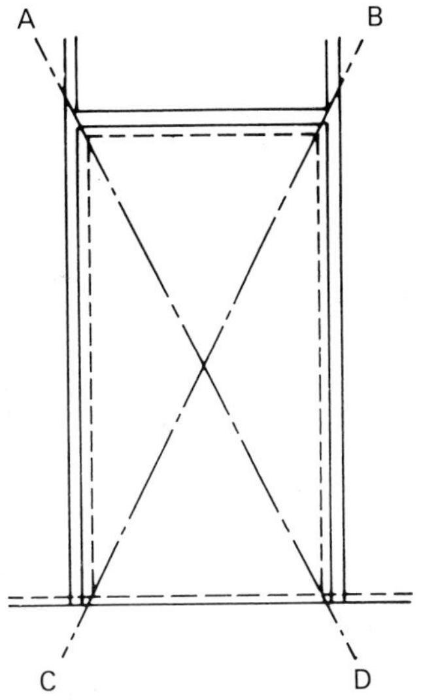
Cup & bow					
Twist	28 one 13 other	40 side 70 side	Any corner in relation to the other three	10.0	
			For fire resistant doorsets	3.0	

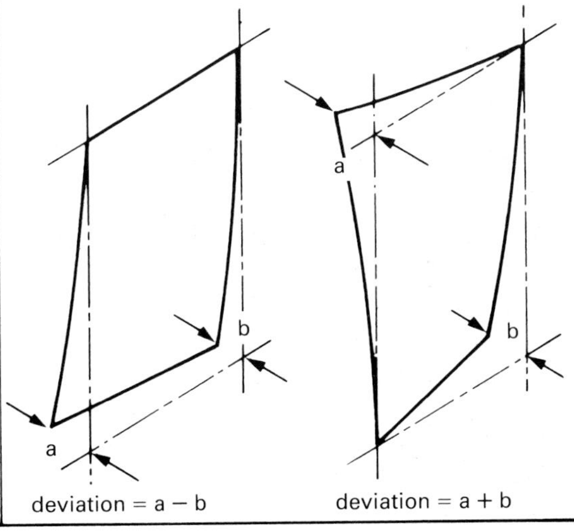

Figure 9.10 *DOE Property Services Agency Method of Building Group pass limits for hygrothermal tests on doors.*

Figure 9.11 *Testing the fire resistance of doorsets.*

'high performance' should be backed by test evidence as to the actual levels of performance achieved.

Doors

The test methods for measuring the squareness and flatness of doors are laid down in BS 5277 and BS 5278. BS 5369 'Methods of testing doors: behaviour under humidity variations of door leaves placed in successive uniform climates' sets the tests to be undertaken. It does not, however, set any performance levels. The DOE Property Services Agency Method of Building group has defined pass levels for hygrothermal tests on doors (Figure 9.10).

Fire performance

The requirements for fire performance of building components are laid down in the Building Regulations. These may include restrictions on the ignitability of materials, surface spread of flame properties (discussed in Chapter 3 and under Finishes) and fire resistance. Fire resistance is most often required for structural elements but is also necessary for some joinery components, particularly fire resisting doorsets (leaf, frame and essential ironmongery). BS 476 'Fire tests on building materials and structures' Part 8 'Test methods and criteria for the fire resistance of elements of building construction' lays down international standard fire conditions which are used to compare the performance of different constructions (Figure 9.11). BS 476 Part 8 is undergoing revision and will be replaced by four separate parts. Doors and partitions will appear in Part 22, although it is unlikely that the revision will radically alter the performance requirements. The current Standard defines four parameters:

Stability	the doorset must not collapse and must remain effective as a significant barrier to fire spread
Integrity	the doorset must not have holes or gaps in the cold condition or develop cracks and fissures during the test such as to cause an oven dry fibre cotton pad to ignite
Insulation	the temperature of any point on the door or frame must not rise by more than $180°C$ above the ambient temperature, nor shall the average temperature of the door rise by more than $140°C$ above ambient
Radiation	there is no criterion of failure relating to the amount of radiation emitting from the unexposed face of a door. However, this can be measured and included in the test report to allow the safe storage distance for materials to be computed

The fire resistance of a doorset when tested to BS 476: Part 8 will therefore be expressed in minutes for the three criteria, with an additional reference to the maximum amount of radiant heat measured at a certain position. In practice the Building Regulations require only stability and integrity; for example, a half-hour fire resisting doorset will be a minimum of 30/30 minutes.

Specifications for fire resisting doorsets should therefore state the required periods of stability and integrity (and insulation and radiation if appropriate). Relevant parts of BS 5588 'Fire precautions in the design and construction of buildings' refer only to integrity and BS 476 Part 22 will reflect this change. The manufacturer or supplier should be able to provide test evidence that the required performance to BS 476: Part 8 has been met.

The Building Regulations (England and Wales) 1976 and the Building Regulations (Northern Ireland) 1977 refer to the BS 476: Part 8 1972 procedure as the main test method, but still allow the use of doorsets tested to the earlier and less stringent standard, BS 476: Part 1 1953, provided they were tested prior to 31 August 1973. The 1980 amendment to the GLC Building (Constructional) Byelaws allows parity between Part 1 and Part 8. The Building Standards (Scotland) Consolidated Regulations still refer only to BS 476: Part 1.

In an ideal world every variation from the tested prototype should be evaluated by test. However this is not practicable, either economically or with the availability of test facilities. Information is available from TRADA giving guidance on modifications which are likely to be deemed acceptable to the regulatory authorities. These cover modifications to size, essential hardware, additional furniture, intumescent seals, facings, glazing and frame.

VERIFICATION

In principle a designer should aim to ensure that anything shown on the drawings or specified is verifiable. It is easy to forget that 'light colour', 'rounded', 'hand carved', 'kiln dried' or even 'true' are not really verifiable on their own without measurements or qualifications. The requirements in British Standards are all intended to be verifiable: BS 0, which describes how standards are to be written states:

'Verification of compliance with specified requirements should always be possible within a reasonable cost. Specifications should be drafted as if a third party were to be called upon to verify compliance.'

It is economic for manufacturers of mass produced joinery to have samples of their products tested to performance standards but for relatively small numbers or one-off items the costs can become excessive in relation to the numbers produced.

Some aspects relating to joinery specification are relatively easy to check; others may require laboratory tests and are likely to be needed only in the event of a dispute. Manufacturers and suppliers of joinery items are subject to normal consumer legislation concerning the supply of goods etc.

Identification of timber species can be carried out by specialist laboratories, such as TRADA and the Building Research Establishment, Princes Risborough Laboratory, or by timber consultants. A sample will need to be provided for laboratory identification of species. In some cases, where groups of very similar species are marketed together, it may not be possible, or even necessary, to identify the individual species. However, the new edition of BS 1186: Part 1 does not require that the timber species be named, since the emphasis is placed on meeting the requirements regarding the class of timber specified, rather than on species.

Verification of the timber class and end use category

as laid down in BS 1186: Part 1 is largely a matter of inspection of knots and defects on finished joinery. These are defined in the Standard and should be measurable.

Each type of board material has its own set of tests to verify the properties claimed for it (see Chapter 2 and list of British Standards). If there is doubt about the identity of the board material, manufacturers will usually identify a sample without making a charge. Tests on the glues used, for example in the manufacture of plywood, can be undertaken by specialist laboratories.

The moisture content of timber or board materials can easily be checked by a moisture meter but remember that the presence of chemicals, glues, preservatives etc can affect the readings (see Chapter 4). BS 1186: Part 1 recommends random checks at the time of handover and lays down the procedure for establishing moisture content in the event of a dispute.

Verification of preservative treatment is a difficult process. Chemical tests to detect the presence of preservatives may need to be carried out in the laboratory since contaminants on building sites can affect results. Tests to discover the penetration and amount of preservative present need sophisticated analytical equipment and complex techniques. Such tests can be performed by TRADA and other specialist laboratories but the best way of ensuring that preservative treatment has been carried out is to witness the process or obtain a certificate of treatment from the processor (see Chapter 3). Finishing treatments should be checked by inspection on site but, in the event of a dispute, samples can be sent for examination under the microscope and chemical analysis.

Compliance with performance specifications is usually verifiable by examination of the test evidence. Manufacturers who have had tests carried out on their products will hold test certificates or reports. Designers are normally only involved in checking that standard tests have been carried out or in comparing results where testing is undertaken against a scale of varying requirements.

Third party quality assurance schemes, where the manufacturing process and product quality is monitored by an organization other than that producing the goods, help the designer with the most difficult aspect of control when he knows that the client could not afford to have the product tested. For example, a fire resistance test to BS 476: Part 8 will involve the destruction of at least two doorsets (one mounted opening into, and one out of, the furnace). TRADA operates a quality assurance scheme for fire resisting doors and doorsets where manufacturers agree to produce doors under controlled conditions and are subject to checks by TRADA inspectors. Doors produced under this scheme are permanently marked with a colour coded plastic plug inserted into the door leaf. The plugs are coded according to the performance of the doorset and whether intumescent seals are necessary to achieve the performance rating.

The British Board of Agrément is concerned with the testing, assessment and certification of products for the construction industry. The subjects for assessment are usually new or innovatory products although some existing products may be assessed if the need arises. Some

large public sector clients arrange their own quality assurance schemes for sophisticated manufacturing processes producing standard joinery components, but generally there are few quality assurance schemes for joinery. Manufacturers may offer their own guarantee of conformity with British Standards. The British Woodworking Federation has set performance and manufacturing standards for its members and products may be offered as complying with these standards.

SPECIFICATION STRATEGIES

A specification is a basis for setting acceptable quality levels and their verification; it is also intended to prevent misunderstandings and to forestall problems. It can be looked at as having three levels:

- the naming of a specific product
- the reference to a standard set of requirements (such as British Standards)
- specific requirements for the job of a higher or different standard from those laid down in British Standards.

It is at this third level that a specification eventually reaches its limit of usefulness; for example it cannot cope with the finer points of appearance or craftsmanship or avoid the misunderstandings which can occur between drawing office, joinery shop and site. When high class purpose made joinery is required, the designer must look to other parts of the contractual arrangements to help where the specification falls short. The quality of the product and the service will depend above all on the joinery firm selected for the job. Previous experience of the firm, references and completed work will form the basis of selection, but for a large order the type of machinery and equipment, quality control in the works, the workforce and order book may all need to be checked. Main contractors can provide assistance in the selection of sub-contractors; some will interview each sub-contractor before selecting those that are to tender, and the main contractor should be given the opportunity to vet sub-contractors. Joinery is almost always fitted towards the end of a job and a sub-contractor who does not deliver on time will cause delay to the whole project and incur additional costs to the main contractor.

For high quality joinery work timber and veneers can be selected in the yard before the joinery is made. When repeated items are ordered a sample can be inspected before the rest of the batch is completed, remembering that the others may not be exactly like the sample. For larger jobs the manufacturer should be asked to include the full range of timber variations and defects that are likely to occur within the whole batch. It is common practice for the designer to inspect partially completed work in the joinery shop where alteration can still be made and finishes agreed.

A further consideration is the relative value of labour (including machining) and materials in different types of joinery. One-off fixtures with specially applied veneers or laminates and shop drawings made from the designer's details will have a relatively high labour content – possibly 70 per cent of the cost being labour and only 30 per cent materials. In these cases the designer should concentrate on the standard of workmanship – it does not make sense for the manufacturer to risk having an item rejected for poor materials when labour is the greater cost. At the opposite end of the scale, mass produced joinery may have only a 30 per cent labour content and the quality of the material, which may account for more than 70 per cent of the cost, is therefore a more critical item.

A common complaint from manufacturers when purpose made joinery is specified is that designers don't necessarily show the relevant details on the drawings. The joinery manufacturer will look first at the drawings and will consult the written specification if the required information does not appear. Materials, dimensions, fixings, ironmongery and glazing should all be shown on the drawings. Specific details related to the construction of the items should only be shown if they are vital to the design. Such aspects of production should be agreed with the manufacturer since the details used may depend on the type of machinery available. Otherwise the draughtsman in the joinery shop has to decide what the designer really considers essential and recast the design to suit the processes in that particular company.

STORAGE, PROTECTION AND HANDLING

The protection, storage and handling of joinery should be specified in detail as British Standards are not specific on this aspect. Manufacturers generally regard this as a contractor's problem and the contractors who may not have allowed for it in competitive tendering are reluctant to incur extra expense later on.

The first point to deal with is the protection to be provided before delivery. Components which are to be painted should be primed before delivery to site. A minimum of one coat of clear finish should be applied before delivery. Protection should be applied to stairtreads and thresholds etc. For some joinery items, other forms of casing, wrapping and protection can be specified and the contractor can be instructed not to remove it until a particular stage in the job (Figure 9.12). However this assumes that the item has already been found acceptable by inspection at the works.

The second point to specify is the storage of joinery (and this should include how, where and when not to store it). The contractor may wish to take early delivery but until the site is fit to receive the joinery it is better to delay manufacture or to arrange storage elsewhere. When joinery is delivered to site it is not sufficient to simply state 'adequate protection'. Joinery has been specified at an appropriate moisture content for its intended use; storing internal joinery outside will allow the moisture content to increase so that the original specification becomes meaningless. A storage shed or space within the building which is dry and can be heated may be a requirement for joinery at a low moisture content.

Figure 9.12 *Windows may be supplied wrapped in polyethylene.* Photograph: Magnet and Southerns Ltd.

EXAMPLE SPECIFICATIONS

Proprietary softwood window

Overall sizes and profiles to be in accordance with schedule on drawing no....

Joinery sections to be manufacturer's standard profiles. Timber to be softwood in accordance with BS 1186: Part 1: 1985,* class 3, apart from sashes and beads which are to be class 2. Moisture content of timber to be 16 per cent ± 3.

All timber to be preservative treated in accordance with BS 5589: 1978 Section 2, with organic solvents by the double vacuum process after all machining has been carried out. Any subsequent cutting on site must be treated with a liberal application of organic solvent preservative. All joints to be glued with WBP adhesive to BS 1204: 1979.

Workmanship to be in accordance with BS 1186: Part 2: 1971.

Windows to be delivered with one coat of decorative stain (type to be selected by the window manufacturer and approved by the architect) to all exposed surfaces, glazing rebates and back faces of the frame.

Window performance
The windows will be required to comply with BS 6375: Part 1: 1983; air permeability 300 Pa, water tightness 300 Pa and wind resistance 1200 Pa. Evidence of satisfactory tests to be provided by the manufacturer.

Protection
Windows are to be delivered with adequate protection which is to be retained until they are fixed. Storage on site to be in accordance with the manufacturer's recommendations, under cover and away from ground contact. Finishing coats of stain to be applied as soon as practicable after fixing.

(NOTE: assuming windows are to be glazed on site, the glazing method specified should be checked for compatibility with the finish selected. Glazing should be in accordance with the recommendations of BS 6262: 1982.)

Internal wood stair – straight flight

Staircase to be the dimensions shown on drawing no....

Stair to be of softwood suitable for painting and shall be fabricated in accordance with BS 585: Part 1: 1984. Timber, plywood and adhesives to comply with section 4 of that Standard.

The moisture content of the timber to be 12 per cent ± 2 at time of delivery.

Fixing to be in accordance with the recommendations given in Appendix A of BS 585: 1984.

Site storage prior to fixing to be under cover and in such conditions that the delivered moisture content of the timber is maintained. Adequate protection must be given to all parts of the stair and balustrade after fixing. Nosings to be protected with timber battens securely held in place. Staircase must not be fixed until the building is sufficiently dried out to maintain its moisture content at the specified figure.

(NOTE: Design of stair should comply with BS 5395: Part 1: 1977 and balustrade should comply with BS 6180: 1982.)

Specialist hardwood external glazed screen

Overall dimensions and profiles to be in accordance with drawings nos....

Timber to be American mahogany (*Swietenia* species), free from sapwood and graded in accordance with BS 1186: Part 1: 1985, Class CSH. Representative samples of timber to be approved for quality and colour prior to commencement.

The moisture content of the timber to be 16 per cent ± 3.

Workmanship to be in accordance with BS 1186: Part 2: 1971. Machined surfaces to be suitable for the intended finish; finger jointing of members will not be accepted.

All joints to be glued with WBP adhesive in accordance with BS 1204: 1979.

The component is to be finished with one coat of 'proprietary clear finish' to all exposed surfaces, backs of rebates and beads and the back face of the frame before delivery.

The component is to be delivered with adequate protection, which is to be maintained until it is fixed in position and final finishing coats are applied. Site storage is to be under cover and in such conditions that the delivered moisture content of the component is maintained.

(NOTE: The glazing method should be specified and reference made to compliance with the recommendations given in BS 6262: 1982.)

---

* The revised edition of BS 1186: Part 1: is due for publication in 1985.

10 Design and manufacture of mass production joinery

Peter J Carr

Peter J Carr is managing director of the John Carr Group of Companies. He worked in the sawmill industry in British Columbia and Finland and for a timber importer in the UK before joining the John Carr Group in 1960. He has been a member of the British Woodworking Federation executive since its inception and is chairman of the Window Marketing and Commercial Committee.

The emergence of large-scale production joinery companies has been a feature of the industry over the last 15 to 20 years. Prior to this most companies were small to medium size joinery manufacturers essentially concentrating on batch production of designs to individual customers' specific requirements.

This pattern of demand placed considerable restraints on the manufacturer as quite clearly he was unable to utilize his resources of plant and buildings effectively if constant changes were required in order to comply with individual requirements. Difference in component size was one major variable; others included ironmongery, which often meant changes of detailing to accommodate the requirements of different manufacturers' ranges, and priming coat variations. Specifications requiring lead based, lead free, oil based, acrylic or aluminium primer all made the task of applying priming coats expensive as the lack of continuity meant that the operation could not be mechanized. The range of timber sections and profiles created many variations and manufacturers found the cost of setting up and special tooling an extravagant cost to bear.

The growth in demand for joinery products in the late sixties and early seventies led to a realization by some companies that the constraints of limited batch production were too restricting and that industrialization and mass production provided the opportunity for improved product performance as well as for expansion. The introduction of performance standards placed the onus on the manufacturer to design and test his product to conform with the levels of performance specified; this is economic for large numbers of similar components.

The large manufacturers now dominate the market in terms of output with a fairly substantial gap between them and the medium and small size manufacturers who provide much of the batch production requirements and the outright specials. This is illustrated by the structure of the British Woodworking Federation (BWF); the representative body for the industry. Whereas there are some 500 members in the architectural and general joinery section, there are only 40 in the windows section and ten in the doors section.

It is estimated that the window manufacturing capacity of the five largest companies accounts for around 75 per cent of the timber window production in the country. The production capacity of a large window manufacturer may be upwards of $\frac{1}{4}$ million items per year. Similarly, out of the approximately 7.5 million doors made in the UK, 80 per cent are made by six companies. Some of these companies have a capacity in excess of one million doors per annum – a daily production of more than 4000 doors, or one door every 7.2 seconds during an eight-hour day. Figure 10.1 illustrates the scale of operations of the large joinery manufacturing companies.

Most manufacturers, other than those who specialize in doors, produce a wide range of joinery components, e.g. windows, doors, staircases and kitchen units. Extensive ranges are available within each component type. Many major joinery manufacturers also produce a variety of other items such as bedroom fitments, timber panelling and mouldings. The production of standard items allows the manufacturer to increase his output whilst maintaining quality control of materials and processing. This provides many advantages to the specifier in terms of improved availability and quality, reliability of service and value for money.

WINDOWS

The earliest form of standardization in the industry was shortly after the Second World War when the English Joinery Manufacturers Association (EJMA, forerunner of the BWF) produced a design for a basic wood window which would satisfy, at modest cost, the needs of the house building industry in its attempt to provide large estates of housing to cope with the effect of the War. This window is still being produced today, albeit in rather modified forms (Figure 10.2). There have been changes in the ironmongery used and, most important of all, windows are now fully preservative treated to avoid decay. However, the basic timber sections and sizes remain similar although the window in its original form satisfies no more than sheltered conditions.

The move towards specification by performance allows manufacturers to design their own profiles which will meet the required performance levels (see Chapter

9). A typical high performance window is shown in Figure 10.3. The BWF has prepared a suggested performance standard for its members' wood windows which requires frames to be Class 3 and opening lights and glazing beads to be Class 2 of BS 1186 Part 1. The classes are described in Chapter 4. This BWF standard applies to windows of maximum dimensions as shown in Table 10.1

Table 10.1 *Maximum overall dimensions of windows in BWF standard*

	Width mm	Height mm
OPENING LIGHTS		
Side hung	600	1350
Side hung projecting	600	1150
Top hung and top hung projecting*	1150	1150
Horizontal pivot	1150	1150
FIXED LIGHTS†	2350	1450

*Top hung projecting windows are not suitable for cleaning from the inside for opening lights greater than 760 mm in height.

†The two maximum dimensions for width and height shall not occur together

Range of sizes

Generally timber windows are available in three size ranges; the equal divide range, the imperial range and the modular or metric dimensionally co-ordinated range. However, many manufacturers produce windows outside these size ranges; these may be available from stock or to order. Manufacturers' catalogues should be consulted to check on the availability of items in the sizes required. BS 644 Part 1 'Wood casement windows', last published in 1951 and now withdrawn, is being revised. The new edition will include the equal divide and modular metric size ranges.

Figure 10.1 *Aerial view of John Carr Joinery Sales Ltd, Doncaster.* Photograph: John Carr Joinery Sales Ltd.

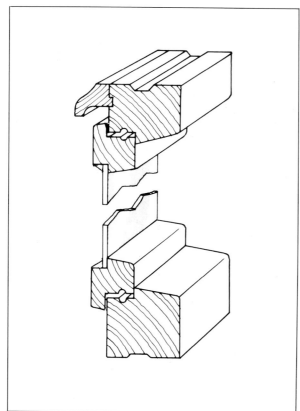

Figure 10.2 *Typical section of EJMA window.*

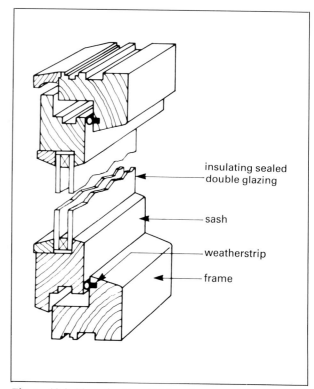

insulating sealed double glazing

sash

weatherstrip

frame

Figure 10.3 *Typical section of high performance window.*

156

Equal divide range

A range of metric sizes with widths based on multiples of standard casement sizes and heights on multiples of 150 mm to align with brick courses. This range of sizes is shown in Table 10.2. Windows in these sizes are available from stock from most manufacturers and include a wide range of types and configurations including high performance and double glazed units.

Table 10.2 *The equal divide range of window sizes*

	Width mm					
	488	631	915	1200	1769	2338
Height mm						
450		★	★	★	★	★
600		★	★	★	★	★
750	★	★	★	★	★	★
900	★	★	★	★	★	★
1050	★	★	★	★	★	★
1200	★	★	★	★	★	★
1350	★	★	★	★	★	★
1500		★	★	★	★	★
2100			★	★	★	★

Imperial range

This is the traditional range of window sizes which has been in existence for over 30 years. Windows in these sizes are widely available from stock in a wide variety of patterns and types in both softwood and hardwood, including high performance windows and the facility for double glazing.

Table 10.3 *Imperial range of window sizes*

	Width mm					
Height mm	438	641	920	1225	1809	2394
768	★	★	★	★	★	
920	★	★	★	★	★	★
1073	★	★	★	★	★	★
1225	★	★	★	★	★	★
1378		★	★	★	★	★
1530			★	★	★	★

Modular metric range

This range is based on heights of 150 mm increments and widths of 300 mm. Windows in these sizes are available ex stock from some manufacturers but may not be as widely available as the other types.

Table 10.4 *Modular metric window sizes*

	Width mm				
Height mm	600	900	1200	1800	2400
450	★	★	★	★	★
600	★	★	★	★	★
750	★	★	★	★	★
900	★	★	★	★	★
1050	★	★	★	★	★
1200	★	★	★	★	★
1350	★	★	★	★	★
1500	★	★	★	★	★

Types of windows

The range of window designs available from the mass production companies is large, with side or top hung

Figures 10.4–10.10 *Stages in the manufacture of windows.*

Figure 10.4 *A 'relieving piece' is cut from the timber before moulding to a window head section. This leaves a rebate in the window head and the relieving piece is re-used for moulding glazing bars.*

Figure 10.5 *The window head blanks have three edges planed square with a splay on the top.*

Figure 10.6 *A gang mortiser is used to make mortise slots in window head and sill blanks.*

casements, pivots, sliding and canopy types. No longer are windows available only off the shelf in softwood with a coat of primer: most companies now produce a range of hardwood windows, and alternative finishes, such as exterior wood stains in various colours, are widely used. Many windows now also incorporate vents within the frame; these may be standard items or additional extras. As an example of the variety available, the John Carr range of 'energy saving' windows has within it as many as 900 standard types. This is achieved by a combination of having a choice of hardwood or softwood, butt or easy clean hinges, handed either as catalogue or opposite, different sizes and types such as arched heads, pivots, vertical sliders, cottage range, top or side hung casements; available in either stained or painted finish with the facility for double or single glazing. Figures 10.4 to 10.10 show stages in the production of window frames.

DOORS

The range of doors available today is extremely wide. Internal flush doors are available in a range of finishes from hardboard or plywood for painting to wood veneers and panel doors in hardwood or softwood for painting or clear finishing (Figure 10.11). Similarly external doors are manufactured in hardwood and softwood as flush or panelled types with a variety of glazing configurations. To cater for non-standard sizes some manufacturers produce door blanks which are designed to be trimmed to size on site.

In addition to the normal range of internal and external doors and doorsets some manufacturers produce ranges of garage doors, gates, vestibule and patio doors.

Doors are, in general, a more standardized item than windows. The range of sizes is laid down in BS 4787 'Internal and external wood doorsets, door leaves and frames' Part 1 'Specification for dimensional requirements'. The Standard covers doorsets, i.e. frame and leaf, and the sizes for door leaves supplied separately. The overall sizes are shown in Table 10.5.

Table 10.5 *Standard sizes for doorsets and leaves (from BS 4787)*

INTERNAL DOORSETS	mm
Height of door leaf height sets	2100
Height of ceiling height set	2300
	2350
	2400
	2700
	3000
Width of all doorsets	600 S
	700 S
	800 S&D
	900 S&D
	1000 S&D
	1200 S&D
	1500 S&D
	1800 D
	2100 D
Door leaf height for all doorsets	2040
Width of door leaf in single sets	526 F
	626 F
	726 F&P
	826 F&P
	926 F&P

Width of one leaf of equal double leaf set	362	F
	412	F
	462	F
	562	F&P
	712	F&P
	862	F&P
	1012	F&P
Door leaf thickness	40	
EXTERNAL DOORSETS		
Height of doorleaf height sets	2100	
Height of ceiling height set	2300	
	2350	
	2400	
	2700	
	3000	
Width of all doorsets	900	S
	1000	S
	1200	D
	1500	D
	1800	D
	2100	D
Door leaf height for all doorsets	1994	
Width of door leaf in single set	806	F&P
	906	F&P
Width of one leaf of a double set with	552	F&P
square meeting stiles and 2 mm clearance	702	F&P
between leaves. For rebated meeting stiles	852	F&P
the leaf should be 6.5 mm wider to allow	1002	FP
for 13 mm rebate		
Door leaf thickness	40	
	44	

S – single leaf   F – flush leaf
D – double leaf   P – panel leaf

Fire resisting doors and doorsets

Fire resisting doors, and doorsets will have been tested to the requirements of BS 476 Part 8 (see Chapter 9) and will be supplied with the backing of a fire test evidence. Most fire door assemblies require the use of intumescent seals unless there is specific test evidence to show that such seals are not required. The types of door leaves available are shown in Table 10.6.

STAIRS

Most joinery manufacturers can supply standard stairs from stock. They may also offer half flights, standard open tread stairs and spiral stairs, with other types being made to order. The range of staircases available can be combined with spindles, newels, rails and fittings to produce a variety of designs from standard components (Figure 10.12).

BS 5395 'Stairs ladders and walkways' Part 1 'Code of practice for the design of straight stairs' lays down the dimensions required for stairs. These are summarized in Table 10.7. The design of staircases is governed by the requirements of the Building Regulations, with manufacturing and performance requirements being included in BS 585 'Wood stairs'.

Figure 10.7 *Window sill blank before moulding (right) and finished sill (left).*

Figure 10.8 *A jamb blank tenoned ready for moulding to finished section.*

Figure 10.9 *Frames are assembled on hydraulic clamps, joints being glued and pinned.*

Figure 10.10 *Sashes and frames are coated separately with acrylic primer using an electrostatic paint machine.*

Table 10.6 *Door leaf construction for fire resisting doorsets*

Type	Notes
30/20 AND 30/30 DOOR LEAVES	
Glazed softwood joinery doors	fully glazed (Pattern 10) 30/20 with centre rail (2XGG) 30/30
Framed up solid core flush doors	softwood frame, infill panels timber or wood based materials, facings wood based sheet materials
Solid timber flush doors	laminated timber strips faced with wood based sheet materials
60/60 DOOR LEAVES	
Glazed joinery doors	difficult to produce to meet one hour fire resistance. Mock joinery doors produced by incorporating large areas of glazing in specially constructed flush doors
Framed up solid core flush doors	as 30/30 doors of this type but with increased density of framing and core often of non-combustible products. Non-combustible boards may be incorporated under the facings of doors constructed for 30/30 performance
Solid timber flush doors	as 30/30 doors of this type with carefully selected core material. 30/30 version may be uprated by incorporation of non-combustible board under facing
Non-combustible cored flush doors	thick boards of non-combustible material with timber based facings
Panelled traditionally styled doors	some proprietary doors available to meet these requirements

LEAVES GREATER THAN 60/60 PERFORMANCE
The longer the period of fire resistance required the greater the reliance placed on non-combustible materials. Some high performance door leaves have non-combustible cores with timber based facings and lippings.

Figure 10.11 *Manufacture of flush doors.* Photograph: John Carr Joinery Sales Ltd.

161

Table 10.7 *Dimensions for stairs (from BS 5395 Part 1)*

Stair type	Rise mm	Going mm	2 R + G mm	Pitch deg	Clear width mm
Private	100 min	225 min	550 min	42 max	800 min
	220 max	350 max	700 max	35 opt	600 min Lim use
	175 opt	250 opt	600 opt		
Semi-public	100 min	250 min	550 min	38 max	1000 min
	190 max	350 max	700 max	31 opt	800 min Lim use
	165 opt	275 opt	600 opt		
Public	100 min	280 min	550 min	33 max	1000 min
	180 max	350 max	700 max	27 opt	1200 min hospitals
	150 opt	300 opt	600 opt		

opt – optimum   Lim use – limited use, as defined in BS 5395

BS 5395 Part 2 'Code of practice for the design of helical and spiral stairs' gives allowable sizes for stairs of this type in various situations.

KITCHEN UNITS

Kitchen units are produced in an extremely wide range of types and finishes (Figure 10.13). BS 6222 'Domestic kitchen equipment' Part 1 'Specification for co-ordinating dimensions' sets out a range of metric sizes as shown in Table 10.8.

Table 10.8 *Co-ordinating dimensions for kitchen units (from BS 6222)*

| | LENGTH mm | | | | | | | | | | WIDTH mm | 300 | 600 |
	300	400	500	600	1000	1200	1500	1800					
Base units	★	★	★	★	★	★				Base units		★	★★
Wall units	★	★	★	★	★	★				Tall units		★	★★
Tall units			★	★						Work tops		★	★★
Sink units					★	★	★	★					
Appliance housings			★										

Figure 10.12 *The use of spindles and mouldings with standard stairs gives scope for a wide range of designs.* Photograph: Magnet and Southerns Ltd.

PRODUCTION AND DISTRIBUTION

The variety of items produced and the fact that they have to be available on very short lead-in times means that good production control is essential. Economics dictate that a change from one type to another cannot be allowed to slow down the production process.

The production of standard products in bulk creates a need for different machinery specifications with efficient workshop layouts and mechanical handling of components for finished products. Many of the production lines are linked together incorporating several different work stations in a continuous flow, resulting often in a component being produced from rough sawn timber in a matter of seconds. The use of computers and numerically controlled equipment allows rapid change from one length to another or one section to another by computer repositioning of cutting heads.

An important aspect of quality control in joinery is the surface finish of the timber. This is determined by the number of cutter marks per inch and is a function of the speed of the cutting head and the speed at which the timber is fed through the machine. Recent developments in machinery have allowed manufacturers to produce a higher standard of finish whilst also increasing the throughput of timber. Improved technology has also speeded the drying time of lacquer finishes for veneered doors. However, such equipment has required large capital investment to achieve the necessary throughputs with the minimum amount of labour, for example the current cost of the door finishing line mentioned above is over half a million pounds.

The major manufacturers all produce catalogues giving details of their products, specifications and prices enabling the specifier to establish the cost and performance of components at an early stage in the design process. Some have their own selling depots whilst others

Figure 10.13 *Standard kitchen units are produced in a wide range of types and designs.* Photograph: Magnet and Southerns Ltd.

Figure 10.14 *Most manufacturers have their own showrooms where products can be inspected.* Photograph: John Carr Joinery Sales Ltd.

Figures 10.15 and 10.16 *Major joinery companies maintain large stocks of standard items for rapid supply to their customers.* Photographs: John Carr Joinery Sales Ltd.

supply a wide range of builders and timber merchants where products can be examined (Figure 10.14).

Modern warehousing techniques and mechanical handling equipment capable of dealing with the very large number of items enable most manufacturers to restock their own depots or merchants on a regular basis with a very short lead-in time, usually less than one week (Figures 10.15 and 10.16). Therefore many products are available 'off the shelf', particularly as many of the large companies service the DIY market in addition to their professional customers.

11 Design and detail of purpose made joinery

David F. Wallis

David F Wallis BA(Cantab) FCIOB, now retired, was director of GE Wallis and Sons Ltd. He was president of the British Woodworking Federation from 1971 to 1981. The drawings in this chapter were prepared from originals by Harry Munn, joinery manager of GE Wallis & Sons Ltd.

The fundamental difference between mass production and purpose made joinery is that the former is a product, or range of products, available to be selected from a catalogue, whereas the latter is a service. Many other differences flow from this distinction, most obviously those of scale, of manufacturing methods, of marketing and sales.

Firms engaged in making purpose made joinery to customers' individual requirements vary widely in size and type. Many of them are part of building firms, more or less independent in their operation, control, administration and finance within those firms, and wholly or largely providing the joinery requirements of the building work. Some, however, are completely independent, although they may have begun as a builder's shop, and find their markets among builders and many other clients. In both categories, the size may range from a very small unit of just a few employees to major companies with a payroll numbered in three figures, and with a correspondingly complex structure and organization.

Those which are within building firms are entirely dependent upon them for their workflow, unless they are given the opportunity to seek a proportion of their work externally, and the smaller units may well have their work priced and even accounts rendered by the estimators and surveyors of the building side, being themselves solely an operational function. Others which are set up as independent departments will probably be in competition with outside suppliers for the orders of their building departments. In evaluating their prices, the builder will be wise to take into acount the benefit of his direct control of quality, delivery and service to his building sites when the work is done in his own shop.

The independent firm has the opportunity, within the limits of the market and its estimating success, of maintaining a steadier workload in its shop, with benefits of economy, and it may be able to obtain nominations for the supply of joinery directly from architects, particularly for work of high quality. Orders may also be sought across a wider range of sources than building contractors alone, and the opportunity taken sometimes

of influencing specification and detail before work is priced.

The information available at the estimating stage is normally just what the builder has received in his tender documents; extracts from a bill of quantities, including specification clauses, supported perhaps by sketch details, and with considerably less time for pricing even than the limited period the builder has himself. There is no time to query anything except a matter of major importance, and assumptions have to be made about uncertainties. Some of these arise even with the new standard method of measurement; for example the sketch or detail provided of some of the items of joinery may not make it clear whether some of the members are separately billed as site framing or are to be provided as part of the joinery, or how far the item is required to be framed in the shop or assembled on site.

The degree of exact repetition is important, for it has a big influence on cost. As an indication, a 'one-off' item which is virtually a 'prototype', may cost as much as four times the price of a mass-produced item of the same specification – consider how much would be charged by a car manufacturer, as a comparison, for a special car exactly like one of his standard models, but just a few millimetres different in dimensions of wheelbase, track width, door opening sizes! The more information provided at estimating stage and the more time available, the keener and more accurate will be the price.

Once an order is received, the joinery manager will need to obtain detail drawings, specification, schedules and programme of deliveries as soon as possible, for the 'lead time' necessary to provide the material is often much larger than is generally realized by the architect and contractor, who are much preoccupied with foundations, structure and other urgent matters on site. Time is needed for checking all this information against site drawings (to eliminate discrepancies); for setting out and obtaining contractors' and designers' approval of shop drawings and rods; for ordering timber, kilning, special preservative or flame retardant impregnation; for obtaining special ironmongery and so forth. It is particularly helpful if the designer and contractor can visit the joinery shop at a very early stage, soon after the

Figures 11.1–11.5 *The manufacture of panelling for the extension to the Central Criminal Court, Old Bailey, completed in 1975.* Architects: McMorran and Whitby.

Figure 11.1 *Assembling faceted panelling in wych elm.*

detailed information has been provided, for a conversation face to face can save many telephone calls and much correspondence later, and establish a confident working relationship. It may also allow for manufacture to be simplified by small adjustments of detail to permit the joiners' preferred methods of jointing and assembly. Details in any case are best confined to the desired profiles and dimensions of the finished items, leaving jointing details for the shop to decide, but they are most likely to be economical and effective if the designer has some knowledge of the jointing techniques usually employed, many of which are illustrated later.

Items will normally be supplied framed up and primed for painting or given a protective sealing coat ready for polish. Some designers consider that some work can be more cheaply framed on site, and it may even be billed as 'sawn framed'. However, any material to be framed should be planed at least on two edges for accuracy, and it is normally more economical in the end to frame up in the shop (Figures 11.1 and 11.2). Exceptions are sometimes made for door linings, supplied 'knocked down' in sets for site assembly, to save bulk on transport, and for items which are too large for access to their final positions in the building through doorways, stairwells or corridors. Access needs early consideration for some major assemblies, where leaving down a wall may be the best solution for access for

panelling, counters, staircases and other large units.

The sequence of operations is very similar in a large or small joinery shop. Setting out always used to be done full size on a paper or plywood 'rod'; in many shops this is still the method, although some have changed to drawings. Once the timber is received in bulk, kilned as specified, the material will be selected for the cutting sheets which have been made up from the rods. After primary machining (sawing, planing and moulding to section) the timber will go to the marker out, who will mark one piece of each kind with details of secondary machining required for jointing and special shaping. It will then go to the spindle, router, tenoner, morticer, and sander, for the aim today is to remove the maximum amount of surplus material by machine, leaving the least possible for manual labour on the bench (Figure 11.3).

If impregnation with preservatives or flame retardant chemicals is necessary at this stage, some degree of distortion can occur, and either time must be allowed for machining replacement pieces for treatment or an extra quantity provided at first to allow for this factor. (N.B. treatment with organic solvent preservatives does not result in distortion.) On the bench, the joiner will finish any shaping operations which could not be completed by machine, e.g. stopped mouldings, mitres and scribes and will finish mating surfaces and edges of components to be jointed, clean up surfaces ready to receive paint or polish and frame up the assemblies. It is at this stage that the extra cost of high quality work is principally incurred; the processes as far as jointing will usually be very similar for all classes of work going through the shop but the special labours of hand assembly and finishing can make a great difference to quality.

A number of hand-held power tools are used by the joiners, including drills with a range of special attachments, and routers, sanders, staplers and screwdrivers. They reduce the manual effort needed, and are suitable for all qualities of work, if properly used. A wide range of adhesives are available to suit different applications, and this has become a complex technology in itself, dealing with a variety of materials now used in association with wood, such as wood-based boards, plastics and metals, to cope with the effects of organic solvents in wood treatment.

The benefits of repetition have already been mentioned, and this is relevant in relatively small batch production as well as in mass production. Similar items in a bill of quantities will have been collected and aggregated for pricing on the assumption that they will be machined in one run of operations, unless the total is very large. It will also be helpful if information about the whole job is available at an early stage in big contracts, so that economic decisions can be taken about the work sequence. A balance has to be struck between the benefits of setting up machines for the longest possible runs and the need for shop storage and the cost of a bigger volume of work in progress. In the largest contracts, the time necessary for manufacture may be much

longer than the overall site programme of calling forward for delivery and fixing. In such cases, storage is necessary for finished work, and it is equitable for the client's professional advisers to provide in the contract for payment on account of finished joinery held at works (Figure 11.4).

Consideration should be given to the care and protection of joinery on site, both in storage and after fixing. Not only can damage occur through mishandling, bad stacking, exposure to weather, and impact damage by site traffic and in the course of the work of other trades, but also through excessive moisture within the building, or excessive heat during the testing and commissioning of the mechanical services.

Timber is sensitive to a combination of temperature and humidity. For any pair of values of these two factors there is an equilibrium moisture content (emc) for wood, which does not vary significantly for different species, although the extent of swelling and shrinkage varies considerably between species as emc is varied (see Chapter 1, and Appendix). For a building in which good quality joinery is to be installed, air conditioning gives the ideal conditions, for the appropriate emc can be calculated from the design data of the mechanical services installation and specified at design stage. Timber may then be ordered kilned to that emc and maintained, so far as possible, reasonably near that value. In other cases, a reasonable assessment may be made of probable emc during the working life of the building (see Chapters 4 and 9).

In any case, valuable finished joinery should not be fixed until the building has dried out sufficiently for

Figure 11.2 *Curved double-headed hung casement in utile.*

167

Figure 11.3 *Routing head mould for faceted panelling in cedar of Lebanon.*

Figure 11.4 *Assembling of court room fittings in cedar of Lebanon.*

conditions to approximate to those to which the desired emc corresponds. This can readily be checked, either by use of thermometer and hygrometer or by placing thin end-grain samples of the timber in the building for a few days and then weighing, oven-drying and re-weighing them (see Chapter 4). It is also important that the conditions should not become too dry for a significant period whilst boilers and heating equipment are being tested under heavy load conditions. In some cases, it may be desirable to take special precautions about emc by using stat-controlled heaters, humidifiers and dehumidifiers in spaces through which air flow is restricted or prevented, so as to obtain the desired conditions before installing special joinery and maintaining it in good condition until the building is taken into occupation. The cost of these measures may well be worth incurring in relation to the value of the joinery protected thereby (Figure 11.5 and Plate 13). Detailed information on this subject may be obtained from TRADA or the Princes Risborough Laboratory of the Building Research Establishment.

JOINTS AND DETAILS

It is possible here to give only a selection of the details most frequently used, both traditional and modern, in contemporary purpose made joinery practice. Further information on this aspect and on purpose made joinery generally is available in many textbooks.

Frames

Figure 11.6 shows the traditional mortice and tenon joint used to frame heads, jambs and sills of door and window frames. The joints of external frames used to be painted with white lead before assembly, but today external joinery should be pressure treated with an organic solvent (OS) wood anti-fungal and insecticidal preservative. The joints should then be glued with resorcinol formaldehyde (RF) or resorcinol phenol formaldehyde (RF/PF) adhesive for maximum strength and water resistance. The joint may be secured by a pair

Figure 11.5 *Faceted and acoustic panelling, and witness box in cedar of Lebanon.*

of wedges or a pair of nails may also be driven diagonally through the head or under the sill into the tenon. Modern practice tends to use a hardwood pin or a non-ferrous metal star dowel from one side.

Figure 11.7 shows the forked or combed joint, made possible by modern machinery and assembly methods. The glue line of modern adhesives can be stronger than the cell structure of timber, so the large joint surface area provides an exceptionally strong joint. A hardwood pin or metal dowel may also be used. This joint dispenses with the extended ends of the head (horns) which used to be built into brickwork for extra strength of fixing.

Figure 11.8 shows the joint of head to jamb of a frame which projects in front of the plaster face. With softwood the edge face of the jamb would run past the head as shown by the dotted line; with hardwood for polish a mitre would be formed.

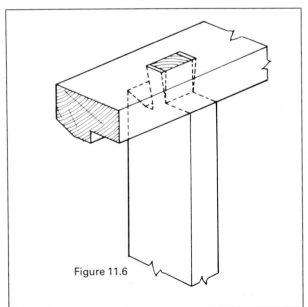

Figure 11.6

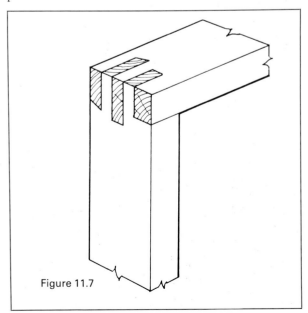

Figure 11.7

Figures 11.6–11.12 *Joints in frames.*

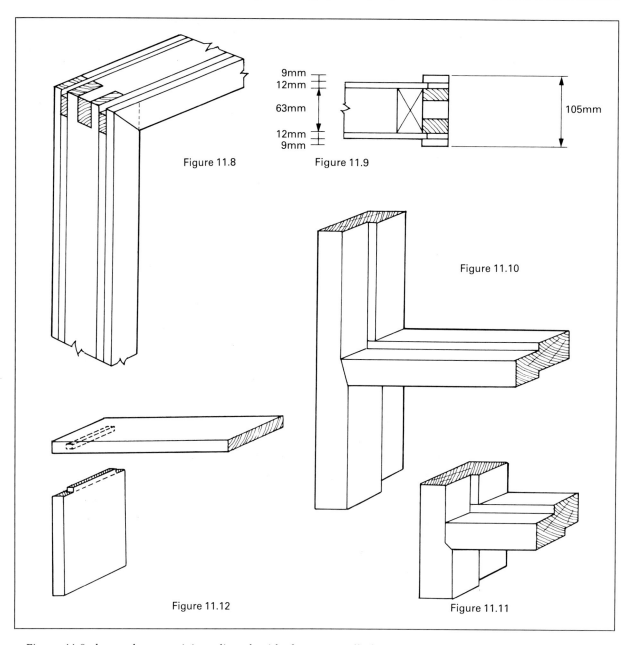

Figure 11.8

9mm
12mm
63mm
12mm
9mm

105mm

Figure 11.9

Figure 11.10

Figure 11.12

Figure 11.11

Figure 11.9 shows the same joint adjusted with the forking to match the dimensions of stud partitioning with plasterboard facings.

Figure 11.10 shows a joint in a softwood frame rebated in the solid, with rebates and splay shoulders on opposite faces, for inward opening door below and outward opening sash above.

Figure 11.11 shows the same joint, two solid stop rebates, but for hardwood to be polished, the angles being formed with mitres instead of splay shoulders.

Figure 11.12 shows the stop housed joint of an internal door lining, with the groove in the head and the barefaced tongue in the jamb, stopped at both ends. Cheap practice would be to run the groove and tongue through, but the ends then show in the angles of the architraves.

Doors

Figure 11.13 shows the arrangement of mortices and tenons in the stiles and rails of a door. The tenons are normally between a quarter and a third of the thickness of the framing and their length not more than five times their thickness. Top and bottom rails have the tenons haunched to enable them to be wedged, and wide rails have vertical pairs of tenons. Lock rails have double tenons within the thickness, to allow a mortice lock to be housed between them; in very thick doors double tenons may be used for all rails.

Figure 11.14 shows that barefaced tenons have to be used in rails below the top one, in the case of framed and ledged doors, to enable the vertical ledges to pass them.

Windows

Figure 11.15 shows the vertical section of a casement window illustrating the requirements for weathering. The sashes are shown with their outer faces flush with the frame; they could be detailed with a rebated or closed joint. Projecting drips are housed into the head and transom enabling the main frame members all to be machined from the same width of material to make the machining of fork joints easier. The top casement is shown putty glazed; the lower casement bead glazed with a projecting bottom bead and the jamb beads stopped short. The sill is shown with an integral drip requiring the use of a tile or brick sub-sill, alternatively a wider sill or planted sill nosing could be specified. However it is considered better practice for the window to be located well back from the face of the wall to improve weathering, necessitating a sub-sill.

Figure 11.16 shows the positions of small V cuts on vertical shoulder joints. Horizontal joints tend to fail before vertical ones if weather is allowed to penetrate, but even the latter are given added protection by the V joint, since it reduces movement in a flat painted surface.

Figure 11.17 shows the upper sash of a double hung cased box frame, with a special forked joint between stile and meeting rail, normally secured after gluing with a screw or star dowel. The sash also has a horn or joggle for ornamentation as well as strength.

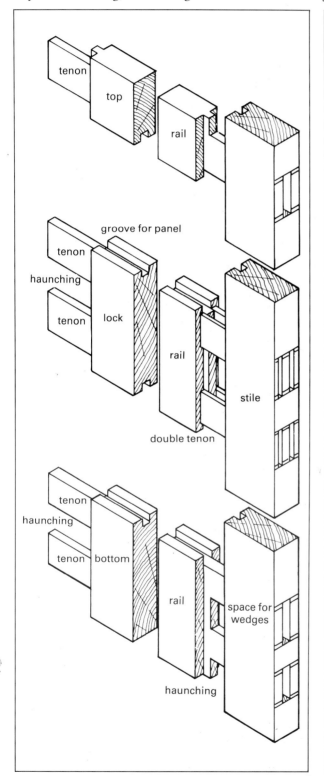

Figure 11.13 *Details of joints in panelled doors.*

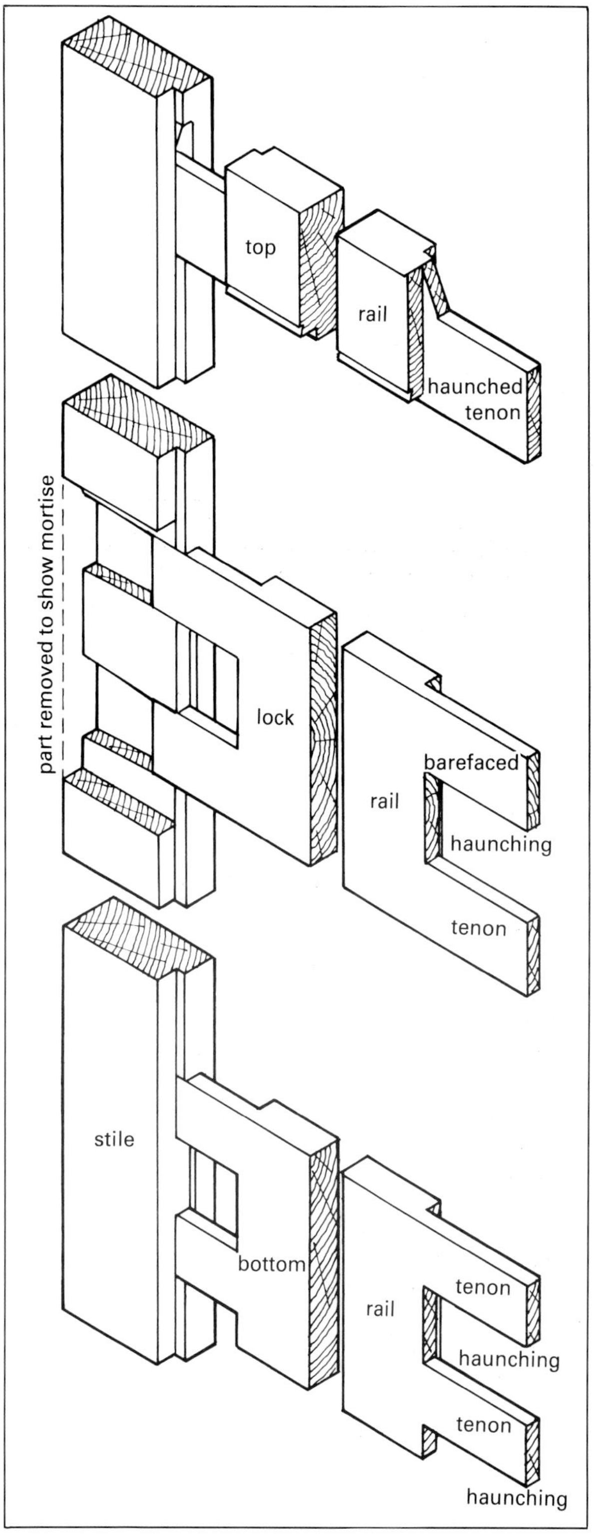

Figure 11.14 *Details of joints in framed and ledged doors.*

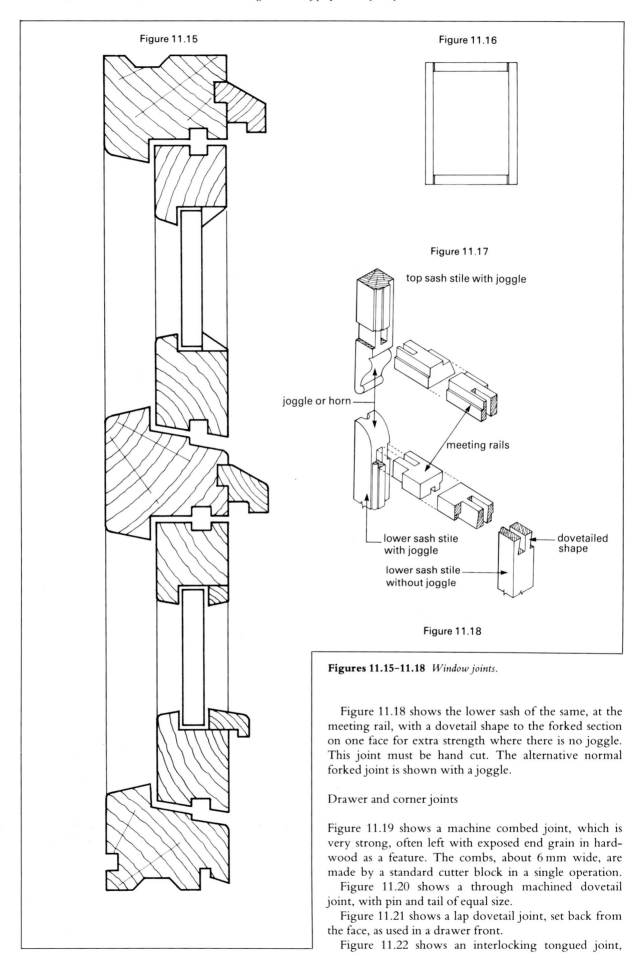

Figure 11.15

Figure 11.16

Figure 11.17

top sash stile with joggle

joggle or horn

meeting rails

lower sash stile
with joggle

lower sash stile
without joggle

dovetailed
shape

Figure 11.18

Figures 11.15–11.18 *Window joints.*

Figure 11.18 shows the lower sash of the same, at the meeting rail, with a dovetail shape to the forked section on one face for extra strength where there is no joggle. This joint must be hand cut. The alternative normal forked joint is shown with a joggle.

Drawer and corner joints

Figure 11.19 shows a machine combed joint, which is very strong, often left with exposed end grain in hardwood as a feature. The combs, about 6 mm wide, are made by a standard cutter block in a single operation.

Figure 11.20 shows a through machined dovetail joint, with pin and tail of equal size.

Figure 11.21 shows a lap dovetail joint, set back from the face, as used in a drawer front.

Figure 11.22 shows an interlocking tongued joint,

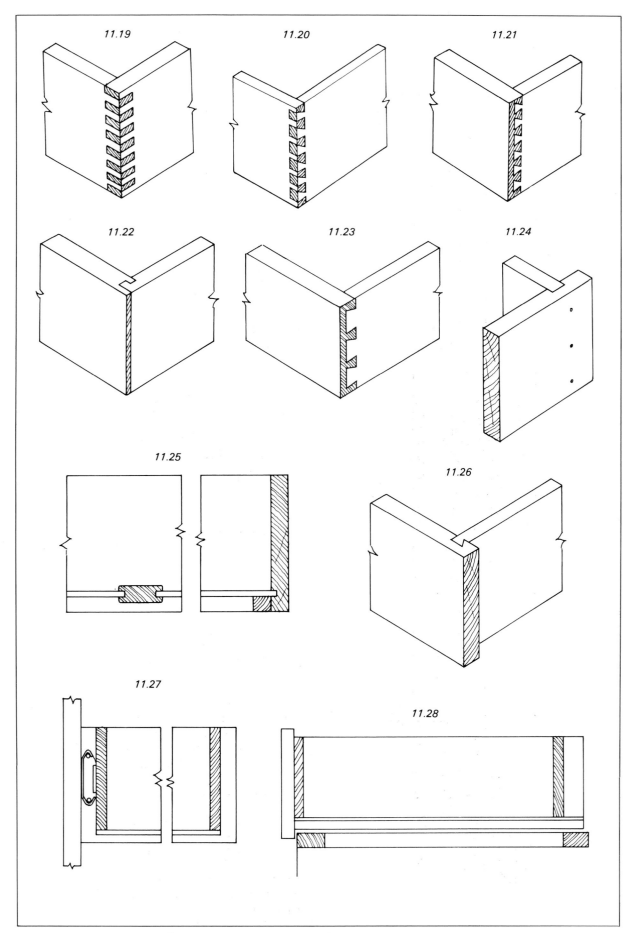

Figures 11.19–11.28 *Drawer and corner joints.*

used alternatively for drawer fronts, and also in the outer casing of fitments.

Figure 11.23 shows a hand made lap dovetail joint. As in all non-machined joints the dovetail is wide and the pin small, with a bevel of one in six.

Figure 11.24 shows the back housed into the sides of a drawer in traditional construction.

Figure 11.25 shows a section of a wide drawer, whose base needs the support of a muntin. The side is also grooved for the base, which is strengthened by a glued runner.

Figure 11.26 shows a slip dovetail joint between drawer side and front, to allow for an extended front where the drawer is suspended from fibre or metal runners.

Figure 11.27 shows a section of a drawer carried by a metal runner. In this case also the base is screwed up to the side, avoiding the use of a groove and glued runner.

Figure 11.28 shows the construction where a projecting laminate covered or veneered front is secured to a four-sided drawer framing from the inside. The normal drawer under-frame is also detailed. In high quality work a ply panel, called a dust board, is fitted within this frame.

Staircases

The joints of staircases are basically very simple – treads and risers are housed or trenched into strings, with tap-ered housings to accommodate wedges, and strings are stub-tenoned into newels. The skill lies in the setting out, and care must be taken to abide by Building Regulations, e.g. for width of stairway, for minimum width of tread at winders. There are basically two types of strings; closed and cut strings. Risers are also omitted in some modern stairs, called 'open stairs'. The basic joints only are illustrated here.

Figure 11.29 shows the principles of construction of treads and risers in relation to both closed and cut strings.

Figure 11.30 shows the joints of strings to newel, and also the housing of ends of tread and riser to newel.

Economic profiles

Figure 11.31 illustrates various standard machine sections, with their descriptive names used in specification, which can be produced economically and which are suitable for scribed or mitred joints. A sill section is also shown which would be specified as having seven labours (two throats, two grooves, one bead, one sunk weathered and round, and one splay rebate).

Panels for doors, panelling and fitments

Figure 11.32 details a section and elevation of a raised and fielded panel, such as would be used in one face work, a wall panel or 'single sided' door, or a fitment. Small panels would be made in the solid, but this would

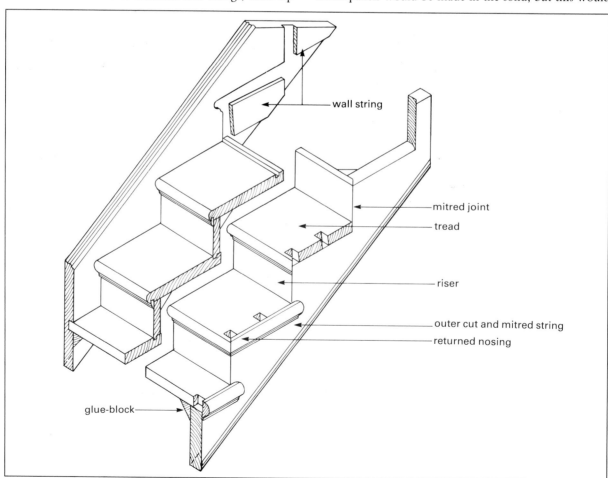

Figure 11.29 *Part of a flight of stairs, showing constructional details.*

174

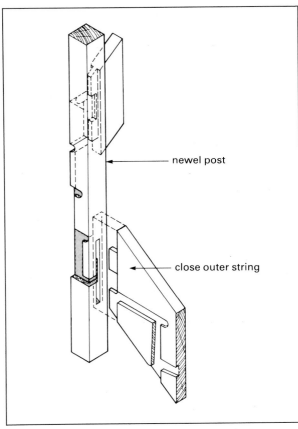

Figure 11.30 *Newel post cut to receive strings, treads, risers etc.*

not be suitable for large panels due to the effects of heating in buildings today, unless air conditioning is very closely controlled. For larger panels the flat centre would be made of board material (ply, block, lamin, chip, etc) and the solid raised margin mitred around.

Figure 11.33 details a raised, sunk and fielded panel, which is a better detail for the method described above with the margin mitred around.

Figure 11.34 details a raised fielded panel used only for small panels; the angle would be too flat to be effective if used in larger panels.

Figure 11.35 details a raised, sunk and raised fielded panel used in joinery of the highest class, mainly in doors or small panels.

Figure 11.36 details the fixing of a raised, sunk and fielded panel to a door of high quality. The panel is not housed directly into the door framing, but a panel frame is fitted to it, and the panel within this framing has freedom of movement. The bolection mould and bed mould (or two bolection moulds) are mitred and screwed to the panel framing but not fixed to the panel itself.

Figure 11.37 shows a section of a door with bead butt panel, which has vertical beads worked in the solid along two parallel edges only, with the grain.

Figure 11.38 shows a section of a door with bead flush panel, where the beads run around all four sides of the panel. It is impractical to work the bead cross grain in the solid, so the panel is deep rebated all round and the beads are mitred and pin fixed to one or both faces.

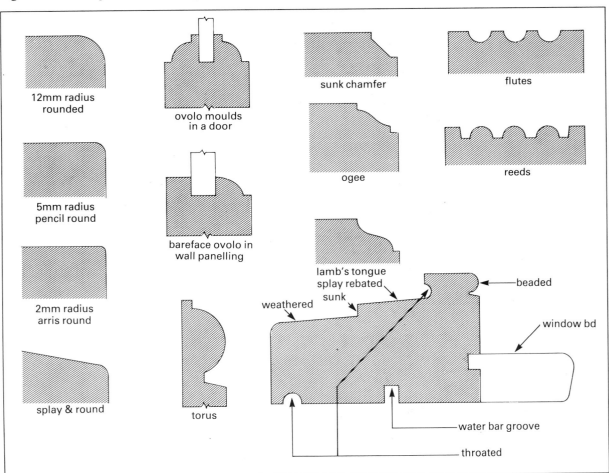

Figure 11.31 *Economic profiles.*

175

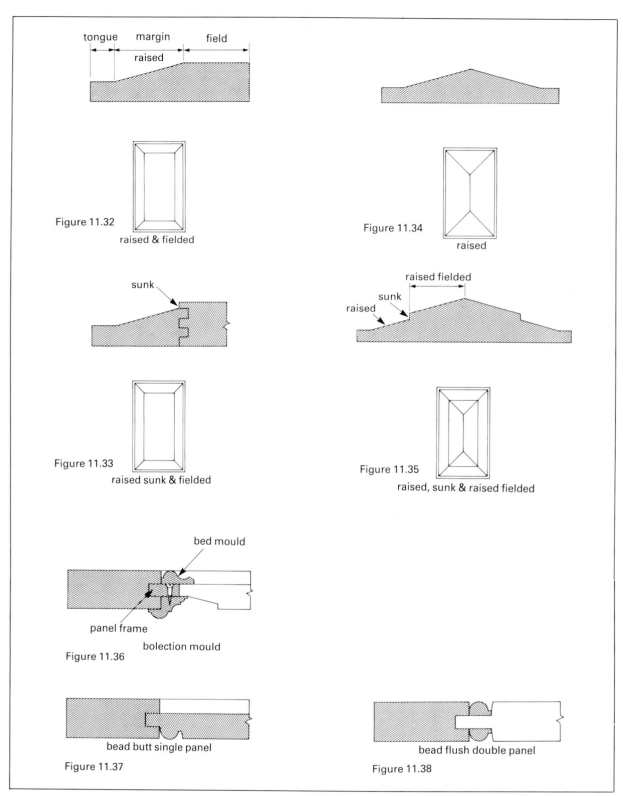

tongue   margin   field
raised

Figure 11.32
raised & fielded

Figure 11.34
raised

sunk

Figure 11.33
raised sunk & fielded

raised fielded
sunk
raised

Figure 11.35
raised, sunk & raised fielded

bed mould

panel frame
bolection mould
Figure 11.36

bead butt single panel
Figure 11.37

bead flush double panel
Figure 11.38

Figures 11.32–11.38 *Panels.*

12 Timber – decorative and practical

Barbara Bedding

Barbara Bedding BSc DipInfSc is publications editor for TRADA. After graduating from University College of North Wales, Bangor, she worked at the Building Research Establishment, Princes Risborough Laboratory, before joining TRADA in 1975.

Although timber is usually considered as a single material it is perhaps better thought of as a family of materials since the range of colour and properties is so wide. The range of timber species available plus the various types of wood based sheet materials means that timber and its derivatives can fulfil almost any function required. Timber provides a huge range of decorative features, ranging in colour from almost white to almost black, with grain and figure varying from relatively plain to striped or highly figured species. The Appendix Plates illustrate the range of species commonly available in the UK. Timber can be used in many forms; solid, laminated or veneered; it can be bent, jointed or carved; it can be varnished, stained or painted; it can be used indoors or out, it can be mixed, matched or used with other materials – the scope is wide – the choice is up to the designer.

The range of species available in the UK is wider than in many of the major timber producing countries of the world; our traditional position as a major international trader still persists in the timber industry and designers therefore have enormous choice in specifying timber for structural and decorative purposes. Balsa is the lightest and weakest of the commercially available timbers and lignum vitae one of the hardest and heaviest. Between these two extremes we find the range of commercially available timbers which are used for structural and decorative purposes in building. Most of the commonly used structural softwoods fall in strength classes SC3 and SC4 according to BS 5268: Part 2: 1984. They are therefore in the lower range of strength properties but allow efficient and attractive design at reasonable cost. Many of our most decorative hardwoods fall into the higher strength classes but they are prized for their appearance and used in decorative situations, often in the form of veneers.

Timber is used structurally for all building elements; walls, floors and roofs. However its decorative properties can also be exploited in these situations, opening up possibilities for exciting designs which are both functional and aesthetic. Other timber properties can also be combined in similar ways, for example its acoustic properties are exploited in many of our most prestigious concert halls and public buildings while the abrasion resistance of some species is used to provide hardwearing floors in domestic, public and industrial situations.

Architectural tradition in the UK means that buildings constructed wholly in timber are comparatively rare. However, throughout our history there have been timber buildings, from the medieval barns to the timber buildings of today. These range from amenity buildings where timber is chosen to blend with the environment, to houses, sports facilities and industrial or farm units.

The versatility of timber is amply demonstrated by two buildings which provide broadly similar amenities in a rural environment. Although the situation and requirements of the buildings are similar, the design approaches adopted are widely contrasting.

A Visitors' Centre at the Bowood Estate, near Calne in Wiltshire, was designed as a low pavilion style building spreading out beneath the overhead tree canopy with a central cruciform column branching out to support the roof, reflecting the structure of the surrounding woodlands. The structural frame was made from prefabricated European whitewood glulam members based on a 3.4 metre module. The major diagonal hip beams are supported on a central cruciform column and sandwiched between double corner perimeter columns infilled with glass. Intermediate double rafters are supported on perimeter columns with prefabricated Columbian pine glazed frames and doors inserted between. The ceiling is European whitewood decking boards which act as bracing to the roof structure upon which is built a ventilated roof covering of cedar shingles. The cedar shingles were cut on site to produce 'laced' hips providing a smooth outline at the mitred junction. The pyramid roof is capped with a large glass lantern light. Unglazed areas of the walls are constructed of stud partitioning, finished externally with softwood boarding and internally with melamine faced interlocking plywood panels. The strong geometry of the building was designed to reflect and merge with the woodlands and the Capability Brown landscape of the Bowood Estate (Plates 14 and 15).

The Tollymore Teahouse, in the Tollymore Forest Park, set in the northern foothills of the Mountains of Mourne in Northern Ireland, on the other hand, is an extrovert design with its brightly stained timber and what the architect calls his 'boy scout' construction of timber poles.

The roof is an independent pyramid arch structure supported on round timber posts of 250 mm diameter at 7.8 m centres with a central post to the slab at first floor level. The perimeter supports are braced externally by diagonal timber poles with bolted 'boy scout' connections. This form of construction is also used for the bridge which provides access from the upper level car park. The poles were treated with preservative and are stained blue-black. This contrasts with the bright red timber cladding and joinery. The tea room is on the first floor of the building with a shop and conveniences below. These are of concrete and masonry construction and are essentially independent of the timber structure. A section through the building shows the roof configuration with four pyramids open to the tearoom. The inverted pyramid in the centre accommodates storage tanks and ducting. Structural softwood decking forms the ceiling, spanning up to 3.9 m between the main arch ribs of sawn softwood – all stained red (Figure 12.1 and Plates 16-18).

In a similar bright vein but put to a very different purpose is the warehouse and office built for a timber company in Tonbridge, Kent. The 875 m² building was designed to reflect the company's activities and act as a colourful 'billboard' for the imaginative use of wood and stain finishes. The site bordered an industrial estate and a riverside conservation area; the local authority therefore wanted a building of some visual quality. The design brief was translated by the architects into a simple but colourful pavilion using exposed laminated rafters and posts forming portals at 5 m intervals, locked together by a ridge beam and perimeter lattice beams. These structural elements are finished with a red exterior wood stain. The non-load-bearing outer panels create further visual interest by the use of dark blue and natural coloured stains and by the use of a variety of softwood

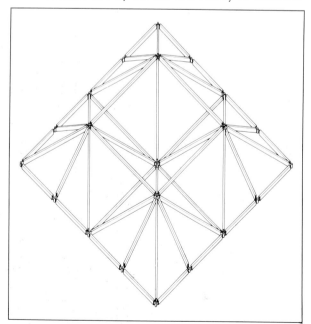

Figure 12.1 _The roof construction of Tollymore Teahouse, County Down, Northern Ireland, consists of four pyramids which are open to the tearoom, with a central inverted pyramid housing storage tanks and ducting._ Architects: Ian Campbell and Partners. Structural engineers: Blyth and Blyth.

cladding – feather edged, shiplap, tongued and grooved and diagonal straight edged boarding. These panels are interchangeable and can be removed and replaced by windows, doors or by panels of other company products. The office/showroom which is connected to the warehouse is an almost totally glazed unit supported in a timber framed structure, stained to match the warehouse behind (Plates 19 and 20).

TRADA's own offices at Hughenden Valley in Buckinghamshire are built using a post and beam structure of a dense South East Asian hardwood, balau, forming a continuous ring beam, central spine frame and floor joists. The use of hardwood for the structural frame allowed joist spans of 7.2 m with office loadings, a much longer span than could have been achieved using softwood and more economical than glulam. The external panels are load-bearing stressed skin panels of 9.5 mm thick red meranti plywood on 50 × 75 mm softwood studs. The panels are butt jointed and weathered with a nailed softwood coverstrip. The plywood panels form the exterior surface of the building and are finished with an exterior wood stain (Figure 12.2 and Plate 21).

Timber is used structurally in a very large number of buildings but in many cases the timber structure is enclosed. This is particularly true of roof structures in both domestic and public buildings. Such structures can, however, form an important part of the overall design and aesthetic impact of a building. The structural form can range from simple posts and beams or rafter and purlin roof structures to elaborate and complex designs built up from large numbers of relatively small size timbers.

The Burrell Museum, Glasgow, is a striking example of simple structural forms being used to highlight and complement the building and its contents. A more elaborate roof design could well have distracted attention from the art treasures the building is designed to show. The museum is situated in the Pollock Country Park and the architects have designed the building to reflect the relationship between art and nature by providing an intimate relationship between the woodland and the gallery. Viewed externally the predominating materials are stainless steel and glass, but once inside, the laminated timber structure becomes apparent. The timber is European whitewood laminated using resorcinol formaldehyde glue. The finger joints used within the beams were also glued with resorcinol formaldehyde. However those finger joints which would be visible on the soffit of the beams were glued with lighter coloured urea formaldehyde adhesive to make them less conspicuous.

The courtyard forms a focal point within the gallery, here the 210 × 616 mm principal rafters are supported on slender concrete columns; steel tension rods are used to complete the structure giving a light airy feel to this area. The north section or terrace has a timber and glass screen giving views of the woodlands beyond. The pre-cambered flat roof beams are 210 × 767 mm with secondary beams set on a 780 mm grid. The tongued and grooved boarding is 33 × 130 mm with a double layer bituminous felt vapour barrier above with a Swedish system stainless steel flat roof incorporating 100 mm insulation. The main members across the daylight galleries are cranked laminated beams with bolted joints through a central concealed steel plate. The pitched roof to the restaurant area utilizes two rows of 'Invar' steel stiffening rods within the beams. This type of steel stiffening was chosen because it does not expand or contract with changes in temperature. The rafters are housed onto a principal perimeter beam 210 × 500 mm which also supports the vertical timbers for the upper storey above (Plates 22–27).

On a domestic scale timber is used both for internal and external decoration and also for structural purposes. Most of the timber frame houses built today have brick external cladding and plasterboard wall linings so that the timber structure is not apparent. However there are examples where the timber structure is featured as part of the building.

Bulls Wood House, built on the South Downs in Sussex, is constructed from Western red cedar beams and columns with the same timber used for the exterior cladding of diagonal boarding. Internal load-bearing beams are laminated timber and the ceilings are also tongued and grooved Western red cedar (Plates 28–29).

There are also many examples of houses where timber is used on a less overt scale, where the basic wall structure is brick and block construction but where the timber roof is highlighted. A house in Essex, designed and built by an architect to accommodate his office as well, features exposed roof trusses with large areas of glazing to take advantage of the views of meadows with woods beyond. The structural timber elements were specified as S2 group timber (according to CP112 Part 2) of SS grade (BS 4978). These comprised collared and common rafters and purlins and the twinned columns and collar ties. The twinned cross beams were specified as Douglas fir. The softwood timber floorboarding is exposed and forms a decorative as well as structural floor in the first floor living area. The exposed timber elements are rough sanded and treated with a wood stain (Plates 30–32).

Moving from the simple forms to more complex structural solutions opens up a wide range of options. The relatively simple roof structures are limited in span and therefore restrict the building shape. They are best suited to rectangular forms, not necessarily limited in length provided adequate longitudinal bracing can be incorporated, but limited in width by the need for vertical supports. More complex structures can result from other plan forms; the ease of working timber makes complex structures feasible in both practical and economic terms.

A Roman Catholic church built at Bourtreehill, Irvine New Town, Scotland uses timber in a highly dramatic roof structure. The roof is an extended octagon on plan with eight main composite 'hip rafters'. The hip rafters are three-chord open girders, each chord being formed from 90 × 40 mm members. These are connected by 150 × 40 mm vertical members and steel rod diagonal ties.

The girders rest on concrete columns and are tied together with a 300 mm deep flitch beam. At the upper level they are connected to a ring beam constructed in a similar way to the girders. Each of the eight roof panels consists of interlaced beams, intersecting diagonally and constructed on the same principle as the main beams using 75 × 40 mm timbers in two double chords connected by 100 × 40 mm vertical struts.

Above the ring beam the roof plane breaks at a steeper angle to form a peak; this is constructed from single solid timber members and incorporates two large glazed panels.

Structural timber is stress graded Oregon pine finished with a clear polyurethane varnish. The roof boarding is tongued and grooved European redwood stained poppy red. All timber to timber and timber to steel connections are bolted with exposed 50 mm diameter washers painted poppy red.

The adjoining church hall can act as an overflow to the church itself for special occasions. Its roof is a diminuendo of the main church with shaped glulam beams forming the hip rafters, with solid Oregon pine rafters laid in a diagonal pattern supporting the clear finished tongued and grooved European redwood boarding. The hip rafter glulam beams are connected by a glulam ring beam surmounted by a glazed rooflight supported on single Oregon pine rafters. The timber theme is continued with beech strips providing the finished floor surface in the hall (Plates 33–35).

In addition to those situations where timber is used to fulfil both structural and decorative functions there are many situations where timber is chosen because of the possibility of combining the decorative features of timber with other functional properties.

The Barbican Centre for Arts and Conferences, in the City of London, provides a dramatic example of the many ways in which timber can be used for decorative and acoustic purposes. The Centre also demonstrates the ways in which timber, a combustible material, can meet the stringent fire regulation requirements demanded in

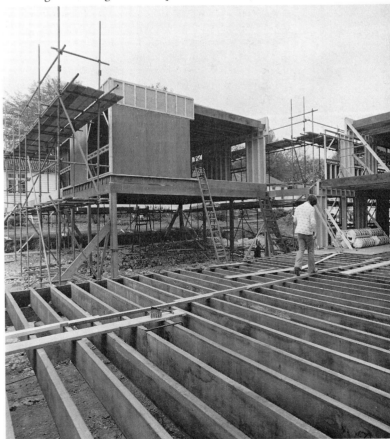

Figure 12.2 *Long span structural hardwoods form the structural frame of TRADA's offices in Buckinghamshire.*

179

Figures 12.3 and 12.4 *Detail of the organ-like sculpted screen forming the stage lining, Barbican Concert Hall.* Architects: Chamberlin Powell and Son. Structural engineers: Ove Arup and Partners.

major public buildings of this type. Flame retardant treatments were used extensively to meet the required Class O performance and in some areas timber veneers were applied to non-combustible substrates.

The largest auditorium, the Barbican concert hall, is lined throughout in timber. The focal point is the acoustic and decorative screen which forms the stage lining. Built in clear Canadian Pacific Coast hemlock, the organ-like sculpted screen incorporating the coat of arms of the Corporation of the City of London is almost 30.5 m long and 15 m high at its extremities. The panelling is carried on a framework which also houses removable sound absorbing and sound reflective boxes which allow the stage to be acoustically tuned. The complex design required the lining to be set out and manufactured in two separate halves and installed on site using a maze of string lines to position accurately the intersections on the sculptured features of the panelling. The stage canopy is designed to be sound reflective and also to house speakers. It is constructed from 30 mm thick fire resistant panels veneered with random selected strips of 100 mm wide European redwood. The forward portion of the canopy conceals an enormous mobile gantry weighing approximately 35 tons. In manufacture, allowances had to be made for vibration and distortion during movement of the gantry.

The stage wings are strips of European redwood, varying in width between 54 mm and 61 mm and in length up to 2.4 m, veneered onto an under veneer on a non-combustible substrate. This strip veneer construction is also used between the acoustic boxes which form the side walls of the hall. The acoustic boxes themselves, in contrast to the stage, are plain in design but the design requirements were perhaps even more stringent. The object was to give the impression of a solid dug out tree trunk. The boxes should be acoustically reflective with the random crown cut aspen veneers spreading to quarter cut veneers at the corners and back to crown cut at the intersection with the walls. The veneers on the side panels were wrapped round 63 mm diameter radiused corners. Most of the boxes were between 2.5 and 5 m in length; this meant that the joinery manufacturers had to develop their own technique for laying long lengths of veneers on radiused corners without joints since the normal lengths achievable are limited to around 2 m by the size of the press.

The stage itself is Canadian maple strips and the hall floors are finished with end grain European redwood blocks. This provides a continuous theme with the stalls foyer where they cover an area of about 3000 square metres. End grain blocks are very hard wearing and have traditionally been used for industrial flooring. However, in this situation they provide a highly decorative and unusual floor.

The stalls foyer also leads into the second main auditorium, the Barbican Theatre. Here, in contrast to the warm golden tones of the concert hall, the walls are dark. The theatre is designed with no central aisles, each row of seats leads to its own door held open by an electromagnet and closed automatically when a performance is in progress. The acoustic doors are manufactured from 44.5 mm thick blockboard faced with 9.5 mm Peruvian walnut veneered plywood. Push plates and pull handles are Brazilian mahogany and their de-

Figures 12.5 and 12.6 *Glazed screens and partitions form the entrance to the London branch of the Shanghai Commercial Bank. A similar system of screens separates the individual offices. The timber used throughout the bank is sycamore, with a specially formulated silver grey stain, which when polished provides a delicate sheen.* Architects: Barbara Chu and Kathleen Morrison (now Iso Tec Partners). Photographs. David Ward.

Figure 12.7 *Specially made doors and frames match the wall panelling, furniture and gates throughout the bank.*

sign is reflected in the light fittings and loudspeaker covers housed in the columns between the doors. The wall linings are also Peruvian walnut veneers, the rich dark brown coloration enhanced by a water-based stain and flame retardant lacquer (Figures 12.3 and 12.4, and Plates 36–38).

Although timber is often chosen mainly for its aesthetic qualities it also offers other properties such as a hard-wearing surface which can be decorated in various ways to achieve the desired effect. This is demonstrated by the London branch of the Shanghai Commercial Bank where the designer's brief was to provide a clear view of the ground floor area with some areas sound-proofed and others which provided a higher degree of privacy. This balance between public and private, transparent and opaque was achieved by evolving a system of screen-like timber partitions which were sometimes glazed and sometimes slatted to control vision. The external elevation has as a result a 20 m long screen made up of vertical blades set at different angles to provide privacy from outside whilst enabling the bank employees to have a view onto the courtyard outside. Sycamore was selected for its fine grain and subtle figuring and a silver grey stain was specially developed which when lightly polished gave the required delicate sheen.

The banking hall features a purpose made counter and receptionist's desk plus individual offices. The kitchen, dining area, cloakrooms and general storage were neatly screened by an ingenious system of sliding cupboards. All panelling is veneered and the requirement for 4 m long posts for the full height screens meant that 12 mm thick facings were applied to a solid timber core (Figures 12.5–12.7 and Plates 39–40).

Timber is a natural material and this can be considered both as a major advantage and as a disadvantage. The natural variation found, even within timber of the same species, can be exploited as a decorative feature, in contrast to the uniformity often associated with man-made materials. The range of timber species available in many forms provides the designer with a range of design possibilities which is not available in any other single material. However this natural variation which makes timber so desirable also means that it needs to be considered in a different way from manufactured materials. Timber use and specification is a matter of selecting and maximizing the material available and careful design and specification is therefore paramount in achieving the desired result. Given an understanding of the material and its behaviour the possibilities are limited only by the imagination of the designer.

13 Timber today and tomorrow

John G Sunley

John Sunley MSc FIStructE FIWSc is director of TRADA. Prior to joining TRADA he was head of the structures division at the Building Research Establishment, Princes Risborough Laboratory.

Man has always had plenty of timber available for his needs. He has ample timber available today and will always have sufficient to meet his requirements.

Current forestry policies in the developed countries and future policies in the developing countries will ensure that adequate supplies of timber are maintained.

About a third of the world's land surface is covered by forest representing a growing stock of around 300,000 million cubic metres of timber, of which some 135,000 million cubic metres are coniferous trees, the remainder being non-coniferous trees producing hardwood lumber (Figure 13.1 and Plates 41–44). The pulp and paper industry takes account of around 40 per cent of the value of world primary forest industries, with sawn wood accounting for more than 38 per cent and wood based panel products around 20 per cent. Set against the vast growing stock the consumption of timber in the UK looks minute; in 1982 it was:

Sawn softwood	7 019 000 cubic metres
Sawn hardwood	954 000 cubic metres
Plywood	937 000 cubic metres
Chipboard	1 227 200 metric tonnes

The role of the forest in man's survival on earth is crucial since the forest itself, plus the products from it, have and always will play a major part in maintaining life. The forest is a complex ecological system. Like all green plants, trees take in carbon dioxide and water and by the process of photosynthesis, convert them into carbohydrates and release oxygen back into the air. Thus the forest plays an essential part in maintaining the earth's atmosphere. In forest areas the trees also regulate the flow of water, preventing flooding by their use of water, preventing silting of rivers by stabilizing the soil, preventing erosion by maintaining the water balance and physically retaining the soil which otherwise could dry and be blown away. The forest provides a physical barrier to landslides and avalanches, provides shade, fodder and shelter for livestock and wildlife in addition to, in some of the less remote areas, providing recreation for man.

The forest therefore could be seen as a natural phenomenon, to be retained and conserved at all costs. However the forest also provides a multitude of forest products which are of major importance in human life today. The advantage which trees have over almost all other resources available to man is that they are a living and therefore renewable source of fuel, paper, sawn wood, panel products, plastics, textiles, rubber, charcoal, medicines, gums, resins, oils, tannins, dyes and a host of other products, used directly or in industry for the manufacture of other products. In nature trees grow and die and are replaced by new ones. Thus timber and other forest products can be grown and harvested as a crop in just the same way as any other form of agriculture, providing an endless supply of material for use.

The need to treat timber as a crop with the attendant requirements of good husbandry and management is becoming recognized worldwide. Forestry had been practised in Europe for about 200 years before it was introduced into the United States in the late nineteenth century. The developing nations, where much of the large expanses of forest exist, are being financed and educated in forest management with the help of developed countries through organizations such as the United Nations Food and Agriculture Organization. This does not mean that all the problems of clear felling in forest areas have ceased – large areas of forest are still being felled in the Amazon basin and in areas of South East Asia. Much of this clear felling is to provide fuel – over half the wood used in the world is for fuel – but perhaps more serious is the indiscriminate felling of the forest to clear areas for agriculture. There are clear indications that this is unproductive, the soil in the Amazon basin, for example, is maintained by the forest itself – the natural processes of regeneration form an ecological cycle which, when the trees are totally removed, is broken down and the land is only able to sustain agricultural crops for a very limited period of a few years. This in turn leads to a cycle of destruction with more and more forest areas being felled each year as those previously cleared become infertile. The danger is recognized and the international organizations, with the backing of the developed countries are carrying out educational programmes and research to encourage replanting and management in the major forest areas (Figures 13.2 and 13.3).

Figure 13.1 *The pine forests in north-east Nicaragua were depleted in the nineteenth century. Since 1959 the government has implemented a reafforestation and fire control programme in the area and United Nations agencies are undertaking technical and economic studies for eventual large-scale investment in the region. The photograph is a view of dawn over the forest.* Photograph: United Nations Y Nagata/PAS.

It is estimated that in tropical forest areas only five per cent of the timber harvested finds it way onto the international hardwood market. However this does not leave room for complacency and an important international agreement is about to be signed for a 20-year plan to encourage substantially more investment in the tropical forest and the more effective use of the available resources in perpetuity. The highly prized hardwoods of the tropical forests are felled selectively with individual mature trees being removed from the forest; this selective felling both allows and encourages the development of younger trees so that they too reach maturity. However over-utilization of some species in the past has led to severe shortages of individual timbers (e.g. the 'true' mahogany, *Swietienia mahagoni*) and the need to utilize a wider range of species. This is still true today and research and development work is being undertaken worldwide, not only to allow the use of a wider range of species but also to maximize the efficient use of the timber currently available.

This process of maximizing the resources available has recently been the subject of worldwide recognition and debate, but a look at the developments in the use of timber in the UK over the years shows that it is a process which has been in operation for a very long time. Like so many other developments the process has speeded up in recent years and seems likely to continue to do so. The changes in timber utilization and supply have been influenced by a number of factors; many of them are economic, brought about by rises in the cost of obtaining, for example, large section timbers. This provides an incentive to seek alternative means of obtaining the desired section for large span structures. Increases in price of the decorative woods have also led to the need to conserve their use.

The bulk of timber used for building in Europe is softwood rather than hardwood (Plates 45–47). The main reason is that in the past softwood has given the best combination of cost and performance and will tolerate a fair amount of abuse and yet still give an acceptable performance. Supply changes in the future mean that it will be necessary to use a wider range of species, both softwoods and hardwoods, with more variable properties than at present. Decorative hardwoods will undoubtedly achieve greater use as we erect more leisure buildings with greater aesthetic appeal.

The large softwood producing areas such as North America and Scandinavia now plan production against raw material availability and are ensuring that supplies will be available for as far ahead as one can see. Other developed countries are following this lead, for example New Zealand. Eventually developing countries, with assistance, will follow and provide guaranteed supplies. Some of these may be species with which we are presently unfamiliar but by the use of modern technology, promotion and marketing, full utilization will be obtained.

DEVELOPMENTS IN TIMBER UTILIZATION

Two broad aspects of changes in utilization can be considered, although there is obviously some interaction and overlap between the two. The first relates to the general use of timber and the second is more specifically concerned with timber structures and timber engineering.

The raw materials which form the basis for man-made products used in building occur in nature in an unusable form and require large quantities of energy to turn them into usable materials (see section on Energy). Timber is already in a usable form as round timber and is easily convertible into a very useful raw material. However, since it is not manufactured like other materials, some form of selection or grading is necessary to ensure that timber is used to best effect.

Over-design and over-specification are wasteful and expensive, both in terms of direct cost and of the overall use of the resource. There is no advantage in using timber that is stronger than required or using highly decorative timbers if they are to be enclosed within a structure or concealed by paint or other finishing treatments. Two methods of grading are required for the two main uses of timber, namely joinery and structural. In the first category appearance is important and in the second, structural performance. One of the most significant developments in this field has been the advent of stress grading timber for structural use (see Chapter 4). This allows the strength of individual pieces of timber to be assessed, thereby obviating the need to allow for uncharacteristically weak pieces in a design.

Stress grading ensures that all pieces assigned to a grade, whether this is done by machine or visually, will

Figure 13.2 *The United Nations agencies are carrying out extensive reafforestation programmes in many parts of the world. In Lebanon an ambitious 'Green Plan' aims to restore the famous cedar forests which once covered the mountains. Workers in a model nursery break up soil which will be mixed with peat and sand and placed in plastic bags for the cultivation of cypress seedlings.* Photograph: United Nations GT/jr.

have a guaranteed minimum stiffness and strength (Figures 13.4–13.6). All stress graded timber is marked with its grade and the grading carried out by companies is often backed by a quality assurance scheme so that the user can have confidence in the grade assessment. The lower stress grades, e.g. the GS grade of British Standard BS 4978, allow a larger number and larger sizes of knots than many specifiers were used to seeing in structural timber. However the stresses and design parameters laid down in the Codes of Practice CP 112 1972 and BS 5268 1984 are based on the quality of timber within that grade so that provided the design calculations were based on the use of GS timber the resulting structure will be more than adequately strong.

Stress grading also allows the use of smaller section timbers as there is less need for conservative design to allow for weak pieces. The choice of whether to use lower grade, larger section timbers or high grade smaller section timbers is of course largely dictated by cost and availability; these will vary with different designs. It is therefore wise to check on the price and supply situation early in the design process. One advantage in using lower grades of timber is that larger sections are used with a consequently more robust structure providing easier fixing for decorative lining materials.

The quality grading systems used in the countries of origin not only ensure that the producers obtain a higher price for high quality timber but also that unnecessarily high qualities are not used where they are not required. The class system laid down in BS 1186 Part 1 for joinery timber is specifically designed with this consideration in mind. There is no advantage in specifying the highest grade intended for a clear finish if joinery is to be painted (see Chapter 4).

The development of panel products of the various types was a great step forward in ensuring the economic use of timber (see Chapter 2). The first stage was the cutting of decorative veneers which were initially applied to lower grades or less prized species of solid timber. This led to the development of veneer plywood which not only allows the use of lower grades of timber but also provides a material of greater dimensional stability and multidirectional strength properties. The particleboards and fibre building boards take the use of lower grade timber still further by utilizing material which was previously regarded as waste. They are essentially reconstituted products where defects in the original timber are eliminated. The use of panel products with decorative timber veneers for internal joinery and cabinet work ensures the best of both worlds – the panel products are dimensionally more stable than solid timber whilst the decorative veneers allow the use of the most exotic timbers at an economic price.

The introduction of laminating techniques was started in the nineteenth century but this did not reach its full potential until durable adhesives were introduced during the Second World War. Lamination allows small dimension timbers to be built up into large sections. Finger jointing timbers within laminated components also means that large spans can be produced and defects in the timber can be distributed throughout the beam so that the strength of the whole can be greater than the sum of its parts. The limitations on laminated components are imposed by transport considerations but even these can be overcome by producing laminated components in sections for jointing on site. Laminating techniques tend to be considered in relation to large structural components but the techniques and the justification

Figure 13.3 *Lebanese women tend the cypress seedlings in the nursery.* Photograph: United Nations GT/jr.

for their use can be equally applied to smaller units such as joinery. Laminated timber provides economic structural sections in the sizes required and also is an extremely attractive form of construction. It is becoming more and more widely used (see Chapters 6 and 12) and this trend is likely to continue and expand.

Timber engineering

The development of timber engineering can be divided into three phases and is essentially a process of industrialization brought about by developments in related fields. The chief influence has been the development of jointing techniques. Because timber is strong in compression and tension but relatively weak in shear it is difficult to transmit the direct stresses that timber is capable of sustaining from one member to another (see Chapters 5 and 6).

The first phase is characterized by the lack of efficient jointing techniques and can be seen as the 'Carpenter's Era'. This began with the utilization of tree trunks split to make cruck frames (see Chapter 5). Greater development of carpentry skills led to the introduction of structures largely based on the 'post and beam' principle (Figure 13.7).

House roofs until 1950 were an orthodoxy of construction using an evolved carpenter's art. They were three-dimensional structures composed of a heterogeneous assemblage of timber of different shapes and sizes cunningly contrived to wedge together under the action of vertical loading and avoiding the need to transmit tensile forces through structural joints (Figure 13.8). Timber was available in relatively large sizes and labour was cheap and very skilled. Jointing was simple, mainly the common wire nail with occasional use of screws and bolts.

The second phase saw the development of synthetic adhesives during and after the Second World War plus the introduction of reasonably efficient jointing devices such as split ring and 'bulldog' connectors. The new adhesives allowed the plywood and glulam industries to develop since the durability of the glues meant that long term use in exterior situations was now possible. Plywood, with its more uniform properties and relatively high shear strength in large widths, made feasible a wide range of stressed skin constructions and other structures requiring efficient diaphragms. Box beams, I beams, stressed skin floors, walls and roofs all became widely used. Glulam structures based on straight and curved members were widely introduced for sports halls, churches and other public buildings. The availability of mechanical connectors led to the design of a large number of 'one off' structures, particularly long span roof trusses, often for industrial use. Chapter 6 describes and illustrates a range of such buildings.

The third phase can be seen more as the substitution of mechanical for manual processes than with the introduction of new materials – a process of industrialization which, although not attracting public attention to the same extent as the newer, more spectacular industries, has nevertheless transformed the use of old materials by applying new industrial techniques. A major transformation in the UK came with the introduction of the trussed rafter from the United States in the 1960s (see

Figures 13.4 and 13.5 *Machine stress grading of timber.*

Figure 13.9 and Chapters 6 and 8). The first truss-making machine was installed in the UK in 1964 and there are now about 120 of these of about six different types. There are differences in the nail plate design between different manufacturers but basically there are three types of machinery used for inserting nail plates to join timber pieces into a trussed rafter:

1 a complete jig where the truss slides or is rolled under a stationary press and out the other side
2 a separate press at each joint position; the truss remains stationary
3 a mobile press, which deals with each joint in turn, while the truss remains stationary

Figure 13.10 illustrates trussed rafter manufacture.

A similar revolution has taken place in the development of the timber frame industry in the UK. In North America most of the timber frame houses continue to

Figure 13.6 *Trainees being instructed in the visual stress grading of timber at TRADA.*

be 'stick built' on site, whereas in the UK we have taken modern timber frame techniques and industrialized them. The degree and sophistication of prefabrication varies from hand-held nailing and staple guns used in a small factory to highly streamlined computer controlled production lines (Figure 13.11). Most timber frame panels are produced with the sheathing material in place but panels can be produced which incorporate the insulation, joinery components, cladding and even the services (Chapter 7). This allows the timber framed house to be erected and weatherproofed on site in a very short space of time, typically three to five days, thus eliminating many of the problems associated with the vagaries of British weather. Quality control during panel production is carried out in the factory – equally strict control should be exercised on site to ensure that what, after all, is now an engineered structure, is erected properly.

The industrialization process has been taken even further with the introduction of volumetric housing where complete house units are made in the factory, including internal fittings, transported to the site and craned into position (Figure 13.12). With services available on site ready to be 'plumbed in' the house can be in use in a day. This form of construction has found a market in areas where there are special problems of needing to provide housing in a short space of time. Many of the portable office accommodation units which are widely used are built using timber frame techniques.

Floors present greater problems in industrialization due to the requirements for dimensional accuracy. Whereas walls can be erected in spite of inaccuracies in building and the roof presents few problems because it is a separate lid, floors have to be dropped into a constrained dimensional system. Variations in tolerances in

brickwork make this operation difficult but the increasing use of accurately manufactured timber frame wall panels opens up the field for new floor designs which make more economic use of materials and which can be produced off site (Figure 13.13).

Timber has certain properties which make it a very useful building material and point the way to the future. These are concerned chiefly with cost, strength, stiffness to weight ratio, ease of working, insulation properties etc. One big advantage of the ease of working is that in the past it has enabled timber to compensate for the faults of other building materials. Thus, whilst it may not be possible to build masonry walls at an exact distance apart, timber can easily be cut to fit between such walls. It is therefore easy to see why timber has evolved as a prime material for constructing house floors and roofs in which it forms a link between masonry walls.

Timber will continue to be used for building since it is always likely to provide a reasonable balance of performance and economy. The performance requirements will increasingly be dictated through national and international standards and regulations and backed by quality assurance. So far as timber is concerned, the technology is available to provide the necessary base for continuous improvement in timber products. With the full utilization of this technology timber will continue to be used as a major building material for as far ahead as one can see. An important trend which may increase the use of timber in buildings is the need to conserve raw materials and energy. Timber has the advantage of being a raw material which can be regenerated naturally and requires little energy to transform it into a usable building material. It is also relatively easy to combine timber with other materials to achieve desirable performance, for example the use of insulation materials in timber frame buildings to obtain high levels of thermal insulation (Figure 13.14).

Wood based sheet materials have, and will continue to expand in structural use since they provide more uniform properties in the form of wide sheets. Their increased use has been linked with changes in design and manufacture, for example wall panels which, instead of expensively framed timber structures, are now built from simply fixed members covered with plywood sheathing making a lighter, stiffer product.

TIMBER TO HOUSE THE WORLD?

The use of timber for constructional purposes varies widely throughout the world. Countries have tended to develop their own methods of construction depending largely on the availability of local raw materials and to a lesser extent on climate. The originally low populated areas in the northern hemisphere obviously used timber construction and have developed designs and constructional methods to meet the material and the climate. Examples are Canada and the Scandinavian countries where timber construction is usual and has become highly sophisticated.

The highly populated areas of western Europe have used stone and masonry constructions, after exhausting most of their timber resources in earlier building and in industry. It is only in recent years that timber construction has seen a revival and this is linked with the easing of transport and other problems.

The requirements of the Third World are somewhat different in that they have a need for more housing and improved standards. A wide range of indigenous timbers is often available but they may be difficult to work and considerable transportation difficulties arise (Figures 13.15 and 13.16). The Third World can therefore benefit enormously from developments in Europe and elsewhere so long as appropriate changes are made to meet local conditions.

The problems of timber utilization in the developing countries have some common elements and some major differences. In South America, for example, there are large quantities of hardwood trees but these tend to be distorted making conversion and use difficult. The huge variety of species makes consistency of quality a problem but perhaps the greatest difficulty which is common to many remote regions of the world is the need to transport timber for long distances over difficult or non-existent road systems. Central America has some excellent timbers with good pine forests in Mexico but the distances from the forests to centres of population create transportation problems (Plates 48 and 49). Southern Africa has better transport but lack of knowledge in the remote areas leaves a considerable education problem.

Africa has similar problems to South America with extremely hard and difficult to work timbers, and in some areas poor quality timber with wavy grain which makes it unsuitable for constructional purposes. The percentage of forest in India is small in relation to the size of the country, little industry exists and what there is, is craft based. Middle Eastern countries tend to be importers of European wood products; they have virtually no trees and very little appropriate technology. Little is known about China but other areas of the Far East have

Figure 13.7 *Post and beam construction.* Photograph: John Lawrence Photography Ltd.

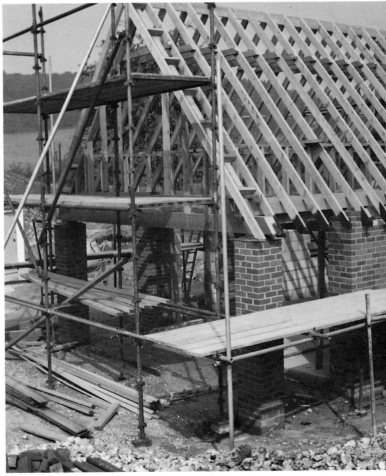

Figure 13.8 *Traditional roof construction.* Photograph: John Challen Sharp, architect.

Figure 13.9 *Trussed rafters are now the most widely used form of construction, particularly for domestic roofs. They are usually erected singly with bracing incorporated during construction but for large contracts they may be assembled into units on the ground and craned into position.* Photograph: Twinaplate Ltd.

Figure 13.10 *Manufacture of trussed rafters.* Photograph: Gang-Nail Ltd.

well developed timber industries and in certain parts there are considerable forest resources of excellent species. Generally there is a lack of skilled tradesmen for timber conversion and for general construction work in the developing countries – this is an area of expertise in which the highly developed nations are well able to help (Figure 13.17).

ENERGY CONSIDERATIONS

Increases in the costs of energy, largely influenced by oil prices, have led to greater attention being paid to energy conservation, particularly in the more highly developed northern countries of the world. Climatically these countries tend to be colder than the developing nations and there is therefore not only a greater requirement for energy for industry but also for space heating in buildings. Building legislation has called for higher insulation levels in buildings, for example in the UK the requirements for insulation in house walls were increased from 1.7 W/m^2 $°C$ to 1.0 W/m^2 $°C$ in 1972 to 0.6 W/m^2 $°C$ in 1981. It is this factor, along with others such as a lack of skilled site labour and the speed of construction giving more rapid cash flow for building firms, which prompted the rapid rise in timber frame construction in the UK. The ease with which insulation can be incorporated into timber frame panels allows houses to be constructed with insulation levels of 0.3 W/m^2 $°C$ within the normal construction.

The production of usable timber is also a low energy

Figure 13.11 *Manufacture of timber frame house panels.* Photograph: Guildway Ltd.

Figure 13.12 *Volumetric house units being craned into position.*

consuming process. Its growth is promoted via solar energy and its processing into a usable form uses relatively low level technology and relatively little energy.

Table 13.1 *Primary energy requirements for the production of building materials*

Material	Primary energy requirement* kWh/m²
Timber†	695
Concrete	736
Concrete blocks	834
Lightweight concrete	834
Bricks	973
Plasterboard	1425
Steel	1.02×10^{10}

* The energy requirement is the total primary fuel used at all stages in the production of the item. Values are average for the UK and have been adapted from a number of UK information sources.
† Timber value is for finished components and includes a substantial transport energy factor as much of the timber is imported into the UK (Figure 13.18).

About half the wood harvested from the world's forests is used as fuel although timber is not a particularly efficient source of energy:

Table 13.2 *Gross calorific values of fuels*

Gross calorific values	MJ/kg
Wood, 25% moisture content	16
Wood, dry	20
Coal	27.5
Fuel oil	44.4

TRENDS IN TIMBER RESEARCH

The last 50 years have seen two major developments in research on the use of timber and there is undoubtedly a third following. In the immediate post-war years most research activity was concerned with the properties of materials and the ways of using them reasonably effi-

Figure 13.13 *Prefabricated floor panels.*

ciently without problems, hence a great deal of time was spent on characterizing species and investigating various finishes and adhesives for use in combination with them.

The second stage was more concerned with applying modern processing methods to timber to reduce the amount of site labour and bring as much work into the factory as possible. It was linked with a period of increasing labour costs – hence the need to save on labour. This resulted, as already explained, in the development of the trussed rafter and the timber frame wall panel for house building.

There is little doubt that the third major change will be more organizational, bringing together work on materials and production to create more organized systems; obviously computers will have a large part to play in this.

191

Figure 13.14 *Insulation of timber frame wall panels.* Photograph: Fibreglass Ltd.

Building trends

Looking at the conditions which will probably prevail in building in the future, it is possible to link these with the properties of timber and timber products. Generally, it can be assumed that building materials and components will have to meet the following broad requirements.

- A reasonable combination of economy and performance
- Minimum maintenance during the life of the building
- Continuing need for quick erection and reduced site work
- Greater flexibility in building to enable the changing needs of occupancy to be met by existing buildings
- Increasing demand for higher quality and better performance
- Continuing demand, particularly in northern climates, for well insulated buildings

These general requirements will be linked to other trends such as:

* Increasing use of performance standards
* General control of building with regard to specification and approval passing more and more into the hands of technical people who are not committed to a particular material
* Increasing demand for guaranteed performance or assurance of quality

Figure 13.15 *Traditional methods of timber extraction are still used in many developing countries; trained elephants being used to move timber in a forest area of Coorg, Karnataka State, India.* Photograph: United Nations J. Isaac (NJ).

192

Figure 13.16 _Logs being transported along a road in Tamil Nadu, India._ Photograph: United Nations J. Isaac.

Most of these requirements will be demanded through national, regional, and international codes, standards and regulations with nationally run quality assurance schemes.

Performance standards and quality assurance

There has recently been a growing use of performance, as distinct from product, standards where the requirements for components are specified in terms of performance, such as adequate structural rigidity, sound insulation, surface protection etc. It will become increasingly necessary to prove that components are capable of meeting the required performance standards, rather than to specify how the components shall be made. There is little doubt that timber based materials will be able to meet all sensible requirements and research will continue to ensure that this is so. Quality assurance schemes already exist for many timber products and these will be extended to provide consumer confidence. It is doubtful if there will be a rapid change to complete specification by performance but there will be increasing dependence on performance-aided documents which also demand quality assurance.

Maintenance

Adequate techniques and preservatives are already available to enable most timber species to give a reasonable guaranteed life in relation to the expected life of a building. However there is a considerable need to apply the available technology in the form of better specification and quality control. Preservative treatment is already required for exterior joinery such as window and door frames in many countries; finishes for external timber have always presented more of a problem but work is in hand to produce better finishes and the ability to apply them in adverse conditions. Again, the technology and materials are available and their application should follow quickly.

Figure 13.17 _Sawing a mahogany log at a sawmill in Sudan._
Photograph: United Nations/FAO F. Mattioli NJ.

193

Figure 13.18 *Much of the timber used in the UK is imported.* Photograph: Seaboard International (Timber and Plywood) Limited.

Flexibility in building

Timber is an ideal material for renovating old buildings because of its ease of working; it can easily be cut on site to fit the existing shapes and desired sizes. Timber buildings are also somewhat easier to adapt than those made of denser materials. There is considerable evidence that at present more renovation and less new building is taking place.

Recent developments, such as trussed rafters and timber frame wall panels, have produced timber components which will give greater flexibility in house building. This is somewhat limited with the trussed rafter since, although it produces a roof which spans from wall to wall without the need for internal load-bearing partitions, it does preclude, to some extent, the future use of the roof space as habitable rooms. However, it is already possible to obtain trussed rafters which will permit a change later, or alternative methods of construction, such as folded plate roofs, may be adopted in the future.

Amenity standards in housing will increasingly demand a greater degree of flexible occupation. Ideally what is needed is greater freedom of internal planning and the facility easily and cheaply to extend or adapt the layout to meet changing family needs. In the limited concept of housing as we know it today, the possibilities for improving the use of internal space are:

- use of the roof space
- provision of basements
- development of clear spans for first floors to allow freedom of planning using non-load-bearing partitions

There is little doubt that high rise housing will not be used much in the future but with an increasing need for single occupation, low rise flats will become more prevalent. These will call for the further development of compartment floors with improved sound and fire resistance between adjacent living areas. Current research will ensure that timber continues to be used.

With regard to the use of the roof space, it is important that components are designed to allow its use without losing the advantages of prefabrication. Basements pose different problems and to date have been less popular in the UK than in many other countries.

Better quality building

There is likely to be an increasing demand for higher quality products in the future compared with the low cost ones which have been used in the past. This will relate to aesthetic and performance qualities, such as thermal insulation and acoustic properties. In future, more care with regard to the drying of timber to suit the environment in which it will be placed, improvement in surface finishing and better use of preservatives will become an essential part of high quality. Materials will need to be combined to achieve the desired performance; thus if timber is capable of providing the main bulk of a component, and a better surface finish can be obtained with other materials, then this is a sensible approach. It is obvious that with continuing energy problems, insulation of walls and double or even triple glazing of windows will become the norm.

Timber and timber products are well able to meet all requirements which can be envisaged at the present time. However, this may need a change of attitude on the part of designers and specifiers who may have been used to providing the cheapest possible product which would meet the most basic requirements.

Appendix

Properties and uses of commonly used timbers

David Sulman AIWSc is TRADA regional officer for Scotland. He joined the association in 1979 as assistant regional officer for the south east, moving to Scotland in 1983. Prior to joining TRADA he was a management trainee and later salesman for a major timber group.

The table shows the broad range of species which are available in the UK. The plate numbers refer to the colour illustrations between pages 144 and 145. The symbol † denotes that the structural properties of a species are included in BS 5268 Part 2. The following properties of each species are described:

Species

Common and botanical names and countries of origin are indicated.

Colour

The colour(s) indicated relate to the heartwood of the species. However most timbers show variation in colour as well as changing colour in use and by the application of finishes. Timber exposed to light will change colour and unprotected timber exposed to the weather will eventually become silvery grey in colour.

Density

Timbers vary in density depending on their species and moisture content. The values quoted are averages at 15 per cent, but the increase caused by moisture can be calculated by adding 0.5 per cent of the given weight for every 1 per cent increase in moisture content. The symbol ★ indicates that density can vary by 20 per cent or more.

Texture

Surface texture is classified as fine, medium and coarse.

Moisture movement in service

This refers to the dimensional changes that occur when dried timber is subjected to changes in atmospheric conditions. (This is not directly related to the shrinkage which occurs when green timber is dried to moisture contents suitable for internal use.) The movement is classed as small, medium and large. For structural pur-

poses the movement category of a timber is not usually significant. For situations where varying humidities are likely to be encountered and the stability of a component is important, then a species exhibiting small movement should be specified.

Working qualities

This refers to the ease of working and is classified as good, medium or difficult. A difficult classification does not mean that a timber is unworkable but indicates that particular care should be taken in machining.

Durability

This relates to the resistance to fungal decay of a species. Durability is expressed by one of five classes based upon the average life of a 50×50 mm section of heartwood in ground contact. This is a particularly hazardous situation and timber used externally, but not in contact with the ground, will have a longer life than that indicated, even without treatment. These ratings refer to the heartwood only. The sapwood of all species tested has been found to be non-durable or perishable; consequently the sapwood of all species should not be used in exposed situations without preservative treatment.

The classes used are:

very durable	more than 25 years
durable	15–25 years
moderately durable	10–15 years
non-durable	5–10 years
perishable	less than 5 years

Preservative treatment should be specified where the timber is not sufficiently naturally durable and is to be used in a situation where there is a risk of decay. See Chapter 3.

Permeability

This refers to the ease with which timbers can be penetrated with preservatives applied by a standard pressure impregnation treatment. See Chapter 3. The permeability categories are:

extremely resistant — absorbs only a small amount

very resistant — difficult to penetrate more than 3–6 mm

moderately resistant — 6–18 mm penetration in 2–3 hours

permeable — absorbs preservative without difficulty

⋆ indicates a provisional classification

Availability

Sawn timbers may be in regular or limited supply depending on the availability from producers and levels of demand. Availability is described as regular, limited or variable.

Veneer availability

A tick (√) indicates that the species is available in veneer form.

Price

The following terms are used to indicate prices:

high over £600 per cubic metre
medium £400–600 per cubic metre
low up to £400 per cubic metre

These prices are for guidance only and are based on parcels of sawn timber not less than 1.5 cubic metres ex yard of a normal fair average specification at 1984 price levels. The prices relate to decorative hardwoods; structural softwoods will normally fall into the cheaper half of the low category. Prices are for kiln dried stock where appropriate.

Remarks

Comments where necessary on sizes, special features such as drying, staining etc.

Uses

The list is not exhaustive, and most timbers can be used for more purposes than those listed.

Sizes

Specific information relating to sizes has not been given for individual timbers, although comments on limited sizes or large dimensions are given.

Information on sizes is given in Chapter 4.

Specifiers and buyers should check on the availability of species and sizes with suppliers.

Species of timber in more limited supply not appearing in the following tables include:—

Albizia	Dahoma	Missanda	Rauli
Alerce	Degame	Muhuhu	Saligna gum
Apple	Elm, Rock	Muninga	Sen
Black bean	Holly	Okwen	Sterculia
Bombax	Hornbeam	Omu	Sucupira
Boxwood	Ilomba	Ovangkol	Tatajuba
Californian redwood	Imbuya	Pear	Tawa
Ceiba	Indian laurel	Persimmon	Tetraberlinia
Celtis	Mansonia	Podo	Zebrano
Cocobolo	Mersawa	Pterygota	

Information on the properties and uses of these timbers is available from TRADA.

Species	Plate No	Colour	Density kg/m³	Texture	Moisture movement	Working qualities	Durability	Permeability	Availability	Veneer available	Price	Remarks	Uses
Abura *Mitragyna ciliata* W Africa	36	Hardwood Light brown	580*	Medium/fine	Small	Medium	Non-durable	Moderately resistant	Variable	✓	Low	Colour variable. Resistant to acids.	Interior joinery, mouldings.
Afrormosia *Pericopsis elata* W Africa	38	Hardwood Light brown	710	Medium/fine	Small	Medium	Very durable	Extremely resistant	Regular	✓	Medium/High	Tends to darken on exposure, stains in contact with iron in damp conditions.	Interior and exterior joinery. Furniture. Cladding.
Afzelia/Doussié *Afzelia* spp W Africa	50	Hardwood Reddish-brown	830*	Medium/coarse	Small	Medium/difficult	Very durable	Extremely resistant	Limited	✓	Medium	Exudes yellow dye in damp conditions.	Interior and exterior joinery. Cladding.
Agba *Gossweilerodendron balsamiferum* W Africa	46	Hardwood Yellowish-brown	510	Medium	Small	Good	Durable	Resistant	Regular	✓	Low	Gum exudation may be troublesome.	Interior and exterior joinery, trim, cladding.
Andiroba *Carapa guianenisis* S America	24	Hardwood Pink to red-brown	640	Medium/coarse	Small	Medium	Moderately durable	Extremely resistant	Limited		Low		Interior joinery.
Ash, American *Fraxinus* spp USA	4	Hardwood Grey, brown	670	Coarse	Medium	Medium	Non-durable	Permeable	Regular	✓	Medium/High		Interior joinery, trim, tool handles.
Ash, European *Fraxinus excelsior* Europe	15	Hardwood White to light brown	710*	Medium/coarse	Medium	Good	Perishable	Moderately resistant	Regular	✓	Medium/High	Selected stock may be tough and be suitable for bending.	Interior joinery, sports goods.
Aspen *Populus tremuloides* Canada, USA		Hardwood Grey, white to pale brown	450	Fine	Large	Medium	Perishable/Non-durable	Extremely* resistant	Variable		Low		Interior joinery. Matches.
Balsa *Ochroma pyramidale* S America		Hardwood White	160*	Fine	Small	Good	Perishable	Resistant	Limited		Medium	High buoyancy value, and good insulating value.	Useful for heat, sound and vibration insulation. Buoyancy aids.
Balau (†) *Shorea* spp SE Asia		Hardwood Yellow-brown to red-brown	980	Medium	Medium	Medium	Very durable	Extremely resistant	Variable		Low	A hard, heavy and strong timber. Obtainable in large sizes.	Heavy structural work, bridge and wharf construction.
Balau, Red *Shorea* spp SE Asia		Hardwood Purplish-red or dark red-brown	880	Medium	Medium	Medium	Moderately durable	Extremely resistant	Variable		Low		Heavy structural work.
Basralocus *Dicorynia guianensis* Surinam & French Guiana		Hardwood Lustrous brown	720	Medium	Medium/Large	Medium	Very durable	Extremely resistant	Limited		Low/medium	Acid resistant. Obtainable in large sizes.	Marine and heavy construction
Basswood *Tilia americana* N America		Hardwood Creamy white to pale brown	420	Fine	Medium	Good	Non-durable	Permeable	Limited	✓	Low		Constructional veneer, turnery, piano keys, woodware.
Beech, European *Fagus sylvatica* Europe	6 18	Hardwood Whitish to pale brown, pinkish-red when steamed	720	Fine	Large	Good	Perishable	Permeable	Regular	✓	Low	Excellent bending properties.	Furniture, interior joinery, flooring. Plywood.
Birch, American *Betula* spp N America		Hardwood Light to dark reddish-brown	710	Fine	Large	Good	Perishable	Moderately resistant	Limited	✓	Low		Furniture, plywood; flooring.
Birch, European *Betula pubescens* Europe, Scandinavia	2	Hardwood White to light brown	670	Fine	Large	Good	Perishable	Permeable	Limited	✓	Low		Plywood, furniture, turnery.
Cedar of Lebanon *Cedrus libani* Europe		Softwood Light brown	580	Medium	Medium/small*	Good	Durable	Resistant	Limited	✓	Medium	Pungent cedar odour.	Joinery, garden furniture, gates.
Cedar, Central/South American *Cedrela* spp Central & S America	20	Hardwood Pinkish-brown to dark reddish-brown	480	Coarse	Small	Good	Durable	Extremely resistant	Limited	✓	Low	Distinctive odour.	Cabinet work, interior joinery. Racing boat-building. Cigar boxes.
Cherry, American *Prunus serotina* USA	33	Hardwood Reddish-brown to red	580	Fine	Medium	Good	Moderately durable	No information	Limited	✓	Medium		Cabinet making, furniture. Interior joinery.

Species	Plate No	Colour	Density kg/m³	Texture	Moisture movement	Working qualities	Durability	Permeability	Availability	Veneer available	Price	Remarks	Uses
Cherry, European *Prunus avium* Europe		Hardwood Pinkish-brown	630	Fine	Medium	Good	Moderately durable	No information	Limited	✓	Medium/High	Inclined to warp. Use in small sections.	Cabinet making, furniture.
Chestnut, Horse *Aesculus hippocastanum* Europe		Hardwood White to pale yellow-brown	510	Fine	Small	Medium	Perishable	Permeable	Limited		Low		Brush backs, fruit trays and boxes.
Chestnut, Sweet *Castanea sativa* Europe	42	Hardwood Yellowish-brown	560	Medium	Large	Good	Durable	Extremely resistant	Limited	✓	Medium	Stains in contact with iron in damp conditions.	Interior and exterior joinery. Fencing.
Danta *Nesogordonia papaverifera* W Africa	57	Hardwood Reddish-brown	750	Fine	Medium	Good	Moderately durable	Resistant	Limited		Low		Flooring, joinery, turnery.
Douglas fir (t) *Pseudotsuga menziesii* N America and UK	34	Softwood Light reddish-brown	530	Medium	Small	Good	Moderately durable	Resistant/ Extremely resistant	Regular	✓	Medium	Marked 'flame-like' growth ring figure. Long lengths and clear grades available.	Plywood, interior and exterior joinery, construction. Vats and tanks.
Ebony *Diospyros* spp W Africa, India, Sri Lanka		Hardwood Black, some grey/black stripes	1030/ 1190	Fine	Medium	Medium	Very durable	Extremely resistant	Limited	✓	High	Generally small sizes only available. Dust may be irritant.	Used primarily for decorative work. Turnery, inlaying.
Ekki/Azobé (t) *Lophira elata* W Africa	63	Hardwood Dark red to dark brown	1070	Coarse	Large	Difficult	Very durable	Extremely resistant	Limited		Medium	Moderately resistant to termite attack. Acid resistant. Obtainable in large sizes.	Heavy construction, marine and freshwater construction. Bridges, sleepers, etc.
Elm, American *Ulmus americana* N America		Hardwood Pale reddish-brown	580	Coarse	Medium	Medium	Non-durable	Moderately resistant	Limited	✓	Medium	Good strength, toughness and bending properties.	Furniture, coffins, rubbing strips.
Elm, European *Ulmus* spp Europe	39	Hardwood Light brown	560*	Coarse	Medium	Medium	Non-durable	Moderately resistant	Limited	✓	Medium		Furniture, coffins, boat building.
Freijo *Cordia goeldiana* S America	43	Hardwood Golden brown	590	Medium	Medium/ small	Medium	Durable	No information	Variable		Medium		Furniture, interior and exterior joinery.
Gaboon *Aucoumea klaineana* W Africa		Hardwood Pinkish-brown	430	Medium	Medium	Medium	Non-durable	Resistant	Limited	✓	Medium		Used principally for plywood and blockboard.
Gedu nohor/Edinam *Entandrophragma angolense* W Africa	58	Hardwood Reddish-brown	560	Medium	Small	Medium	Moderately durable	Extremely resistant	Limited	✓	Low		Furniture, exterior and interior joinery.
Geronggang *Cratoxylon arborescens* SE Asia		Hardwood Pink to red	550	Coarse	Medium	Medium	Non-durable	Permeable	Variable		Low		Interior joinery.
Greenheart (t) *Ocotea rodiaei* Guyana	45	Hardwood Yellow/olive green to brown	1040	Fine	Medium	Difficult	Very durable	Extremely resistant	Variable		Medium	Available in very large sizes.	Heavy construction, marine and freshwater construction. Bridges, etc.
Guarea *Guarea cedrata* W Africa	28	Hardwood Pinkish-brown	590	Medium	Small	Medium	Very durable	Extremely resistant	Variable	✓	Medium	Fine dust may be irritant. Resin exudation may occur.	Furniture, interior joinery, cabinet making.
Hemlock, Western (t) *Tsuga heterophylla* N America	41	Softwood Pale brown	500	Fine	Small	Good	Non-durable	Resistant	Regular		Low	Obtainable in large sizes.	Construction, joinery.
Hickory *Carya* spp N America		Hardwood Brown to reddish-brown	830	Coarse	Large	Difficult	Non-durable	Moderately resistant	Limited		Medium	Good steam bending properties. Good shock resistance.	Striking tool handles, ladder rungs, sports goods.
Idigbo *Terminalia ivorensis* W Africa	11	Hardwood Yellow	560*	Medium	Small	Medium	Durable	Extremely resistant	Variable	✓	Low/ Medium	Stains yellow in contact with water, is acidic and may corrode ferrous metals, also stains in contact with iron when wet.	Interior and exterior joinery, plywood.
Iroko (t) *Chlorophora excelsa* W Africa	49	Hardwood Yellow brown	660	Medium	Small	Medium/ difficult	Very durable	Extremely resistant	Regular	✓	Medium	Occasional deposits of stone may occur.	Exterior and interior joinery, bench tops, constructional work.

Species	Plate No	Colour	Density kg/m³	Texture	Moisture movement	Working qualities	Durability	Permeability	Availability	Veneer available	Price	Remarks	Uses
Jarrah (t) *Eucalyptus marginata* Australia	31	Hardwood Pink to dark red	820*	Medium	Medium	Difficult	Very durable	Extremely resistant	Limited		Low/Medium		Heavy constructional work. Flooring.
Jelutong *Dyera costulata* SE Asia	13	Hardwood White to yellow	470	Fine	Small	Good	Non-durable	Permeable	Regular		Low	Latex ducts may be present.	Pattern making, drawing boards.
Kapur (t) *Dryobalanops spp* SE Asia	29	Hardwood Reddish-brown	770*	Medium	Medium	Medium	Very durable	Extremely resistant	Variable		Low	Camphor-like odour.	Exterior joinery, decking, constructional use.
Karri (t) *Eucalyptus diversicolor* Australia	61	Hardwood Reddish-brown	900	Medium	Large	Difficult	Durable	Extremely resistant	Limited		Medium		Heavy construction.
Kauvula *Endospermum macrophyllum* Fiji	5	Hardwood Pale cream to straw yellow	480	Medium to coarse	Small	Medium	Perishable	Permeable	Limited		Low/Medium		Mouldings. interior joinery.
Kempas (t) *Koompassia malaccensis* SE Asia		Hardwood Orange-red to red-brown	880	Coarse	Medium	Difficult	Durable	Resistant	Limited		Low	Slightly acidic and may encourage corrosion of ferrous metals.	Heavy constructional use.
Keruing, Apitong, Gurjun, Yang (t) *Dipterocarpus spp* SE Asia	30	Hardwood Pinkish-brown to dark brown	740*	Medium	Large/Medium	Difficult	Moderately durable	Resistant	Regular		Low	Liable to resin exudation.	Heavy and general construction. Decking, vehicle flooring.
Larch, European (t) *Larix decidua* Europe		Softwood Pale reddish-brown	590	Fine	Small	Medium	Moderately durable	Resistant	Regular	✓	Low/Medium		Boat planking, pit props, transmission poles.
Larch, Japanese (t) *Larix kaempferi* Europe		Softwood Reddish-brown	560	Fine	Small	Medium	Moderately durable	Resistant	Regular		Medium		Stakes, general construction
Lauan see Meranti													
Lignum vitae *Guaiacum spp* Central America		Hardwood Dark green/brown	1250	Fine	Medium	Difficult	Very durable	Extremely resistant	Limited		High	Obtainable in small sizes only.	Bushes and bearings, sports goods and textile equipment.
Limba/Afara *Terminalia superba* W Africa	7	Hardwood Pale yellow brown/straw	560*	Medium	Small	Good	Non-durable	Moderately resistant	Limited	✓	Low/Medium		Furniture. interior joinery.
Lime, European *Tilia spp* Europe		Hardwood Yellowish-white to pale brown	560	Fine	Medium	Good	Perishable	Permeable	Limited		Low/Medium		Carving. turnery. bungs. clogs.
Mahogany, African *Khaya spp* W Africa	26	Hardwood Reddish-brown	530	Medium	Small	Medium	Moderately durable	Extremely resistant	Regular	✓	Low/Medium		Furniture, cabinet work. boat building. joinery.
Mahogany, American *Swietenia macrophylla* Central and S America especially Brazil	35	Hardwood Reddish-brown	560	Medium	Small	Good	Durable	Extremely resistant	Regular	✓	Medium		Furniture, cabinet work, interior and exterior joinery. Boat building.
Makoré *Tieghemella heckelii* W Africa	59	Hardwood Pinkish-brown to dark red	640	Fine	Small	Medium	Very durable	Extremely resistant	Variable	✓	Medium	Fine dust may be irritant.	Furniture, interior and exterior joinery. Boat building. Plywood.
Maple, Rock *Acer saccharum* N America	14	Hardwood Creamy white	740	Fine	Medium	Medium	Non-durable	Resistant	Regular	✓	Medium/High	High resistance to abrasion.	Excellent flooring timber. Furniture. Sports goods.
Maple. Soft *Acer saccharinum* N America		Hardwood Creamy white	650	Fine	Medium	Medium	Non-durable	Moderately resistant	Limited	✓	Medium		Furniture. Interior joinery. Turnery.
Mengkulang *Heritiera spp* SE Asia	22	Hardwood Red, brown	720	Coarse	Small	Medium	Moderately durable	Resistant	Limited	✓	Low		Interior joinery. Construction. Plywood.

Species	Plate No	Colour	Density kg/m³	Texture	Moisture movement	Working qualities	Durability	Permeability	Availability	Veneer available	Price	Remarks	Uses
Meranti, Dark Red/ Dark Red Seraya/ Red Lauan Shorea spp SE Asia	23	Hardwood Medium to dark red-brown	710*	Medium	Small	Medium	Variable, generally moderately durable to durable.	Resistant to extremely resistant	Regular	✓	Low		Interior and exterior joinery, plywood.
Meranti, Light Red/ Light Red Seraya/ White Lauan Shorea spp SE Asia	40	Hardwood Pale pink to mid red	550*	Medium	Small	Medium	Variable, generally non-durable to moderately durable	Extremely resistant	Regular	✓	Low		Interior joinery. Plywood.
Meranti, Yellow/ Yellow Seraya Shorea spp SE Asia		Hardwood Yellow brown	660*	Medium	Small	Medium	Variable, generally non-durable to moderately durable	Extremely resistant	Limited	✓	Low		Interior joinery, plywood.
Merbau (t) Intsia spp. SE Asia	53	Hardwood Medium to dark red brown	830	Coarse	Small	Moderate	Durable	Extremely resistant	Variable	✓	Low	Liable to stain when in contact with iron in damp conditions.	Joinery, flooring, structural work.
Nemesu Shorea pauciflora Malaysia		Hardwood Red brown to dark red	710	Medium	Small	Medium	Moderately durable to durable	Resistant to extremely resistant	Regular	✓	Low/ Medium		Interior and exterior joinery. Plywood.
Niangon Tarrietia utilis W Africa	21	Hardwood Reddish-brown	640*	Medium	Medium	Good	Moderately durable	Extremely resistant	Variable	✓	Medium		Interior and exterior joinery. Furniture.
Nyatoh Palaquium spp SE Asia	54	Hardwood Pale pink to red-brown	720	Fine	Medium	Medium	Non-durable to moderately durable	Extremely resistant	Variable	✓	Low/ Medium		Interior joinery, furniture.
Oak, American Red Quercus spp N America	25	Hardwood Yellowish-brown with red tinge	790	Medium	Medium	Medium	Non-durable	Moderately resistant	Regular	✓	Medium		Furniture. Interior joinery.
Oak, American White Quercus spp N America	44	Hardwood Pale yellow to mid-brown	770	Medium	Medium	Medium	Durable	Extremely resistant	Regular	✓	Medium	Due to acidic nature, may stain when in contact with iron under damp conditions. May also corrode metals.	Furniture, cabinet work. Tight cooperage.
Oak, European Quercus robur Europe	10	Hardwood Yellowish-brown	670/ 720	Medium/ coarse	Medium	Medium/ difficult	Durable	Extremely resistant	Variable	✓	Medium/ High	Iron staining may occur in damp conditions, similarly corrosion of metals.	Furniture. Interior and exterior joinery. Flooring. Tight cooperage. Fencing.
Oak, Japanese Quercus mongolica Japan	48	Hardwood Pale yellow	670	Medium	Medium	Medium	Moderately durable	Extremely resistant*	Variable	✓	High		Furniture. Interior joinery.
Oak, Tasmanian Eucalyptus delegatensis Eucalyptus obliqua Eucalyptus regnans Australia & Tasmania		Hardwood Pale pink to brown	610/ 710	Coarse	Medium	Medium	Moderately durable	Resistant	Limited	✓	Medium		Furniture, interior joinery.
Obeche Triplochiton scleroxylon W Africa	12	Hardwood White to pale yellow	390	Medium	Small	Good	Non-durable	Resistant	Regular	✓	Low		Interior joinery, furniture. Plywood.
Opepe (t) Nauclea diderrichii W Africa	27	Hardwood Yellow to orange yellow	750	Coarse	Small	Medium	Very durable	Moderately resistant	Variable	✓	Medium		Heavy constructional work. Marine and freshwater use. Exterior joinery. Flooring.
Padauk Pterocarpus spp W Africa, Andamans, Burma		Hardwood Red to dark purple brown	640/ 850	Coarse	Small	Medium	Very durable	Moderately resistant to resistant	Limited	✓	High	Dust may be irritant.	Interior and exterior joinery, turnery. Flooring.
Parana Pine (t) Araucaria angustifolia S America	37	Softwood Golden brown with bright red streaks	550	Fine	Medium	Good	Non-durable	Moderately resistant	Regular	✓	Medium/ High	Distortion may occur in drying.	Interior joinery. Plywood.

Species	Plate No	Colour	Density kg/m³	Texture	Moisture movement	Working qualities	Durability	Permeability	Availability	Veneer available	Price	Remarks	Uses
Pau marfim *Balfourodendron riedelianum* S America	8	Hardwood yellow	800	Medium	Large	Good	Non-durable	No information	Limited	✓	Medium	Dust may be irritant.	Interior joinery, furniture. Flooring.
Plane, European *Platanus hybrida* Europe		Hardwood Mottled red-brown	640	Fine	No information	Medium	Perishable	No information	Limited	✓	Medium		Decorative purposes. Inlay work.
Pine, Corsican (†) *Pinus nigra* Europe		Softwood Light yellowish-brown	510	Coarse	Small	Medium	Non-durable	Moderately resistant	Regular		Low		Joinery, construction.
Pine, Maritime *Pinus pinaster* Europe		Softwood Pale brown to yellow	510	Medium/coarse	Medium	Good	Moderately durable	Resistant	Regular		Low		Pallets and packaging.
Pine, Pitch (†) *Pinus palustris Pinus elliottii* Southern USA		Softwood Yellow-brown to red-brown	670	Medium	Medium	Medium	Moderately durable	Resistant	Regular		Low	Also known as longleaf yellow pine or longleaf pitch pine or American pitch pine.	Interior and exterior joinery, heavy construction.
Pine, Radiata *Pinus radiata* S Africa, Australia		Softwood Yellow to pale brown	480	Medium	Medium	Good	Non-durable	Permeable*	Regular		Low		Furniture, packaging.
Pine, Scots (†) *Pinus sylvestris* UK		Softwood Pale yellowish-brown to red, brown	510	Coarse	Medium	Medium	Non-durable	Moderately resistant	Regular	✓	Low		Construction, joinery.
Pine, Southern (†) A number of species including *Pinus palustris, P. elliotti, P. echinata, P. taeda,* Southern USA		Softwood Pale yellow to light brown	560*	Medium	Medium	Medium	Non-durable	Moderately resistant	Regular		Low		Construction, joinery. Plywood.
Pine, yellow *Pinus strobus* N America		Softwood Pale yellow to light brown	420	Fine	Small	Good	Non-durable	Moderately resistant	Regular		Low/Medium	Also known as Quebec yellow pine.	Pattern making, drawing boards, doors.
Poplar *Populus* spp Europe		Hardwood Grey, white to pale brown	450	Fine/Medium	Large	Medium	Perishable/non-durable	Extremely resistant	Variable	✓	Low		Pallet blocks, box boards, turnery. Wood wool.
Purpleheart *Peltogyne* spp Central & S America		Hardwood Purple to purplish brown	880	Medium	Small	Medium/difficult	Very durable	Extremely resistant	Limited		High		Heavy construction. Flooring. Turnery.
Ramin *Gonystylus* spp SE Asia	16	Hardwood White to pale yellow	670	Medium	Large	Medium	Non-durable	Permeable	Regular	✓	Medium		Mouldings. furniture.
Redwood, European (†) *Pinus sylvestris* Scandinavia/USSR	9	Softwood Pale yellowish-brown to red-brown	510	Medium	Medium	Medium	Non-durable	Moderately resistant	Regular	✓	Low		Construction, joinery, furniture.
Rosewood *Dalbergia* spp S America, India	62	Hardwood Medium to dark purplish-brown with black streaks	870*	Medium	Small	Medium	Very durable	Extremely resistant	Limited	✓	High	Sizes may be limited.	Interior joinery, cabinet work, turnery.
Sapele *Entandrophragma cylindricum* W Africa	60	Hardwood Medium reddish-brown with marked stripe figure	640	Medium	Medium	Medium	Moderately durable	Resistant	Regular	✓	Medium		Interior joinery, furniture, flooring.
Sepetir *Sindora* spp SE Asia		Hardwood Golden brown	640/830	Medium	Small	Difficult	Durable	Extremely resistant	Limited	✓	Low		Joinery, furniture.

Seraya – see meranti

Species	Plate No	Colour	Density kg/m³	Texture	Moisture movement	Working qualities	Durability	Permeability	Availability	Veneer available	Price	Remarks	Uses
Spruce, Canadian (†) *Picea* spp Canada		Softwood White to pale yellow	400/500	Medium	Small	Good	Non-durable	Resistant	Regular		Low		Construction, joinery.
Spruce, Sitka (†) *Picea sitchensis* UK		Softwood Pinkish-brown	450	Coarse	Small	Good	Non-durable	Resistant	Regular		Low		Construction, packaging, pallets.
Spruce, Western white (†) *Picea glauca* N America		Softwood White to pale yellow/brown	400/500	Medium	Small	Good	Non-durable	Resistant	Regular		Low	Large sizes available.	Construction, joinery.
Sycamore *Acer pseudoplatanus* Europe	1	Hardwood White or yellowish-white	630	Fine	Medium	Good	Perishable	Permeable	Limited	✓	Medium/High		Turnery, textile equipment. Joinery.
Taun *Pometia pinnata* SE Asia		Hardwood Pale pinkish-brown	750	Coarse	Medium	Medium	Moderately durable	Moderately resistant	Limited	✓	Low		Structural work, turnery, joinery, furniture.
Teak (†) *Tectona grandis* Burma, Thailand	55	Hardwood Golden brown, sometimes with dark markings	660	Medium	Small	Medium	Very durable	Extremely resistant	Regular	✓	High	Fine dust may be irritant. Good chemical resistance. Resistance to termites.	Furniture, interior and exterior joinery. Boat building.
Utile *Entandrophragma utile* W Africa	56	Hardwood Reddish-brown	660	Medium	Medium	Medium	Durable	Extremely resistant	Regular	✓	Medium/High		Interior and exterior joinery. Furniture and cabinet work.
Virola Baboen *Virola* spp *Dialyanthera* spp S America	19	Hardwood Pale pinkish-brown	430/670	Medium	Medium	Medium	Non-durable	Permeable	Limited	✓	Low		Carpentry, furniture, plywood, mouldings.
Wallaba *Eperua falcata E grandiflora* Guyana		Hardwood Dull reddish-brown	910	Coarse	Medium*	Medium	Very durable	Extremely resistant	Limited		Medium	Gum exudation likely.	Transmission poles, flooring, decking, heavy construction.
Walnut, African *Lovoa trichilioides* W Africa	47	Hardwood Yellowish-brown, sometimes with dark streaks	560	Medium	Small	Medium	Moderately durable	Extremely resistant	Variable	✓	Medium		Furniture, cabinet work. Interior and exterior joinery.
Walnut, American *Juglans nigra* N America	52	Hardwood Rich dark brown	660	Coarse	Small/Medium*	Good	Very durable	Resistant	Variable	✓	High		Furniture, gun stocks.
Walnut, European *Juglans regia* Europe	51	Hardwood Grey-brown with dark streaks	670	Coarse	Medium	Good	Moderately durable	Resistant	Limited	✓	High	Staining likely if in contact with iron under damp conditions.	Furniture, turnery, gun stocks.
Wenge *Millettia laurentii M stuhlmannii* Central & E Africa	64	Hardwood Dark brown with fine black veining	880	Coarse	Small	Good	Durable	Extremely resistant	Limited	✓	High		Interior and exterior joinery. Flooring, turnery.
Western red cedar (†) *Thuja plicata* N America	17	Softwood Reddish-brown	390	Coarse	Small	Good	Durable	Resistant	Regular	✓	Medium	An acidic timber which may corrode metals under damp conditions and cause iron staining	Shingles, exterior cladding, greenhouses, beehives.
Whitewood, European (†) *Picea abies* and *Abies alba* Europe. Scandinavia. USSR	3	Softwood White to pale yellowish-brown	470	Medium	Medium	Good	Non-durable	Resistant	Regular	✓	Low		Interior joinery, construction, flooring.
Willow *Salix* spp Europe		Hardwood Pinkish-white	450	Fine	Small	Good	Perishable	Resistant	Limited		Medium/High		Cricket bats, boxes, crates.
Yew *Taxus baccata* Europe	32	Softwood Orange brown to purple brown	670	Medium	Small/Medium*	Difficult	Durable	Resistant	Limited	✓	High	Sizes may be limited.	Furniture, turnery. Interior joinery.

References

BRITISH STANDARDS

BS0 A standard for standards
  Part 3: 1981 Drafting and presentation of British Standards
BS144: 1973 Coal tar creosote for the preservation of timber
BS459 Doors
  Part 3: 1951 Fire-check flush doors and wood and metal frames (half hour and one hour type) (Proposed for withdrawal)
BS476 Fire tests on building materials and structures
  Part 7: 1971 Surface spread of flame tests for materials
  Part 8: 1972 Test methods and criteria for the fire resistance of elements of building construction (to be replaced by BS476 Parts 20-23)
BS584: 1967 Wood trim (softwood)
BS585 Wood stairs
  Part 1: 1984 Specification for straight flight stairs and stairs with quarter or half landings for domestic use
BS644 Wood windows
  Part 1: 1951 Wood casement windows. (Withdrawn, under revision)
BS745: 1969 Animal glue for wood (joiner's glue) (dry glue jelly or liquid glue)
BS881 and 589: 1974 Nomenclature of commercial timbers, including sources of supply
BS913: 1973 Wood preservation by means of pressure creosoting
BS1088 and 4079: 1966 Plywood for marine craft
BS1088 Marine plywood manufactured from selected untreated tropical hardwoods
BS4079 Plywood made for marine use and treated against attack by fungi or marine borers
BS1142 Fibre building boards
  Part 2: 1971 Medium board and hardboard
  Part 3: 1972 Insulating board (softboard)
BS1186 Quality of timber and workmanship in joinery
  Part 1: Revision due: 1985 Selection of timber species; moisture content; classification of timber
  Part 2: 1971 Quality of workmanship
BS1187: 1959 Wood block for floors
BS1202 Nails
  Part 1: 1974 Steel nails
BS1203: 1979 Synthetic resin adhesives (phenolic and aminoplastic) for plywood

BS1204 Synthetic resin adhesives (phenolic and aminoplastic) for wood
  Part 1: 1979 Gap filling adhesives
  Part 2: 1979 Close contact adhesives
BS1210: 1963 Wood screws
BS1282: 1975 Guide to the choice, use and application of wood preservatives
BS1297: 1970 Grading and sizing of softwood flooring (confirmed 1980)
BS1336: 1971 Knotting (confirmed 1982)
BS1444: 1970 Cold-setting casein adhesive powders for wood
BS1455: 1972 Plywood manufactured from tropical hardwoods
BS1579: 1960 Connectors for timber
BS2832: 1957 Hot applied damp resisting coatings for solums
BS3051: 1972 Coal tar creosotes for wood preservation (other than creosotes to BS144)
BS3444: 1972 Blockboard and laminboard
BS3452: 1962 Copper/chrome water-borne wood preservatives and their application
BS3453: 1962 Fluoride/arsenate/chromate/dinitrophenol water-borne preservatives and their application
BS3583: 1963 Information about blockboard and laminboard
BS3842: 1965 Treatment of plywood with preservatives
BS4024: 1966 Pentachlorophenyl laurate
BS4050 Specifications for mosaic parquet panels
  Part 1: 1977 General characteristics
  Part 2: 1966 Classification and quality requirements
BS4071: 1966 Polyvinyl acetate (PVA) emulsion adhesives for wood
BS4072: 1974 Wood preservation by means of water-borne copper/chrome/arsenic compositions
BS4169: 1970 Glued laminated timber structural members
BS4261: 1968 Glossary of terms relating to timber preservation
BS4471 Dimensions for softwood
  Part 1: 1978 Sizes of sawn and planed timber
  Part 2: 1971 Small resawn sections
BS4756: 1971 Ready mixed priming paints for woodwork
BS4787 Internal and external wood doorsets, door leaves and frames
  Part 1: 1980 Dimensional requirements

BS4978: 1973	Timber grades for structural use
BS5056: 1974	Copper naphthenate wood preservatives
BS5082: 1974	Water thinned priming paints for woodwork
BS5268	Code of practice for the structural use of timber
Part 1	Limit state design, materials and workmanship (to be published in the future)
Part 2: 1984	Permissible stress design, materials and workmanship
Part 3: Publication due 1985	Trussed rafter roofs
Part 4	Fire resistance of timber structures
Section 4.1: 1978	Method of calculating fire resistance of timber members
Section 4.2	Method of calculating the fire resistance of timber stud walls and joisted floor constructions (to be published in the future)
Part 5: 1977	Preservative treatments for constructional timber
Part 6	Timber frame wall design (to be published in the future)
Part 7	Calculations basis for span tables
Section 1	Domestic floor joists (to be published in the future)
other sections	will include ceiling joists, joists for flat roofs, purlins and common or jack rafters
BS5277: 1976	Doors. Measurement of defects of general flatness of door leaves
BS5278: 1976	Doors. Measurement of dimensions and of defects of squareness of door leaves
BS5291: 1984	Finger joints in structural softwood
BS5358: 1976	Specification for low-lead solvent-thinned priming paint for woodwork
BS5368	Methods of testing windows
Part 1: 1976	Air permeability test
Part 2: 1980	Watertightness test under static pressure
Part 3: 1978	Wind resistance tests
BS5369: 1976	Methods of testing doors; behaviour under humidity variations of door leaves placed in successive uniform climates
BS5395	Stairs, ladders and walkways
Part 1: 1977	Code of practice for the design of straight stairs
Part 2: 1984	Code of practice for the design of helical and spiral stairs
BS5407: 1976	Classification of adhesives
BS5442	Classification of adhesives for use in construction
Part 1: 1977	Adhesives for use with flooring materials
Part 3: 1979	Adhesives for use with wood
BS5450: 1977	Sizes of hardwoods and methods of measurement
BS5531: 1978	Code of practice for safety in erecting structural frames
BS5588	Fire precautions in the design and construction of buildings
Part 1	
Section 1.1: 1984	Code of practice for single-family dwelling houses
Part 3: 1983	Code of practice for office buildings
BS5589: 1978	Code of practice for preservation of timber
BS5606: 1978	Code of practice for accuracy in building
BS5669: 1979	Specification for wood chipboard and methods of test for particleboard
BS5707	Solutions of wood preservatives in organic solvents
Part 1: 1979	Specification for solutions for general purpose applications, including timber that is to be painted
Part 2: 1979	Specification for pentachlorophenol

	wood preservative solution for use on timber that is not required to be painted
Part 3: 1980	Methods of treatment
BS5756: 1980	Specification for tropical hardwoods graded for structural use
BS5977	Lintels
Part 2: 1983	Prefabricated lintels
BS6100	Glossary of building and civil engineering terms
Part 4	Forest products
Section 4.1: 1984	Characteristics and properties of timber and wood based panel products
Section 4.2: 1984	Sizes and quantities of solid timber
Section 4.3: 1984	Wood based panel products
BS6150: 1982	Code of practice for painting of buildings
BS6180: 1982	Code of practice for protective barriers in and about buildings
BS6222	Domestic kitchen equipment
Part 1: 1982	Specification for co-ordinating dimensions
BS6229: 1982	Code of practice for flat roofs with continuously supported coverings
BS6262: 1982	Code of practice for glazing for buildings
BS6375	Performance of windows
Part 1: 1983	Classification for weathertightness
BS6446: 1984	Manufacture of glued structural components of timber and wood based products
BS6566: Publication due 1985	Plywood
CP112	The structural use of timber (being replaced by BS5268)
Part 2: 1971	Metric units (superseded by BS5268 Part 2)
Part 3: 1973	Trussed rafters for roofs of dwellings (to be replaced by BS 5268 Part 3)
CP153	Windows and rooflights
Part 1: 1969	Cleaning and safety
Part 2: 1970	Durability and maintenance
CP201: 1951	Timber flooring (under revision)
CP209	Care and maintenance of floor surfaces
Part 1: 1963	Wooden flooring
CP2004: 1972	Foundations

OVERSEAS AND INTERNATIONAL STANDARDS

Canada	Canadian Standards Association
	CSA0121 – 1978 Canadian Douglas fir plywood
	CSA0141 – 1970 Softwood lumber
	CSA0151-M 1978 Canadian softwood plywood
	National Lumber Grades Authority (NLGA)
	Standard grading rules for Canadian lumber 1980 + 1981 supplement
Finland	Suomen Standardisomislitto
	SFS 2416 Testing of the characteristics of birch plywood 1972
	SFS 4091 Finnish birch-faced plywood 1977
Malaysia	Standards and Industrial Research Institute
	Standard 3.360 Specification for timber and plywood 1976
Singapore	Singapore Institute of Standards and Industrial Research
	Standard 1 Specifications for plywood for general purposes 1970 amended 1976
Sweden	Sveriges Standardsiseingskommission
	SIS 23–42 05 Plywood – sizes and form
USA	National Bureau of Standards
	PS1-83 Construction and industrial plywood
	PS 20-70 American softwood lumber standard
	National grading rules for softwood dimension lumber (NGRDL) 1975

Europe	Economic Commission for Europe (ECE) Recommended standard for stress grading of coniferous sawn timber 1982
International	ISO 2428: 1974 Plywood – Veneer plywood with rotary cut veneer for general use – Classification by appearance of panels with outer veneers of birch
	ISO 2429: 1974 Plywood – Veneer plywood with rotary cut veneer for general use – Classification by appearance of panels with outer veneers of broadleaved species of tropical Africa
	ISO 834: 1975 Fire resistance tests – Elements of building construction

REFERENCES

Materials: Chapters 1–4

Timber – properties and uses

BROWN, W.H. Timbers of the world. Timber Research and Development Association Red booklets. Hughenden Valley, TRADA.
 RB1 Africa 1978
 RB2 South America 1978
 RB3 Southern Asia 1978
 RB4 South East Asia 1978
 RB5 Philippines and Japan 1978
 RB6 Europe 1978
 RB7 North America 1978
 RB8 Australasia 1978
 RB9 Central America and the Caribbean 1979
BUILDING RESEARCH ESTABLISHMENT. Handbook of hardwoods, revised by R.H. Farmer. London, HMSO. 1972.
BUILDING RESEARCH ESTABLISHMENT. A handbook of softwoods. BRE Report. London, HMSO. 2nd edition. 1977.
BUILDING RESEARCH ESTABLISHMENT. The natural durability classification of timber. Technical Note 40. Princes Risborough, BRE. 1979.
DESCH, H.E., revised J.M. Dinwoodie. Timber – its structure, properties and utilization. London, Macmillan. 6th edition. 1981.
RENDLE B.J. World timbers. London, Ernest Benn Ltd.
 Volume 1, Europe and Africa. 1969.
 Volume 2, North and South America. 1969.
 Volume 3, Asia and Australia and New Zealand. 1970.
RENDLE B.J., revised J.D. Brazier. The growth and structure of wood. Forest Products Research Laboratory. Bulletin 56. London, HMSO. 1971.
PANSHIN A.J. and C. de Zeeuw. Textbook of wood technology. 4th edition. New York, London etc, McGraw-Hill Book Co. 1980.
TSOUMIS G. Wood as a raw material. London, Pergamon Press. 1968.
TRADA Wood Information sheets:
 1– 6 Introduction to the specification of glulam members
 1–11 Timber building elements of proven fire resistance
 2/3– 5 Guide to the specification of structural softwood
 2/3– 6 Wood decorative and practical
 2/3–15 Basic sizes of softwoods and hardwoods
 2/3–19 Timbers – their properties and uses
 4– 7 Guide to stress graded softwood
 4–11 Timber and wood based sheet materials in fire
 4–14 Moisture content in wood

Board materials

TRADA Plywood – its manufacture and uses. TBL 7. Hughenden Valley, TRADA. 1981.
TRADA Wood Information Sheets
 2/3– 7 Low flame spread wood based board products
 2/3–11 Specification and treatment of exterior plywood
 2/3–17 Wood based sheet materials for formwork linings
 2/3–20 Edge sealants for wood based boards
Publications are issued by the associations representing panel products in the UK:
 American Plywood Association
 Association of British Plywood and Veneer Manufacturers
Chipboard Promotion Association
Council of Forest Industries of British Columbia
Fibre Building Board Organization
Finnish Plywood International
United Kingdom Particleboard Association

Protection

TRADA/BWPA Timber Pests and their control. TBL 25. Hughenden Valley, TRADA. 1984.
TRADA Wood Information Sheets
 2/3– 1 Finishes for exterior timber
 2/3– 3 Flame retardant treatments for timber
 2/3–14 Seals for timber floors
 2/3–16 Preservative treatment for timber – a guide to specification
 2/3–21 Wood preservation – processing and site control

Supply statistics

FOOD AND AGRICULTURE ORGANIZATION. 1982 Yearbook of forest products. Rome, FAO. 1984.
NORMAN, C.K. UK Yearbook of timber statistics 1980–82. London, Timber Trade Federation. 1983.

Structural Uses: Chapters 5–8

Regulations

The Building Regulations (England and Wales). London, HMSO 1976
The Building Standards (Scotland) Regulations. London, HMSO 1981
The Building Regulations (Northern Ireland). Belfast, HMSO 1971

Note: The Building Regulations are undergoing alteration. See page 12.

Historic Structures

BOURNE J.C. Bourne's Great Western Railway. London, David Bogue. 1846. Reprinted: Newton Abbot, David and Charles Reprints. 1970.
BRANDON R. and BRANDON J.A. The open timber roofs of the Middle Ages. London, David Bogue. 1849.
VIOLLET-LE-DUC M. Dictionnaire raisonné de l'architecture. Tome troisième. Paris, A Morel. 1868.
WREN Christopher. Parentalia. London, T. Osburn and R. Dodsley. 1750.

Modern Structures

BAKER J.F., HORNE M.R. and HEYMAN J. The steel skeleton. Volume 2. Plastic behaviour and design. Cambridge, University Press. 1965.
BUILDING RESEARCH ESTABLISHMENT. Flat roof design; the technical options. Digest 221. London, HMSO. 1980.
CURRY W.T. Grade stresses for structural laminated timber. Forest Products Research Laboratory Bulletin 53. London, HMSO. 1970.
DINWOODIE J.M. Timber – its nature and behaviour. Wokingham, Van Nostrand Reinhold Co. 1981.
GORDON J.E. The new science of strong materials or Why you don't fall through the floor. Harmondsworth, Penguin Books. 1974.
GORDON J.E. Structures or Why things don't fall down. Harmondsworth, Penguin Books. 1978.
INTERNATIONAL TRUSS PLATE ASSOCIATION Bulletins. Halesowen, ITPA.
 No 1 Roof bracing for fink and fan trusses 1974.
 No 2 Erection procedure 1974.
 No 3 Site storage and handling 1974.
 No 4 Tank supports: details and limiting spans 1974.
 No 5 Ventilation and condensation 1981.
OZELTON E.C. and BAIRD J.A. Timber designers' manual. London, Crosby Lockwood Staples. 1984.
PROPERTY SERVICES AGENCY. Flat roofs technical guide. Croydon, PSA 1979.
 Volume 1 Design

PROPERTY SERVICE AGENCY (_continued_)
Volume 2 Construction (site control)
Volume 3 Post-construction (maintenance)
ROSSMAN W.E. The Ensphere. Acta Univ. Oulu 1980, Series C
Technica 16, Artes Construction 3, pp 127-137.
TRADA PUBLICATIONS
DESIGN AIDS
To BS5268 Part 2
DA 1 Design examples to BS5268 Part 2 1984
DA 2 Span tables for domestic purlins 1984
DA 3 Span tables for floor joists 1984
DA 4 Load tables for nailed ply-box beams 1984
DA 5 Load tables for glued ply-box beams 1984
DA 6 Joist span tables for domestic floors and roofs
To CP112
TBL 34   Span charts for solid timber beams 1976
TBL 38   Span tables for floor joists 1976
E/IB/17   Span tables for ridged farm portals in solid timber
          1970
E/IB/27   Span tables for industrial purlins 1977
STANDARD DESIGN SHEETS Domestic roof designs
Type A 40 deg pitch

Imperial Span	Metric to CP112 Span		Metric to BS5268 Span	
SDS77 17'0"	SmDS77	5100 mm	SDS500	5000–6000 mm
SDS78 20'6"	SmDS78	6300 mm	SDS501	6000–7000 mm
SDS79 23'0"	SmDS79	6900 mm	SDS502	7000–8000 mm
SDS80 26'0"	SmDS80	7800 mm	SDS503	8000–9000 mm
SDS81 30'0"	SmDS81	9000 mm		

Type B 35 deg pitch

SDS83 20'9"	SmDS83	6300 mm	SDS508	5000–6000 mm
SDS84 24'3"	SmDS84	7500 mm	SDS509	6000–7000 mm
SDS85 26'0"	SmDS85	8100 mm	SDS510	7000–8000 mm
SDS86 30'0"	SmDS86	9300 mm	SDS511	8000–9000 mm

Joint arrangements for Type A and B trusses
SDS82   SmDS82   SDS507
Type C 22–30 deg pitch

	SDS200	6000 mm	SDS515	5000–6000 mm
	SDS201	7200 mm	SDS516	6000–7200 mm
	SDS202	8400 mm	SDS517	7200–8400 mm
	SDS203	9600 mm	SDS518	8400–9600 mm
	SDS204	10800 mm	SDS519	9600–10800 mm
			SDS520	10800–12000 mm

Type D 25 deg pitch

	SDS205	6000 mm
	SDS206	6900 mm
	SDS207	8100 mm
	SDS208	9000 mm
	SDS209	10200 mm
	SDS210	11100 mm

Type E 30 deg pitch   Pitch 27.5–40 deg

	SDS211	6000 mm	SDS527	5000–6000 mm
	SDS212	6900 mm	SDS528	6000–7000 mm
	SDS213	8100 mm	SDS529	7000–8100 mm

STANDARD DESIGN SHEETS (continued)

Imperial Span	Metric to CP112 Span		Metric to BS5268 Span	
	SDS214	9000 mm	SDS530	8100–9000 mm
	SDS215	10200 mm	SDS531	9000–10200 mm
	SDS216	11100 mm	SDS532	10200–11100 mm

Type F 15 deg pitch   Pitch 15–25 deg

	SDS217	6000 mm	SDS533	6000 mm
	SDS218	7200 mm	SDS534	7200 mm
	SDS219	8400 mm	SDS535	8400 mm
	SDS220	9600 mm	SDS536	9600 mm
	SDS221	10800 mm	SDS537	10800 mm
	SDS222	12000 mm	SDS538	12000 mm

TBL39 Fire and timber in modern building design. Revised 1977
Wood Information sheets
0- 9 Timber bridges
1-10 Principles of pitched roof construction
1-16 TC1 Specification and recommendations for the use of
     polyethylene ground cover for suspended timber ground
     floors
1-17 Structural use of hardwoods to BS5268 Part 2
1-20 External timber cladding
2/3- 9 Mechanical fasteners for structural timberwork

Timber Frame Construction

NATIONAL HOUSE-BUILDING COUNCIL Timber-framed
dwellings and external timber framed wall panels in masonry cross
wall dwellings. Practice Note 5. Amersham, NHBC. 1982.
TRADA
TBL52 Timber frame housing – structural recommendations 1979.
TBL56 Site guidance – timber frame houses 1981.
Wood Information sheets
0- 3 Introduction to timber framed housing
0- 5 Timber framed housing – specification notes
0- 7 Low energy timber frame housing – a checklist
0- 8 Timber frame construction site checklist
0-10 Structural surveys of timber frame houses
1-18 Calculations for the racking resistance of timber framed
     walls
1-19 TC2 Timber frame separating walls
4-15 Condensation control in timber frame dwellings

Joinery: Chapters 9–11

BOWYER J. Handbook of building crafts in conservation. London,
Hutchinson Publishing Group Ltd. 1981.
BRITISH WOODWORKING FEDERATION. BWF
performance standard for wood windows. Outlook on Wood
Windows No 9. London, BWF. 1984 pp 3-9.
EASTWICK-FIELD J. and STILLMAN J. The design and practice
of joinery. London, The Architectural Press with TRADA. 4th
edition 1973.
MITCHELL G.E. Carpentry and joinery. London, Cassells. 1982.
MUNN H. Joinery for repair and restoration contracts. Orion
Books. 1983.
MUNN H. Joinery detailing. Orion Books, 1984.
RILEY S.W. A manual of carpentry and joinery. London,
Macmillan. 1936.
TRADA publications
Fire resisting doorsets – Quality assurance scheme
Wood Information sheets
1-11 Timber building elements of proven fire resistance D1-4
     Doors
1-13 Technology of fire resisting doorsets

Sources of further information

American Plywood Association
101 Wigmore Street
London W1H 9AB
Telephone 01-629-3437
Telex 296009

Association of British Plywood and Veneer Manufacturers
23-35 City Road
London EC1Y 1AR
Telephone 01-628-5801/5

British Adhesive Manufacturers Association
2A High Street
Hythe
Southampton SO9 6TW
Telephone 0703 (Hythe) 842765

British Board of Agrément
PO Box 195
Bucknalls Lane
Garston
Watford
Herts WD2 7NG
Telephone 0923 670844

British Standards Institution
2 Park Street
London W1A 2BS
Telephone 01-629-9000   Head office: counter service for sales
Telex 266933   of British Standards

Linford Wood   Postal sales and information
Milton Keynes MK14 6LE
Telephone 0908 (Milton Keynes) 320066
Telex 825777

British Wood Preserving Association
Premier House
Southampton Row
London WC1B 5AL
Telephone 01-837-8217
Prestel 35116163

British Woodworking Federation
82 New Cavendish Street
London W1M 8AD
Telephone 01-580-5588
Telex 265763

Building Research Station
Garston
Watford
Herts WD2 7JR
Telephone 0923 674040

Chipboard Promotion Association
Stocking Lane
Hughenden Valley
High Wycombe
Bucks HP14 4NU
Telephone 0240 24 (Naphill) 5265
Telex 83292
Prestel 35116164

Council of Forest Industries of British Columbia
Tileman House
131-3 Upper Richmond Road
Putney
London SW15 2TR
Telephone 01-788-4466
Telex 25695
Prestel 35116166

Fibre Building Board Development Organisation Ltd
1 Hanworth Road
Feltham
Middlesex TW13 5AF
Telephone 01-751-6107
Telex 24800
Prestel 35116165

Finnish Plywood International
PO Box 99
Welwyn Garden City
Herts AL6 0HS
Telephone 043-879-746

Furniture Industries Research Association
Maxwell Road
Stevenage
Herts SG1 2EW
Telephone 0438 313433
Telex 25102

Glass and Glazing Federation
6 Mount Row
London W1Y 6DY
Telephone 01-409-0545

International Truss Plate Association
c/o Twinaplate Ltd
Threemilestone
Truro
Cornwall TR4 9LD
Telephone 0872 (Truro) 79525

National House-Building Council
Chiltern Avenue
Amersham
Bucks HP6 5AP
Telephone 02403 (Amersham) 4477

Princes Risborough Laboratory
Building Research Establishment
Princes Risborough
Aylesbury
Bucks HP17 9PX
Telephone 08444 (Princes Risborough) 3101
Telex 83559

Swedish Finnish Timber Council
21 Carolgate
Retford
Notts DN22 6BZ
Telephone 0777 (Retford) 706616
Telex 56494
Prestel 35116162

Timber Research and Development Association
Stocking Lane
Hughenden Valley   Head office and laboratories
High Wycombe   London and South East office
Bucks HP14 4ND
Telephone 0240 24 (Naphill) 3091
Telex 83292
Prestel 3511615

Stirling Enterprise Park   Scottish office
John Player Building
Players Road
Stirling FK7 7RS
Telephone 0786-62122

115 Portland Street   North West and Northern Ireland
Manchester M1 6DW   office
Telephone 061-236-3740

Manchester House   North and North East office
48 High Street
Stokesley
Middlesbrough
Cleveland TS9 5AX
Telephone 0642 712452

91 High Street   Midlands office
Evesham   Bristol Channel and South Wales
Worcs WR11 4DT   office
Telephone 0386 49132

149 St Neots Road   Eastern office
Hardwick
Cambs CB3 7QJ
Telephone 0954 (Madingley) 211377

5-7 South Street   South West office
Wellington
Somerset TA21 8NR
Telephone 082-347-5296

10 Orwell Road   Irish Republic office
Rathgar
Dublin 6
Telephone Dublin 962819

United Kingdom Particleboard Association
Stocking Lane
Hughenden Valley
High Wycombe
Bucks HP14 4NT
Telephone 0240-24-2381
Telex 83292
Prestel 35116161

US Softwood Lumber Associations
(Southern Forest Products Association & Western Wood Products
Association)
69 Wigmore Street
London W1H 9LG
Telephone 01-486-7488/9

Acknowledgements

TRADA is pleased to acknowledge support from the members listed below, without which this venture would have been impossible.

ORDINARY MEMBERS

Afro Timber & Plywood Ltd
Ahlstrom Products Ltd
Alexanders' Sawmills Ltd
J. Alsford Ltd
Anglo-Norden (Timber) Ltd
Ashdar Joinery
Askern Saw Mills Ltd
ASSI Timber (UK) Ltd

J. Baird & Co (Falkirk) Ltd
H. G. Barham Ltd
Boise Cascade Sales Ltd
Bowater Ripper Ltd
Wm Brandts (Timber) Ltd
British Plywood Manufacturers Ltd
British Gypsum
Brooks Bros (Ilford) Ltd
Brownlee plc
Bullock & Driffill Ltd
Burt Boulton (Timber) Ltd
E. O. Burton & Co Ltd
G. H. Buttle & Co Ltd

Canvey Wharf Co Ltd
Carroll System Building (1970) Ltd
Chadwicks
A. W. Champion Ltd
Christie & Vesey Ltd
Churchill & Sim
Ciba-Geigy Plastics (Kirkoswald) Ltd
B.M.M.K. Cotterell
Cottingham Joinery Co Ltd
Cox Long (Investments) Ltd (DBY) Ltd
G. & T. Crampton Ltd
Crest Homes plc
Crosby Doors Ltd
A. W. Cushion Ltd

Karl Danzer Ltd
Dask Timber Products Ltd
James Davies (Timber) Ltd
Dean & Furbisher (Darrington) Ltd
James Donaldson & Sons Ltd
J. T. Dove Ltd

East Asiatic Timber Ltd
East Kent Timber Ltd
Eastern Counties Timber Co Ltd
Edwards & Co (Wandsworth) Ltd
Ellis & Booth Ltd
Ellis & Powell Ltd
Enso Marketing Co Ltd

John Fleming & Co Ltd
Fleming Timber Buildings (Scotland)
Forest Service, Belfast
Forestry Commission
Frame Homes (South West) Ltd
Paul Frost Ltd

William Gimson & Sons Ltd
Graham-Reeves (Timber) Ltd
Grays Construction Supplies Ltd
Gribbinhouse Company
E.C. Griffiths & Co Ltd
Joseph Griggs & Co Ltd
G. Gruneberg (Timber & Veneers) Ltd
GWI Ltd

Hare Buildings
Roger Haydock & Co Ltd
H.D.L. (Waterhouse) Ltd
Highland Forest Products plc
W.F. Hollway & Bro Ltd
W.W. Howard Bros (Investments) Ltd
Howarth Timber Group Ltd

Imperial Chemical Industries plc

T.P. Jordeson & Co Ltd

Robert Keys & Co Ltd

James Latham plc
Arnold Laver & Co Ltd
Walter Lawrence Trading Ltd
John Lenanton & Sons Ltd
Lesser System Build
James Littler & Sons Ltd
Llewellyn Homes Ltd
Nevill Long Group

Macfarlane, Burchell & Co Ltd
Mallinson-Denny Ltd
Marlow & Co Ltd
R. May & Son Ltd
Thomas McDonogh & Sons Ltd
Medina Ltd
Meyer International plc
Miller Bros (Hull) Ltd
George Mixer & Co Ltd
Moelven (UK) Ltd
F.W. Morgan Ltd

R.A. Naylor Ltd
Nectar Homes Ltd
John Nicholas & Sons (Port Talbot)
Noberne Doors Ltd
Northern Ireland Timber Importers Association

David Patton Ltd
F. Peart & Co Ltd
The Phoenix Timber Group plc and
    Alexander Gourvitch
Pinnacle Homes
Albert Plaut Ltd
Powell Duffryn Timber Ltd
Prestoplan Homes Ltd
Price and Pierce Ltd

Quiggin & Co Ltd

Rainham Timber Engineering Ltd
Rauma Repola (UK) Ltd
Rawle, Gammon & Baker (Holdings) Ltd
E. Rea & Son Ltd
Reema Construction Ltd
Cyril Ridgeon & Son Ltd
Robison & Davidson Ltd

The Sabah Timber Co Ltd
Sandell Perkins plc
J. Scadding & Son Ltd
Schauman (UK) Ltd
Seaboard International (Timber & Plywood) Ltd
F.R. Shadbolt & Sons Ltd
Shapland & Petter Ltd
W.S. Shuttleworth (Timber) Ltd
A.J. Smith & Son (Benfleet) Ltd
Thomas Smith & Sons (Kirkoswald) Ltd
Sodra Timber Products Ltd
M.H. Southern & Co Ltd
Southerns Evans Ltd
Sterling International Timber Homes
Stoners Buildings Ltd
Stoners Appliances Ltd
Simon Summers (Timber) Ltd

Swiftplan Ltd
J.T. Sydenham & Co Ltd
George Sykes Ltd

Thanet Timber Frames Ltd
Timber & Plywood Co (Cheshire) Ltd
Timbmet Ltd
Tingdene Homes Ltd
Torwood Homes Ltd
Tower Timber Group Ltd
Travis & Arnold plc
Trend Homes Northern Ltd
Tru Homes Ltd
Tukan Timber Ltd

UCM Timber plc

Henry Venables Ltd

James Walker (Leith) Ltd
Wates Built Homes Ltd
James Webster & Bro Ltd
Wellgrove Timber Systems Ltd
G.F. Wells Ltd
John Woyka & Co Ltd
John Wright (Panel Products) Ltd
Wyckham Blackwell Group of Companies

Yeomans & Partners Ltd
Yeovil Timber Co Ltd
Ystwyth Homes (Aberystwyth) Ltd

ASSOCIATE MEMBERS

J.W. Bollom
Bostitch Division of Textron Ltd
City of Bradford Metropolitan Council
British Waterways Board

Chipboard Promotion Association
Control (Chemical South Eastern) Ltd

Derbyshire County Council
Devon County Council
Dorset County Council

Falkirk College of Technology
Fibre Building Board Organisation
Fibreglass Ltd
Finlandia Construction
Finnish Plywood International
Furniture Timber & Allied Trades Union

Glasgow School of Art
Gwent College of Higher Education
Gwynedd County Council

Hertfordshire College of Building
Hickson's Timber Products Ltd
W.W. Hill Son & Wallace Ltd
Hydro-Air International (UK) Ltd

International Forest Science Consultancy

K.C. Renovation Treatments
William Kenyon & Sons Ltd

Lancashire County Council
Lauder Technical College
Leicester Building Society
Central London Polytechnic

Central Manchester College
Middlesbrough Borough Council
C.D. Monninger Ltd
Mosford Joinery Ltd

City of Newcastle upon Tyne
Norfolk County Council
University College of North Wales
Nottingham University

Pass & Co Timber Preservation UK Ltd
Pass & Co Haywards Heath
Polycell Products Ltd
Portakabin Ltd
City of Portsmouth Department of Architecture &
Design

Queens University Belfast

Rentatherm (London) Ltd
Resin Bonded Repairs Ltd
Rickards Timber Treatment Ltd
Rycotewood College

Sadolin (UK) Ltd
Ron Sammons Ltd
Scottish Special Housing Association
South East London Technical College
R.E.Y. Slater
Southend-on-Sea College of Technology
Spey Control System Ltd
Stafford Borough Council
Harry Stanger Ltd
Surrey County Council
East Surrey College
Swedish Finnish Timber Council Ltd

Terenure College
Tinsley Building Products Ltd
Trade Coaters (Retroflame) Ltd
Twinaplate Ltd

UK Particleboard Association
Ulster University

Terry Waters French Polishing Ltd

Yorkshire Dampcourse & Woodwork Co Ltd

PROFESSIONAL MEMBERS

AA Associates
Richard Adams

Adie Button & Partners
Allsop Sellers
Andrews Kent & Stone
Astley Samuel Leeder & Son
W.S. Atkins (Services) Ltd
Ayshford & Sansome

Barnes Dickins & Associates
Beaumont Structural Consultants
Pat Bellay Ltd
Benefield & Cornford
George Bennett Mitchell & Son
Bickerdike Allen & Partners
C.J.M. Blackie
George M. Bramall & Partners
Gordon C. Britton
Brock Carmichael Associates
Broughton Beatty Partnership
John A. Brown & Associates
John Brunton Partnership
Bruton Knowles & Co
Budgen & Partners
Building Consultancy Services
Building Design Partnership
Building Design Services
Steve Burke
Buro Happold
Leslie Buxton & Partners

Carlson Somers & Partners
Carr Bedford
Carter Jonas
Cassidy & Ashton Partnership
CEP International
De Leuw Chadwick O hEocha
J. Clark & Partners
Clifton Scannell Emerson Associates
Cochrane McGregor Partnership
Desmond Cody Associates
Coffin Jones & Roden
Cogswell Cornick Associates
Jack Collier Partners
A.J. Comben
F. Cooper & Son
Cornwall County Council (Architects)
Costello Murray & Beaumont
Covell Matthews Wheatley Partnership
J.K. Craig
Michael Cronin Associates
Cross & Associates
Leslie Cudmore
Culpin Partnership
W.G. Curtin & Partners
Cuthbert Lake Drew Pearce

A.L. Daines & Partners
J. Kenneth Dancer
Peter Dann & Partners
Robert Davies John West Associates
William T. Davie & Associates
Dick Young & Webb
Dinardo & Partners
C.H. Dobbie & Partners
Drivers

Design Office Dusoswa

Elliott & Brown
Geoffrey M. Evans & Co
Ewbank Preece Engineering Consultants Ltd.

W.A. Fairhurst & Partners (Aberdeen)
W.A. Fairhurst & Partners (Glasgow)
W.A. Fairhurst & Partners (London)
W.A. Fairhurst & Partners (Newcastle)
Farmer & Dark
The Featherstone Austin Partnership
Feilden & Mawson
Fitzroy Robinson Partnership
E.P. Flanagan & Associates
Floyd Slaski
Frameform Limited
David French & Partners
Fuller Horsey Wills

Thomas Garland & Partners
B.E.G. Gibbs
Gifford & Partners
W. & M. Given
Glenister Green
Godman & Kay Partnership
Good & Tillotson
Alex Gordon Partnership
Frank Graham & Partners
Arthur G. Griffith & Sons
D.R. Griffiths

T. Harley Haddow & Partners
Alan Harper
James Harrington Associates
Graham Harris Partnership
Neil Harris Associates
Harris & Sutherland Ltd
Hawkins Heath Partnership
Michael J. Heard & Associates
Hedley Greentree Partnership
Lawrence J. Hewitt & Partners
Hilbery Chaplin & Co
H.J.T. Management Company
Hobbs Architects
Hodgson Wrathall
Holford Associates
Hollier Son & Co
Holmes Grace & Associates
HSD Building Consultants Ltd
Anthony Hunt Associates
Hunter & Partners
Husband & Company

J.R. Illingworth
E.H.C. Inskip & Son
M.R. Isaac
Isherwood & Ellis

D.C.R. James
R.T. James & Partners
Jenkins & Gosby
Jenkins & Marr
Jenkins & Potter

Jolliffe & Flint
Keith Jones

Kenchington Little & Partners (Cambridge)
Kenzie Lovell Partnership
Dennis R. Kightley
King Co
King & King
John Knevitt
Knight Morrish & Partners
Leonard R. Knott & Associates
Peter Knowles

Michael Laird & Partners
Lamb & Edge
W.A.R. Lanham
Lewis & Duviver
Mr D.M. Longbottom
Lorne Brown

Sir M. MacDonald & Partners
Maddocks Lusher & Matthews
Malachy Walsh & Partners
Mallagh Luce & Partners
Manning Clamp & Partners
Peter Manton
Marment Simons
Michael J. Marsh & Partners
Masini Franklin Partnership
J. Maxwell Aylwin
Sir Robert McAlpine & Sons Ltd
Jim McColl Associates
T.A. McKenna & Partners
W.B. McLaughlin
A.J. McLay & Partners
Frederick McManus & Partners
R. Mead
Mercer Blaikie
Merz & McLellan
T.M. Miller & Partners
Peter Minett & Partners
Geo. E. Mitchell
Mitre Drawing Services
Modern Decor Ltd
Montgomery Forgan Associates
Montgomery-Smith & Partners
Morgan Associates
Thomas Morgan & Partners
Philip Morris
L.G. Mouchel & Partners

Norfolk Design Centre Ltd

T.J. O'Connor & Associates
W. O'Neill & Partners
O. Riordan Wilson & Staehli
Ove Arup Partnership
Oxford Polytechnic

Parfitt & Forbes
Parkman Group Professional Services Ltd
Patrick Parsons & Associates
Charles B. Pearson Son & Partners
John D. Peek

Phillips Consultants Limited
Pick Everard Keay & Gimson
Pike Smith & Kemp
Sir Francis Pittis & Son
Norman Plough
Portland Associates
Posford Pavry & Partners
Robert J. Potter & Partners
Poulters
Povall Worthington Associates
Powell Tolner & Associates
Robert H. Preston
Probe Associates

Raffety Buckland
Redditch Development Corporation
Reiach & Hall
Remi Adelaid Partnership
Remmers & Partners
Renaissance Specialists
Riches & Blythin Partnership
Ridge & Partners
H.R. Rix Limited
Ross Gower & Bate
Rother District Council
Roth & Partners
Roughan and O'Donovan
Kenneth Rowe Associates
Andrew Russell Associates

Derick Sampson & Partners
F. J. Samuely & Partners
Messrs Sandberg
Paul Scantlebury
Scarlett Burkett Associates
Walter Scott & Partners
Shepherd Design Group
Sibley Robinson Partnership
Sinclair MacDonald & Son
Bernard H. Skinner & Co
Sir Frederick Snow & Partners
Somerset County Council (Architects)
Somerset & Walsh
Stanislaus Kenny & Partners

P.J. Steer
Stevens Partnership
S.L. Stevenson
Stewart Lyons Partnership
Stone & Partners
Strawberry Hill Estates
Robin Swain

Taylor Boyd & Hancock
Percy Thomas Partnership (Cardiff)
Percy Thomas Partnership (Manchester)
W.H. Thomas & Partners
Thomson Buckle Partnership
S.B. Tietz & Partners
Toleman & Sheridan
Tompkins Robinson & Partners
Gordon L. Torpy
Austin Trueman Associates
Turner & Holman
Turner Wright & Partners
Michael Twigg Brown & Partners

Veryard & Partners
Vidler & Co
K.J. Virgin

Ms Susan Walker
Wann McLaren & Partners
Anthony Ward Partnership (Hants)
Watson Salmond & Gray
Weller Eggar
Wheeler & Jupp
O. N. Wheeler & F. A. Wheeler
Wheelers of Ealing Ltd
Michael White
White Young Consulting Engineers
Mr & Mrs K. A. Whittington
Wilde & Associates
W. M. Wilson & Partners
Winning & Fulton
Peter Woodcock
Wren & Bell
R.E.B. Wyllie
Wythe Holland Udall Partnership

Index

Note: Italic type denotes pages on which illustrations appear.